Law of Wills and Succession

Law of Wills and Succession

Edward Stone

CILEX | Education

Disclaimer

To request permissions, contact the publisher at https://www.cilex.org.uk/contact_us

ISBN: 978-1-911713-34-0
E-ISBN: 978-1-911713-35-7

First paperback edition 2024

Layout by codemantra U.S. LLC

British Library Cataloguing in Publications Data
A catalogue record for this book is available from the British Library

Printed by CILEX Education in the United Kingdom.
CILEX Education
2nd Floor,
The Pinnacle,
Midsummer Boulevard,
Milton Keynes,
MK9 1BP

Cover image: Andrey Danilovich/iStock

www.cilex.org.uk

CILEX titles are printed by Mimeo, who are very proud to be a part of the Woodland Trust's Woodland Carbon Capture Scheme via Premier Paper. Mimeo partner with Woodland Carbon because 100% of the money they give is spent on planting deciduous trees in the UK. Papers are from sustainable sources and waste is recycled. Mimeo continue to use only Forest Stewardship Council accredited paper in their printed items.

About Edward Stone

Edward Stone is a qualified solicitor who has worked as a private client solicitor in Cirencester, preparing wills and administering estates. He has also lectured at Gloucestershire College of Arts and Technology in Cheltenham and Gloucester on a variety of CILEX courses. He is currently a Publisher at CILEX.

Guide to the Book

This textbook contains a range of features which have been developed to help support your learning and reinforce your understanding. The guided tour below explains how to use these features to get the most from your study.

Aims of the Chapter:

By the end of this chapter, you should be able to:

- explain what succession means;
- define technical terms relating to wills and succession that you will come across in this textbook;
- explain the circumstances and property types that wills or the intestacy rules cannot give away;
- explain a *donatio mortis causa*.

Aims

These are the aims of the chapter, which are the learning outcomes of the CILEX syllabus. They may appear in more than one chapter. You will be able to meet these aims by the end of the course. ("The learner will…")

Scenario

Connie and Jim are a married couple in their 60s. They have four children. Connie is convinced, despite the disbelief of all her friends and family that, as soon as she dies, Jim will find another woman and leave everything he owns to her in his will. Nonetheless, Connie still wants to leave all her property to Jim with a proviso that if he predeceases her, her property will pass to their four children. Jim, who always leaves financial affairs to Connie anyway, is quite happy to make a will giving all his property to Connie or to their children if she has predeceased him. How can Connie be reassured that her wishes will be followed after her death if she predeceases Jim?

Scenario

This indicates a scenario or story which explains a point of law or is used as the basis for test yourself questions.

Self-assessment Question

In the light of the difficulties with the case law on mutual wills, do you think that the doctrine should be retained? If it should be retained, how do you think it should be reformed?

Self-assessment Questions

These are questions designed to test your understanding of the part of the manual which you have just studied. The answers can be found at the back of the manual.

Key cases

Can there be a *donatio mortis causa* of registered land?

In ***Sen v Headley [1991]*** and ***King v Dubrey [2015]*** the land which was being given was unregistered. The title deeds were therefore required in order to carry out any transfer of ownership (the Land Registry would subsequently need them in order to turn it into registered land). The situation is different in the case of registered land. The Land Registry now holds all the essential documentation and no longer issues land or charge certificates following transfers of land. It seems unlikely that handing over the title information document (a short document provided by the Land Registry after land is transferred) would be enough to show that the donor had parted with the means of transferring ownership.

Key cases

These are the most important cases discussed in the chapter. You will, however, need to learn additional cases in order to illustrate the application of principles in your answers.

In the News

NEWS

The following article in the *Standard* describes how two brothers of a wealthy ex-model inherited huge sums from their sister, Janet Baird, who had died without a will https://www.standard.co.uk/hp/front/found-longlost-brother-of-exmodel-who-left-ps4m-7205018.html.

News

These are newspaper headlines that illustrate law in real life.

Link to Practice

What is a friendly society?

The following link to the Foresters Friendly Society describes how friendly societies work, including their tax status https://www.foresters-friendlysociety.co.uk/about-us/what-is-a-friendly-society/.

Link to practice

These are useful tips on how procedures work in practice.

1.4 Summary

(1) For an effective *donatio mortis causa* to be created, three requirements must be met:

- the gift is made in contemplation of death;
- it is made on the condition that it is perfected on the death of the donor and is revocable until that time; and
- delivery of the subject matter or sufficient evidence of title amounting to parting with dominion.

Chapter Summaries

At the end of each chapter the key points are summarised, allowing you to reinforce your understanding before moving on to study the next topic. The summaries can also be used for quick revision.

Francis — Hilary
Deirdre — Paul
Lisa

Figures

Figures have been designed to help define complex issues and clearly illustrate key concepts.

Reflective Questions

Consider how relevant the test in ***Banks v Goodfellow [1870]*** is in the 21st century. Is it a straightforward and practical test for lawyers to apply or should the more sophisticated approach in **MCA 2005** be used?

Is the rule in ***Parker v Felgate [1883]*** a helpful way to deal with testators whose mental capacity varies from day to day? Are there any risks?

Reflective Questions

All course books contain reflective questions, positioned at key points throughout the text. These allow you to take time to reflect on what you have learnt, ensure that you have understood the concepts, and contextualise your learning.

Case Study

Greenacre

A house called Greenacre is given to John absolutely. Later in the will, Greenacre is given to trustees to hold on trust for John for life and then for John's children. The residue of the will is given to Sheena. John outlives the testator and, when he dies, he has no children.

The rule states that in this situation, where the trust of the property fails (when John dies childless), the property will pass to the beneficiary who was given the initial absolute gift. Greenacre would pass to John (and his estate on his death) and not pass to the residuary beneficiary, Sheena.

Case Study

An example will be used to contextualize the situation to explore outcomes of legal concepts and real life situations.

Online Resources

For Students:

To access the online resources that have been developed to support this textbook, please visit https://cilexportal.cilexgroup.org.uk/CILEX-Education/Student-Materials.

For Lecturers:

Please contact publishing@cilex.org.uk to request access.

This edition states the law as it is believed to be at January 2024, although in some areas later changes may have been incorporated.

Preface

Welcome to the fascinating topic of succession. In your studies you will find that this area of law mixes detailed statute law with some colourful case law. The **Wills Act 1837** dates from the year Queen Victoria came to the throne and although it has been amended a number of times, its core approach to the rules for making wills has been retained. Other key statutes you will encounter include the **Administration of Estates Act 1925** which deals with the rules on how property is distributed on intestacy (deaths where there is no will) and the **Inheritance (Provision for Family and Dependants) Act 1975** which allows claims in the courts by certain categories of relatives and dependants who believe that they have not received a fair share of an estate under a will or under the rules of intestacy. Key cases which you will study include ***Banks v Goodfellow [1870]*** which sets out the basic test for assessing whether or not a testator has sufficient mental capacity to make a will.

Despite the current focus of the law on 19th and 20th century statutes and case law, change is coming in the law of succession. The Law Commission's Consultation Paper *Making a will* (Consultation Paper 231) http://www.lawcom.gov.uk/project/wills/#related was published in July 2017 and has made wide- ranging proposals. The key proposals are discussed in this textbook. Students are strongly recommended to read the consultation documents and consider whether or not they agree with the proposals discussed.

The consultation considers the possible benefits and problems which could arise if the law were changed to allow **electronic wills**. Advantages include making it easier for testators to make wills and change them in a world where carrying out complex transactions online is increasingly common. Testators with limited capacity may well find them easier to take advantage of. Difficulties include validating electronic signatures and witnessing documents, as well as issues relating to long-term electronic storage. The issue of forgery would need to be addressed.

In October 2023 the Law Commission launched a supplementary consultation paper focussing specifically on electronic wills. It also reviewed whether the rule that entering into a marriage or civil partnership automatically revokes (ends the validity of) a will should be changed to reflect concerns over "predatory marriages" and to protect the children of first marriages. For further details see https://lawcom.gov.uk/project/wills/.

Contents

Table of Statutes

Bill before Parliament

Table of Secondary Legislation

Code of Conduct/Practice Rules

Table of Cases

Australian cases

Irish case

New Zealand case

CHAPTER 1

Introduction to the Law of Succession

Aims of the Chapter:

By the end of this chapter, you should be able to:

- explain what succession means;
- define technical terms relating to wills and succession that you will come across in this textbook;
- explain the circumstances and property types that wills or the intestacy rules cannot give away;
- explain a *donatio mortis causa*.

1.1 Succession

> "Live every day as if it were your last and one day you will be right."
>
> Anon

This textbook deals with death and its aftermath. It does not consider religious and philosophical questions relating to an afterlife, which are inherently uncertain. Instead, it explains how the law of England and Wales governs the transfer of property from the dead to the living.

Underlying the law of succession is a key principle of the law in England and Wales: testamentary freedom. Under this principle, everyone is entitled, but not forced, to state who they want to inherit their property on death, usually through a written will. Succession in these circumstances is described as **testate**. This principle has been weakened by the **Inheritance (Provision for Family and Dependants) Act 1975** (see **Chapter 11**), which allows those who are dependent on the person who has died to go to court to claim a share of the deceased's property, but it is still fundamental to English law. By contrast, in other countries, such as France or Spain, the law dictates that large proportions of a person's assets **must** pass to their relatives, regardless of the wishes of that person.

A will is a written document made by the testator before death that is intended to reflect their wishes as to which relations or other beneficiaries will inherit their property. Making a will does not hasten death (although it does inevitably follow!), and in many cases the testator will live for many years afterwards. In this time, the testator's assets and family circumstances may change radically. Nonetheless, the will must be applied to the changed circumstances on death and is described as "ambulatory" as a result. Much of the complexity of will drafting arises from the implications of this characteristic. Those who draft wills attempt, so far as they can, to provide for likely changes in the testator's circumstances and family between the date of the will and the date of death.

Of course, the best way to cater for future changes is to make a new will as circumstances change – for example, when entering into a new relationship, on the birth of a child, on the death of an existing beneficiary, changes in finances, and so on. Consequently, a person is perfectly entitled to change the terms of their will as many times as they like before they die, provided that they still have the necessary legal capability to make a will. The law lays down strict requirements not just for anyone making a will but for anyone intending to amend or revoke an existing will, as will be seen later.

Where someone dies without a will, the law of England and Wales states that their relatives should benefit in fixed proportions. Succession is described here as **intestate**. Where a will fails to deal with all the person's property, a **partial intestacy** occurs under which the terms of the will are carried out and remaining property is distributed among the deceased relatives in the same fixed proportions as a full intestacy.

1.2 Technical terms

To aid your understanding of the law of succession, here is a list of the main technical terms you will come across during your reading of the textbook.

(1) A **will** sets out a person's instructions as to how they want their property to be disposed of on their death.

(2) A **testator** (female: **testatrix**) is the person making the will.

(3) A **codicil** is a document which makes small changes to a will and is executed in the same way as a will.

(4) An **executor** (female: **executrix**) is a person appointed by the will to deal with an estate. An executor is responsible for collecting in the deceased person's assets, paying their debts and transferring their assets to the beneficiaries named in the will.

(5) An **administrator** (female: **administratrix**) administers the estate where there is no executor, the named executor is unwilling or unable to act, or the person has died intestate.

(6) **Personal representatives** (PRs) is the collective name for executors and administrators.

(7) A grant of **probate** is a court order obtained by the executors to enable them to administer the estate.

(8) A grant of **letters of administration** is a grant obtained by the administrators to enable them to administer the estate.

(9) A **civil partner** is a person who has entered into a formal civil partnership with another person under the **Civil Partnership Act 2004** (**CPA 2004**). Before 2 December 2019, only same-sex couples could register as civil partners but under the **Civil Partnership (Opposite-sex Couples) Regulations 2019** persons of the opposite sex may now enter into a civil partnership as an alternative to marriage. A civil partner has the same rights on the death of the other civil partner as a widow or widower on the death of their spouse.

(10) A **power of appointment** is a right which may be given to a beneficiary under a will to decide who should receive property of the testator.

1.3 Property that wills or the intestacy rules cannot give away

While this textbook concentrates on the rules relating to the transfer of property under a will or under the intestacy rules, you must always bear in mind that not all property in which a deceased person might have had an interest at death is capable of being dealt with in that way. So, even though making a will is a vital step in ensuring that someone's wishes are met, not everything that a person apparently "owns" can be disposed of by will. There are certain types of property, or interests in property, that will pass on death according to different rules and irrespective of whether a person makes a will or not. Also, there are some alternatives to giving away property on death other than by making a will.

These situations are discussed in the following paragraphs. As you read through them, there is one important practical point worth mentioning. Just because certain property in which the deceased had an interest is not capable of being given away by will or passes irrespective of whether or not there is a will, it does not necessarily mean that such property escapes any claim by the government for inheritance tax. In other words, dealing with property in any of these ways will not necessarily save tax on someone's death.

1.3.1 Donatio mortis causa

A *donatio mortis causa* (plural: *donationes mortis causa*) is a conditional gift made in contemplation of death and which is only perfected (completed) on death. Suppose, for example, your Aunt Baljeet believes she is dying. She knows that you have always admired her ring and hands it over to you saying "I am going and don't need this any more – when I am gone it is yours." When Baljeet dies, the *donatio mortis causa* is completed and it becomes valid.

To establish a valid *donatio mortis causa* three requirements must be met, according to Lord Russell CJ in ***Cain v Moon [1896]***.

(1) **Gift in contemplation of death**

The donor must be contemplating death in the near future from some particular reason which they believe to be impending (approaching) (***Re Craven's Estate (No. 1) [1937]***). The actual death may come later than anticipated. In ***King v Dubrey [2015]*** the Court of Appeal held that, for a *donatio mortis causa* to be established, a donor had to be contemplating her own death. However, that requirement was not satisfied just because an elderly donor was approaching the end of her natural life span but did not have a reason to anticipate death in the near future from a known cause. The case involved an 81-year-old aunt who presented her nephew with the title deeds to her unregistered house, saying: "This will be yours when I go." He claimed that her use of the words and the way she looked at him made it clear that she knew that her health was failing and that her death was approaching. The court found that, while it was obvious that most of her life was behind her, there was no evidence that she was suffering from any specific illness. It could not be said that she was contemplating her imminent death at the relevant time. There was no reason why she should not have gone to her solicitors and made a new will. If she had taken that course, the solicitors would have ensured that she understood the consequences of the new will. To have upheld what she had said and done as a *donatio mortis causa* would be to bypass all of the safeguards provided by the **Wills Act 1837**. The Court of Appeal held that ***Vallee v Birchwood [2013]*** (where the donor died four months after the gift) had been wrongly decided because the donor in that case had not been contemplating death in the near future from a known cause.

The evidence of this belief by the donor may come from their words, for example "I am done for" (***Re Lillingston [1952]***). Alternatively, they may be inferred if they are made during a last illness shortly before death, as in ***Gardner v Parker [1818]***.

It is not necessary that the donor actually dies from the illness which they expect to be fatal. In ***Wilkes v Allington [1931]*** the donor knew he was dying from cancer but, in fact, died from pneumonia – the gift was valid.

(2) **Gift is conditional on donor's death**

The gift must be distinguishable from an *inter vivos* (lifetime) gift where the intention is that the gift is immediate and absolute. The court will look at the circumstances at the time the gift was made. For example, if property is handed over during the last days of a donor's final illness, it is more likely to be treated as a *donatio mortis causa* (***Gardner v Parker [1818]***).

Since the gift is conditional on death, the gift will take effect retrospectively from the date of the gift, once the condition, death, has taken place. The donor must have intended that the gift be unconditional on death (***Re Beaumont, Beaumont v Ewbank [1902]***). If the donor recovers from the specific illness or threat of death which they are fearing (such as a particular air journey) the gift will be revoked.

(3) **Donor must "part with dominion"**

This means that the subject matter of the gift must be physically handed over or its means of control. A simple handover of an item rarely causes problems but the issue of the means of control can cause more difficulty. In ***Reddel v Dobree [1839]*** a cash box was handed over but the key was retained by the donor. Here, the means of control did not pass to the donee and the gift was not valid. By contrast, in ***Woodard v Woodard [1995]*** the keys to a car were handed to the donee. Although the donor retained a duplicate set of keys, his words (a few days before his death from cancer) "you can keep the keys, I won't be driving it any more" were sufficient to indicate that he intended to part with dominion over the car.

Gifts of bonds, insurance policies and National Savings certificates can be made as the paper documents are needed as essential items of title. In ***Birch v Treasury Solicitor [1950]*** bank and Post Office passbooks were handed over to one donee as gifts to her and her husband. She was treated as having received her husband's share as his agent – the couple were treated as a single entity.

Difficulties have arisen over gifts of land. Owners of land who are approaching death and want to make a gift of it will rarely have the time to complete the normal conveyancing and Land Registry documentation required to transfer the title. In ***Sen v Headley [1991]*** the Court of Appeal considered a gift by the donor of the keys to a steel box. The donor had said "the house is yours . . . You have the keys. They are in your bag and the deeds are in the steel box." It held that the PRs held the house on a constructive trust for the donee. In ***Vallee v Birchwood [2013]*** the donor gave the deeds to the donee, together with the house keys, although he continued to live in it. The court held that he had parted with the means of transferring the house elsewhere and this was enough to show that he had parted with dominion

Key cases

Can there be a *donatio mortis causa* of registered land?

In ***Sen v Headley [1991]*** and ***King v Dubrey [2015]*** the land which was being given was unregistered. The title deeds were therefore required in order to carry out any transfer of ownership (the Land Registry would subsequently need them in order to turn it into registered land). The situation is different in the case of registered land. The Land Registry now holds all the essential documentation and no longer issues land or charge certificates following transfers of land. It seems unlikely that handing over the title information document (a short document provided by the Land Registry after land is transferred) would be enough to show that the donor had parted with the means of transferring ownership.

(4) **Gift is given to an agent of the donee**

Gifts may be handed over to an agent of the donee. In ***Mills v Shield [1948]*** the donor gave a parcel of share certificates to a priest to be passed on to the donee. The gift will not be a valid *donatio mortis causa* if the donor gives the item to the **donor's** agent – for example, their employee (***Trimmer v Danby [1856]***).

1.3.2 Joint property

Property, whether it is land or personalty (such as a bank account), held by a co-owner under a beneficial joint tenancy will pass automatically to the surviving joint tenant and is therefore unaffected by the will or the intestacy rules. A joint tenancy can be severed *inter vivos*, thereby converting the holding to a beneficial tenancy in common which can then be disposed of by will. However, a joint tenancy cannot be severed by a statement in the will itself.

1.3.3 Life assurance policies and pension scheme benefits

Money arising under policies of life assurance can be directed to a third party with the minimum of formality. Under **s11 Married Women's Property Act 1882** (as amended), the policyholder can create an implied trust in favour of the spouse or civil partner and/or children. Alternatively, to benefit others, an express trust of the policy proceeds may be declared.

In these cases, effectively, the money belongs to the beneficiaries under the trust from the date of the declaration and does not form part of the estate of the deceased at death. So, it cannot pass by the deceased's will and, instead, the proceeds go directly to the beneficiaries. The money is not, therefore, available for the payment of the debts of the deceased (***Re Flavell [1883]***). Such policies may be set up to provide cash to pay a mortgage or inheritance tax. Where a policy is taken out purely to benefit the beneficiaries, since the policy money is paid on proof of death, the money may be paid out without the need for a grant of representation that is usually required before assets can be obtained under a will.

This applies only to policies of life assurance assigned to or directed to be held in trust for a third party. Not all such policies are dealt with in that way, so if the deceased had taken out a policy on their own life without having assigned the benefit or imposing a trust, the proceeds will be paid by the life assurance company to the PRs. Those proceeds will devolve as part of the deceased's estate under the terms of the will (or under the intestacy rules if there is no will).

Many occupational pension schemes for employees are so drafted that the benefits do not form part of the employee's estate on their death. Instead, they are payable at the discretion of the trustees of the scheme. Consequently, unless paid to the deceased's estate, the amount payable is not dealt with by the deceased's PRs as property that passes under any will; instead it can be paid by the pension scheme trustees direct to one or more beneficiaries designated by the scheme. The scheme beneficiaries are usually within the immediate family of the employee, so the pension payment enables funds to go to those who might be financially dependent on the deceased employee without having to wait for a grant of probate or letters of administration. In most cases the employee will be asked by the trustees of the scheme to indicate their wishes as to whom payment should be made, though this is not binding on the trustees. This is sometimes referred to as a "nomination of a preferred recipient", but should not be confused with a "statutory nomination" of certain types of property.

1.3.4 Nominations

The **statutory nomination** removes the need for a will for limited types of property. A person aged 16 or over and entitled to certain types of investment can nominate a third party to receive them on their death. The property will then not vest in the nominator's PRs on death, but will be paid directly to the person nominated. Nominations can be made in respect of deposits in certain friendly societies and industrial and provident societies. The requirements vary according to the particular statutory provisions but, in general, there are four requirements for a valid nomination:

- it must be in writing;
- it must be signed by the nominator in the presence of one witness;
- the witness must attest; and

- the document must be sent during the lifetime of the deceased to the society holding the money.

Until the death of the nominator, the money remains their property and all benefits accrue to them. The nomination is revocable until death and lapses if the nominee predeceases the nominator (***Re Barnes [1940]***).

There is a limit on the amount; for example, **ss66–67 Friendly Societies Act 1974** allow up to £5,000 to be distributed by the nominator. The subject matter passes directly to the nominee on the death of the nominator, even if there is a valid will (***Bennett v Slater [1899]***).

Statutory nominations are no longer applicable to National Savings and trustee savings accounts.

Link to Practice

What is a friendly society?

The following link to the Foresters Friendly Society describes how friendly societies work, including their tax status https://www.foresters-friendlysociety.co.uk/about-us/what-is-a-friendly-society/.

A **non-statutory nomination** – for example, in respect of death benefits under superannuation pension schemes run by employers – operates as a direction to the trustees of the pension scheme to pay the benefits to the nominated person on the death of the nominator. Since the scheme makes payments on death discretionary, the direction is not binding on the trustees, although, in practice, they will follow it. This means that the payment is not subject to any will that the deceased may have made or to the intestacy rules, and is not subject to inheritance tax. Also, the payment will be made on proof of death without waiting for the grant.

1.3.5 Trust interests and property held in a fiduciary capacity

In addition to having an interest in a life policy trust as mentioned in **1.3.3**, a person may have an interest under a different type of trust. For example, Georgina might have an interest as a **life tenant** under a trust set up many years ago by her Uncle Harry. As such, she has a right to the income from the trust property or a right to enjoyment of property in the trust, such as a house, held by the trustees. When Georgina dies, her life interest will come to an end but the devolution of the property will be governed by the terms of the trust that Uncle Harry set up. In other words, it is not possible for Georgina to pass on the rights she has been enjoying to someone else named in her will (unless, exceptionally, the terms of the trust gave Georgina a power of appointment over the trust property which is capable of being exercised by her in her will).

Another type of trust is a **discretionary trust**, where a trust beneficiary has no right to receive anything as such from the fund but is merely the object of a discretion held by trustees to favour the beneficiary with trust property from time to time if they decide to do so. With this type of trust, the beneficiary clearly has nothing that can be left by will in any event.

Note that some trust interests **are** capable of passing by will and so can be given away on death. For example, suppose that under Uncle Harry's trust mentioned above, his nephew Norman is entitled to the trust capital after the death of Georgina, the life tenant. While Georgina is still alive, Norman is said to have a **remainder interest** under the trust (you may also see this described as a "reversion" or "reversionary interest"). As long as Norman's interest is vested when he dies (meaning that it is not capable of being defeated by any expressed condition or contingency, such as requiring him to still be alive when Georgina dies, or attaining a specific age which he has not yet reached) then his remainder interest is an asset that will pass under Norman's will if he dies before Georgina. So a gift in Norman's will of "all my estate to my wife" would be effective to include the vested remainder to which he would have been entitled on Georgina's death if he had still been alive at that time.

A person may also have an interest in property but not as someone who is beneficially entitled to it. Instead, they may own it in a fiduciary capacity, most commonly as a trustee or a PR, either alone or with others. In one sense the property belongs to them but in another it does not because, although they may own the legal title, they hold the beneficial interest for a third party. As such, the interest they hold is one that they are not free to dispose of by will.

1.4 Summary

(1) For an effective *donatio mortis causa* to be created, three requirements must be met:

- the gift is made in contemplation of death;
- it is made on the condition that it is perfected on the death of the donor and is revocable until that time; and
- delivery of the subject matter or sufficient evidence of title amounting to parting with dominion.

(2) Property held on a beneficial joint tenancy will automatically pass to the other joint tenant on death.

(3) Life assurance policies can be directed to a third party, so will not pass by will. Pension payments made at the discretion of the scheme trustees will not pass into the estate to pass by will.

(4) A person aged 16 or over who is entitled to certain investments on death can nominate third parties to receive them on death, provided that:

- the nomination is in writing;
- it is signed by the nominator in the presence of a witness;
- the witness attests;
- the documents are sent during the life of the deceased to the organisation holding the money.

(5) Trust interests are generally not capable of passing by will unless the deceased had a vested entitlement to a remainder in the trust fund.

CHAPTER 2
The Mind of the Testator

Aims of the Chapter:

By the end of this chapter, you should be able to:

- explain the test for assessing mental capacity to make a will and relevant case law;
- list the precautions to use when preparing a will;
- explain the requirement of intention to make a will, including knowledge and approval of a specific will;
- explain in what circumstances the courts will be prepared rectify mistakes made when drafting a will; and
- describe how evidence of force, fraud and undue influence is treated when assessing the validity of a will.

2.1 Introduction

An inevitable result of the freedom that English law gives to testators to distribute their assets as they wish in their wills is that, sometimes, they will make decisions that seem to others to be perverse or irrational.

Assessing whether a person has the required level of mental capacity is one of the most difficult parts of a private client lawyer's work. In most cases, of course, the client very clearly has mental capacity. Other elderly or disabled people quite clearly do not have the mental ability to respond to questions or to give clear instructions. The practical difficulties lie in assessing those whose mental state is marginal.

This chapter describes how English law assesses a person's mental capacity to make a will. It also describes the requirements that the testator had knowledge of, and approved the contents of, the will and that there was no fraud or undue influence.

NB Many of the cases dealing with mental capacity date from the 19th century or earlier. The language used in them to describe mental illness would make doctors and consultants in geriatric medicine today wince. In particular, the word "insanity" was commonly used to describe what would nowadays be considered a range of mental illnesses of varying severity.

2.2 Capacity to make a will

There are two aspects to the capacity to make a will. One is physical and simply relates to the age of the testator. The other concerns the testator's mental competence, which is not so straightforward to assess and, needless to say, is often the source of litigation when the validity of a will is disputed.

2.2.1 Age

The testator must be at least 18 years old (**s7 Wills Act 1837** (**WA 1837**)) unless they are entitled to make a privileged will (see **Chapter 4**). So, on the death of a minor, their estate passes in accordance with the rules of intestacy. A person aged 16 years and over, however, can make a valid statutory nomination of certain types of property (see **1.3.4**).

Law Commission Consultation Paper 231 – *Making a will*

The Law Commission proposes that the minimum age for writing a will be lowered to 16 years. It argues that this will tie in better with the **Mental Capacity Act 2005** and other legislation which treats 16-year-olds as being capable of making valid decisions in certain circumstances.

2.2.2 Mental competence

The courts have traditionally applied established case law to determine whether a person has testamentary capacity, that is, the necessary mental capacity to make a will. They still do so, despite the coming into force of the **Mental Capacity Act 2005** (**MCA 2005**) on 1 October 2007.

MCA 2005 deals with general aspects of a person's mental capacity to carry out acts, as well as dealing with a range of issues about the mental capacity of vulnerable people in a wide range of situations involving their medical treatment, finances, accommodation and other important aspects of their care. The legislation was not aimed specifically at those making wills. We should first consider what **MCA 2005** says about mental capacity generally.

s1 MCA 2005 sets out the following core principles which are relevant to someone making a will.

(1) A person must be assumed to have capacity unless it is established that they lack it.

(2) A person is not to be treated as unable to make a decision merely because they have made an unwise decision.

s2(1) MCA 2005 provides that a person lacks capacity in relation to a matter *if at the material time he is unable to make a decision for himself in relation to the matter because of an impairment of, or a disturbance in the functioning of, the mind or brain.* **s2(3)** provides that lack of capacity cannot be established just by reference to a person's age, condition or aspect of behaviour which might lead others to make unjustified assumptions about their capacity.

s3(1) provides that *a person is unable to make a decision for himself if he is unable to:*

(a) understand the information relevant to the decision;

(b) retain that information;

(c) use or weigh that information as part of the process of making the decision; or

(d) communicate his decision (whether by talking, using sign language or any other means).

s3(3) states that *the fact that a person is able to retain the information relevant to a decision for a short time only does not prevent him from being regarded as able to make the decision.*

Of most importance in looking at these principles is **s2(1)**, which refers to a person's ability to make a decision at the *material time* about a *matter,* and **s3(1)** which talks about understanding *information relevant to the decision.* Taken together, they mean that a person's capacity must be assessed with reference to the particular decision or act in question – and in our case, this means making their will.

The courts have looked at the provisions of **MCA 2005** in the context of the established test for mental capacity set out in ***Banks v Goodfellow [1870]***. This test requires that the testator must have understood:

- that they were making a will which would come into effect on their death and not some other document;
- the extent of their property;
- the moral claims on their generosity.

In addition, the testator must not have been suffering from an "insane delusion".

In ***Scammell v Farmer [2008]*** the judge held that the test in ***Banks v Goodfellow*** should be followed because the testatrix had died before **MCA 2005** had come into force. It was held that ***Banks v Goodfellow*** should be followed in any case since **MCA 2005** was not intended to supersede this test. In ***Re Walker [2014]*** the court directly addressed the question of the extent to which (if at all) **MCA 2005** replaced or superseded the test for mental capacity set out in ***Banks v Goodfellow***. The judge said that the outcome of the case *"may depend on whether the common law as to testamentary capacity* [i.e. ***Banks v Goodfellow*** and similar cases] *has been replaced by the provisions of the* **Mental Capacity Act 2005** *. . . My first impression of this issue . . . was that* ***Banks v Goodfellow [1870]*** *had indeed been replaced by the provisions of the Act, but* [counsel] *has now persuaded me that this is wrong"*. (Emphasis added.)

It is interesting to note that the judge himself was initially unclear as to what impact **MCA 2005** and ***Banks v Goodfellow*** had on each other, and that he changed his view in the light of comments provided by counsel during the hearing. In doing so, he seems to have followed ***Scammell v Farmer [2008]***.

Despite the fact that the main points dealt with in ***Elliott v Simmonds [2016]*** were mental capacity and the allocation of legal fees, the case made it all the way to the national press, with headlines featuring terms like "multi- millionaire", "mistress" and "secret daughter".

The facts were that the deceased (who, having left an estate of £2 m was technically a "multimillionaire", but only just) had made a will in 2010, leaving £100,000 to his daughter, Ruth, from a relationship which dated back long before his marriage. The rest of the estate passed to his wife and his children from the marriage.

In 2012, having fallen out with his wife and children (and having, by then, entered into a relationship with his "mistress", Bernice), the deceased made a new will in which the entire estate passed to Bernice.

The deceased died in 2014. Ruth, who stood to lose her £100,000 legacy, claimed that the 2012 will was invalid on the ground of lack of capacity. When the will was made, the deceased was gravely ill and was staying in a nursing home. The solicitor did not take any medical advice as to capacity and had only a very sparse attendance note of his meeting with the deceased (it was described in court as "more of an aide-memoire than an attendance note").

In considering whether the deceased had testamentary capacity, the court applied the test in ***Banks v Goodfellow [1870]***. No significant reference was made to the **Mental Capacity Act 2005** (**MCA 2005**). This was in keeping with the approach adopted in ***Re Walker [2014]*** suggesting that, at most, **MCA 2005** is being regarded by the courts as of secondary importance in assessing testamentary capacity.

The will was held to be valid.

There is no requirement that the testator should have a perfectly balanced mind, and a will can still be upheld even if the testator was moved by capricious, frivolous, mean, or even bad motives (***Fuller v Strum [2002]***).

Where a testator was held to have been incoherent and confused on the day they purported to execute a will, those arguing that the will was valid were held not to have discharged the burden of proving that they had testamentary competence (***Wood v Smith [1992]***). The testator's confusion had taken the form of not being able to remember names and addresses and not being clear about the names of the people he wished to benefit.

2.2.2.1 Making a will

A testator must be able to appreciate that they are making a will, as opposed to carrying out some other kind of transaction. They must understand that they are disposing of their property on death. It is not necessary to establish that they understand the precise **legal effect** of the provisions of the will.

2.2.2.2 The extent of their property

The testator must be able to recall the property they own. They do not need to have a perfect recollection and are not expected to produce a detailed list of every item owned. It is sufficient to establish this aspect of mental capacity that they should have a broad understanding of the extent of their property.

In ***Schrader v Schrader [2013]*** one of the deceased's sons, Bill, alleged his mother's will was invalid. He based his claim on a number of arguments, the first of which was lack of testamentary capacity. At the time she made the will, she was aged 96, and Bill claimed there was no evidence that she had been aware of the value of her house (given to the other son, Nick).

The court held that the will was rational on its face, giving rise to a presumption of testamentary capacity (see **2.3**). Further, the evidence of what the mother had been like showed that she did have testamentary capacity. She had been in possession of her faculties and she had been able to give clear and full instructions to the will-writer. Although she might not have known the value of her house, this was likely to be the case with many testators, and knowing the value of the house was not a requirement of capacity. It was highly likely that she knew it was her most valuable asset by a long way, and that was good enough. Although Bill failed on this ground, you will see in **2.6.2** how he got on with other aspects of his claim.

2.2.2.3 The moral claims on their generosity

Assessing the moral claims owed to another person may not be straightforward. Family members are usually beneficiaries under wills and generally the law expects a testator to have at least considered whether or not to leave them property in the will, particularly close family relatives. There may also be moral claims owed to close friends and those to whom the testator has given some financial support in the past.

Although the testator should **understand** the moral claims upon them, they do not have to distribute their estate to those who have a moral claim on them. As Sir James Hannen said in ***Boughton v Knight [1873]***, provided that a testator has mental capacity they *"may disinherit . . . the children, and leave property to strangers in order to gratify spite, or to charities to gratify pride"*.

This statement is clearly an illustration of the right to testamentary freedom, and is still good law, but it must now be considered in the light of the **Inheritance (Provision for Family and Dependants) Act 1975** (**I(PFD)A 1975**) (see **Chapter 11**). Consequently, a testator wishing to disinherit their children today must be advised of the consequences which could follow if their aggrieved children decide to make a claim under **I(PFD)A 1975**.

2.2.3 Cases illustrating how mental competence has been assessed in practice

The circumstances in which the mental competence of a testator has been doubted vary considerably. Ultimately, because the testator is no longer available to be questioned, the judge has to make a decision on the available evidence from friends, family and surrounding circumstances. The following cases illustrate how the courts have interpreted such evidence in the light of the ***Banks v Goodfellow*** test.

In ***In the Estate of Park (Deceased) [1954]*** the elderly and wealthy testator married for the second time. On the same day he made a new will which gave a £1,000 legacy (a significant gift in 1949) to his new wife and the remainder of his estate to his nephew and other beneficiaries, who were the same as those named in an earlier will. The new will was fairly complicated. The Court of Appeal held that while the capacity to marry and the capacity to make a simple will were effectively the same, a greater degree of mental capacity was required to make a more complicated will. The court held that the will was invalid and the intestacy rules would therefore apply.

In ***Ewing v Bennett [2001]*** a will was made by a solicitor for a woman who was very deaf, suffered from dizziness and was in the early stages of dementia. The Court of Appeal nonetheless held that the testatrix had the required level of mental capacity.

In ***Sharp v Adam [2006]*** the Court of Appeal held that the testator, who was suffering from severe multiple sclerosis, had *"crossed an imprecise divide"* and lacked the capacity to arrive at a reasonable judgment.

The court has now not only confirmed ***Banks v Goodfellow*** as the test for testamentary capacity, but has apparently extended it. In ***Key v Key [2010]*** a will was executed by a testator within a few days of his wife's death. He had been married to her for 65 years. In his judgment, Briggs J said:

"Without in any way detracting from the continuing authority of Banks v Goodfellow, it must be recognised that psychiatric medicine has come a long way since 1870 in recognising an ever widening range of circumstances now regarded as sufficient at least to give rise to a risk of mental disorder, sufficient to deprive a patient of the power of rational decision making, quite distinctly from old age and infirmity. The mental shock of witnessing an injury to a loved one is an example recognised by the law, and the affective disorder which may be caused by bereavement is an example recognised by psychiatrists."

Key v Key was subsequently followed in ***Re Wilson (Deceased) [2013]***, where the court held that at the time of making her will, the testatrix was suffering an affective disorder brought about by her deep grief at the recent death of her brother combined with her continuing fragile mental state and her grief following the earlier death of her husband. She did not have the mental capacity to make the will.

2.2.4 The lucid interval

Mental illness does not always result in a constant level of mental capacity. In some cases a patient may "have a good day" and experience a lucid interval. The following cases show how the courts have considered claims of a lucid interval.

In ***Cartwright v Cartwright [1793]*** the testatrix was insane from 1774 until 1793 when she died. She had made a will before the onset of insanity, but had destroyed it. In November 1793, she asked for a pen and paper and produced a well-written, clear will, leaving property to named relatives.

The will was valid. There was no evidence of mental disorder affecting the wording and the court accepted that it had been made in a lucid interval.

In ***Richards v Allan [2000]*** the testatrix was elderly and in poor health. The defendant suggested that the testatrix make a will appointing the defendant sole executrix and beneficiary. Instructions were given to a solicitor by the defendant and the will was drawn in accordance with those instructions. The will was signed when the sister of the testatrix was absent. On the day the will was signed, the testatrix was visited by her doctor and by her friend, and both found her to be confused.

The defendant claimed that the will had been validly executed in a lucid period between the visits. It was held that the will was not valid, as the state of confusion was continuing and it was not plausible that the will had been signed in a lucid interval.

In ***Simon v Byford [2014]*** the testatrix was an elderly lady suffering from mild to moderate dementia which varied to some extent in its effects: there were "good days" and "bad days". The will was challenged on the basis of lack of capacity. The court held that the will was executed on one of the testatrix's "good days" and that she understood the nature of a will, the arrangements she was making, the scope of her property and the claims other people had upon her. Despite her illness, she therefore had capacity on the day on which the will was made. It was held that the testatrix's failure to remember why she had made a previous will in the terms she had did not mean she lacked capacity.

The case highlights how dependent upon very precise facts decisions about lack of capacity are; even the presence of a recognised illness which would often affect capacity will not automatically lead to a finding of a lack of capacity.

2.2.5 Insane delusions

A delusion is a belief in something in which no rational person would believe. Where a delusion has had an influence on the gifts made in the will, it must be held fatal to its validity. In ***Banks v Goodfellow*** the testator had suffered from the delusion that he was being molested by evil spirits. The will was held to be valid, for the delusions had no bearing on the gifts in the will.

In ***Dew v Clark [1826]***, where the testator excluded his only daughter from benefit, the will was set aside as it was shown that he had had an irrational aversion to her from birth, including refusing even to see her for the first three years of her life. The irrational aversion had clearly affected the way in which he had made his will.

In ***Kostic v Chaplin and Others [2007]*** the deceased had previously made two wills and a codicil leaving all his property to his son. He made later wills in 1988 and 1989 leaving his entire estate of £8.2 m to the Conservative Party. He suffered from a delusional disorder that led him to believe that only the Conservative Party, through the then Prime Minister, Margaret Thatcher, could save the country from dark forces (and that his son was part of these forces). It was held, applying ***Banks v Goodfellow***, that the later wills were invalid. This meant that the son took the estate.

In ***Re Ritchie [2009]*** the deceased made a will leaving her £2.5 m estate to charity, disinheriting her four children. She was a difficult woman with some elements of obsessive compulsive disorder. The solicitor draftsman of the will, when giving evidence at the trial, said the deceased had told him that her sons were stealing from her and taking advantage, one of her sons was violent to her and had tried to throttle her, and her daughters never came to see her and gave her no help. These allegations were strenuously denied by the children. The judge accepted the allegations were delusions and, pronouncing against the will, accepted the deceased would not have disinherited her children if she had not suffered from these delusions.

In ***Ramsey v Ramsay [2015]*** the testator had made a will in 2008 after she had suffered a stroke. Her son, Roynel, had been living with her as a carer, but relations between the two had deteriorated. Her will was prepared by a solicitor and gave 50 per cent to one daughter, Ericka, whom she described as the most caring of her seven children. The other 50 per cent was split between the other six, with Roynel receiving a very small share, as did another daughter, Lova. The will gave reasons for her distribution: Roynel had *"bullied and harassed me and attempted to steal from me to the extent that the police have an Order that he is not to approach me again on pain of arrest"* while Lova had *"made provision for herself from my money in the past"*.

In 2007, Mrs Ramsay had undergone a formal assessment, the result of which suggested she was suffering from moderate to severe dementia. Despite this, the judge accepted, largely on the evidence of the solicitor who prepared the will, that the first three elements of the ***Banks v Goodfellow*** test – understanding that she was making a will, the extent of the property she owned and the claims that she ought to consider – were satisfied.

So, the case turned on the further requirement of the ***Banks v Goodfellow*** test, namely that Mrs Ramsay must not have been subject to any form of insane delusion which might have influenced the terms of her will. Mrs Ramsay had clearly explained her reasons for discriminating between her children, but was she suffering from delusions as a result of impairments of her memory and understanding produced by her dementia?

Expert medical evidence, which the judge accepted, said Mrs Ramsay was *"vulnerable to the development of false and unshakeable ideas about people"*. The expert also said: *"If these beliefs are found to be untrue, then it would be my opinion that they probably constituted insane delusions that arose in Mrs Ramsay as a consequence of the impairments . . . produced by her dementia."*

The judge said that whether or not the beliefs were true was a mixed question of fact and opinion, which the court had to determine. Ultimately, the judge decided that there was a rational basis for Mrs Ramsay's beliefs, even if she might have placed too much weight on certain incidents. Consequently, Mrs Ramsay's will was held to be valid.

The case is a reminder that making a will does not require capacity to be 100 per cent. So, even though the court accepted that Mrs Ramsay had been assessed as suffering from moderate to severe dementia, this did not necessarily mean that she lacked capacity to make her will at the time she executed it.

Where the testator has left a will together with several codicils, some testamentary documents could stand where it is shown that the delusion only affects, for example, one codicil. This approach of part deletion was applied in ***In the Estate of Bohrmann [1938]***. By a later codicil, the testator altered the direction of a charitable gift where he was under the delusion that the London County Council was attempting to take away his land. The remaining documents were admitted to probate.

2.2.6 The time to apply the test

As a general rule, the testator must have had testamentary capacity at the time they executed the will although, where a will has been drafted by a solicitor, under the rule in ***Parker v Felgate [1883]*** a testator can be regarded as having sufficient mental capacity if:

- they had capacity at the time they gave instructions to the solicitor for the preparation of the will; and
- the will was prepared in accordance with the instructions; and
- at the time of executing the will, they were capable of understanding, and did, in fact, understand that they were executing a will for which they had previously given instructions.

This rule was extended in ***In the Estate of Wallace [1952]*** to apply to a will drafted by a solicitor on the basis of a client's **written** instructions. In ***Battan Singh v Amirchand [1948]*** the Privy Council warned that the rule in ***Parker v Felgate*** should be applied with caution, especially where the testator was relying on a third party to convey their instructions to the solicitor.

The rule in ***Parker v Felgate*** was considered in ***Perrins v Holland and Others [2010]*** by the Court of Appeal. Here, the testator had given instructions in April

2000 but did not execute the will until September 2001, by which time he had lost capacity. The rule was approved and the *"usual preference of the court . . . to uphold transactions"* was affirmed and the will was held to be valid.

Reflective Questions

Consider how relevant the test in ***Banks v Goodfellow [1870]*** is in the 21st century. Is it a straightforward and practical test for lawyers to apply or should the more sophisticated approach in **MCA 2005** be used?

Is the rule in ***Parker v Felgate [1883]*** a helpful way to deal with testators whose mental capacity varies from day to day? Are there any risks?

2.3 The burden of proof and presumptions relating to mental capacity

Traditionally, the propounder of the will (i.e. the person, usually the executor, seeking to have it admitted to probate) had the **legal burden of proof** to establish the existence of capacity. However, two rebuttable presumptions were applied which affected the **evidential burden**.

(1) **Rational will**

If a duly executed will appeared rational (i.e. it contained nothing out of the ordinary or unexpected), capacity was presumed. Only if evidence was produced by the will's "attacker" to rebut the presumption did the propounder then have to prove capacity.

(2) **Continuing mental state**

If the testator generally lacked capacity (e.g. as a mental patient), it was presumed that this state of affairs continued up to the time when they made the will (the presumption of continuance). Therefore, the propounder had to rebut the presumption by showing that the testator had either recovered by the time the will was executed, or that the will was made during a lucid interval.

However, **s1(2) MCA 2005** now states that a person is *presumed to have capacity* unless it is established that they do not. So, the onus of proving lack of capacity is now on the person who alleges it in all cases, although evidence of lack of capacity in other areas and also, perhaps, the irrational terms of a will may make it easier to prove in some cases than in others.

In ***Burgess v Hawes [2013]*** the Court of Appeal said that strong evidence was required to find that a testatrix lacked testamentary capacity when an experienced solicitor had prepared the will and contemporaneously recorded his view that she had capacity. The case arose as a result of one of her children being omitted from a will.

The court said it should not too readily upset, on the grounds of lack of mental capacity, a will that had been drafted by an experienced, independent lawyer. In this case, the solicitor was independent and experienced in drafting wills. His attendance note stated that the testatrix was "*entirely compos mentis*". Such a will should be set aside only on the clearest evidence of lack of mental capacity. The court had to be cautious about acting on the basis of evidence of lack of capacity given by a medical expert after the event, particularly when that expert had neither met nor medically examined the testatrix, and particularly in circumstances when that expert accepted that the testatrix understood that she was making a will and also understood the extent of her property.

In this case there was evidence from a professor of old age psychiatry that the testatrix had been suffering from vascular dementia, which had impaired her ability to understand the moral claims to which she ought to give effect. Although it had been for the trial judge to decide what weight should be given to the evidence that she had heard, the Court of Appeal had doubts about whether the judge's findings justified the conclusion that the testatrix lacked the mental capacity to understand the claims to which she ought to give effect regarding the child whom she omitted from her will.

Although the Court of Appeal overruled the trial judge's decision on capacity, it supported the trial judge in finding on the facts that the will was invalid for want of knowledge and approval (see **2.6**).

2.4 Precautions

Where a person who is given instructions to prepare a will is concerned whether the testator has mental capacity, various precautions are suggested in ***Kenward v Adams [1975]***.

It is recommended that they should have the client examined by a doctor who, ideally, should prepare a written report on the client's condition. The will should be witnessed by medically qualified persons (hospital rules may not permit this, but may provide for an administrator to act as witness). Finally, the person who prepared the will should prepare a full file note of the circumstances. In this way, evidence of the testator's mental capacity will be available if the issue should be raised after their death.

In ***In the Estate of Ellen Jane Wilkes (Deceased) [2000]*** the applicant claimed that his mother was not of sound mind when she made her will, that she did not know or approve the content of the will, or that it was made under the undue influence of the first defendant.

The testatrix was elderly and in poor health. Before the will had been signed, the solicitors had contacted the testatrix's general practitioner, and had obtained a letter confirming that she was of sound mind and that she would understand the implications and effect of signing her will. It was held that the testatrix was of testamentary capacity when the will was made. There was no finding of undue influence and the applicant's claims were dismissed.

The courts use the term "Golden Rule", a phrase first used by Templeman J in ***Kenward v Adams***, when referring to the duties of practitioners in doubtful capacity cases. In addition to obtaining the medical approval mentioned above, solicitors should ensure that:

- they discuss any previous will with the client and the reasons for wanting to change its terms; and
- they take instructions in the absence of anyone who stands to benefit or who may have some influence over the testator.

While non-compliance with the "Golden Rule" does not mean that the will is invalid, in ***Cattermole v Prisk [2006]*** it was observed:

"This 'Golden Rule' provides clear guidance as to how, in relevant cases, disputes can be avoided, or minimised (with the material relevant to the determination of the dispute contemporaneously recorded and preserved). The 'Golden Rule' is not itself a touchstone of validity and is not a substitute for the established tests of capacity and of knowledge and approval."

Similarly, in ***Allen v Emery [2005]***:

"It is undoubtedly a desirable precaution, and one which can save a great deal of trouble in the future, for a solicitor to observe the 'Golden Rule' where there is the possibility of dispute as to testamentary capacity. Failure to do so, however, is not in my judgment determinative; . . . Ultimately, capacity is a question of fact like any other which the Court must decide on the evidence as a whole."

Clearly, complying with the rule provides contemporaneous medical evidence which may assist in the avoidance of a dispute, or minimise the chance of a dispute arising.

Key v Key [2010] (see **2.2.3**) shows that the ability to make rational decisions can be affected by mental disorders, such as the effects of bereavement, which might not be easily recognised by lawyers and non-medical professionals. This can make it increasingly difficult for practitioners to realise that they are dealing with a case where they should follow the "Golden Rule", particularly if the will, as in ***Key v Key***, is a rational one. One aspect of this case was the criticism made by the trial judge of the way in which instructions were taken. In giving his judgment, Briggs J said:

"[A] *significant element of responsibility for this tragic state of affairs lay with the solicitor who accepted instructions for the preparation of* [the will] *from an 89-year old testator whose wife of 65 years' standing had been dead for only a week, without taking proper steps to satisfy himself of Mr Key's testamentary capacity, and without even making an attendance note of the meeting.*"

The solicitor in question had seen the testator a few months before when dealing with the dissolution of his farming partnership and so saw no reason to question his client's capacity to make a will that appeared to be a rational one. However, the judge criticised the solicitor for failing to comply with the "Golden Rule", which "*greatly increased the difficulties to which this dispute has given rise*".

Is it always justified for judges to criticise practitioners in this way, given the practical difficulties, not to say the possible embarrassment, of having to raise questions of mental capacity with the client? In ***Wharton v Bancroft [2011]*** the High Court did at least acknowledge the practical difficulties in trying to follow the "Golden Rule". In making the will of a 78-year-old man, who had only days to live, the solicitor did not arrange for a medical practitioner to satisfy himself of the testator's capacity and understanding. Norris J considered that, in this particular case, the solicitor had acted correctly in making his own assessment of his client's testamentary capacity and then proceeding to make the will. He said:

"*I consider the criticism of* [the solicitor] *for a failure to follow 'the Golden Rule' to be misplaced. His job was to take the will of a dying man. A solicitor so placed cannot simply conjure up a medical attendant. He must obtain his client's consent to the attendance of and examination by a doctor. He must procure the attendance of a doctor (preferably the testator's own) who is willing to accept the instruction. He must make arrangement for any relevant payment (securing his client's agreement). I do not think* [the solicitor] *is to be criticised for deciding to make his own assessment (accepted as correct) and to get on with the job of drawing a will.*"

In ***Williams v Wilmot [2012]*** the court considered if the testator's last will was invalid on the ground of lack of testamentary capacity. A feature of the case was its consideration of the weight of evidence available, both from medical experts and the testator's solicitor.

The testator (T) made a will in December 2003 in which the claimant, C, was entitled. In January 2007, solicitors, who were not T's normal solicitors or local to him, were requested to attend T to take instructions and prepare a new will. They commissioned a medical report from a doctor, who was not T's usual GP but someone who practised some way away. His report, as the trial judge commented, ran to just six lines and said:

"I have seen and carried-out a mental state examination and assessment of capacity and cognitive function on [T] *at 6.15 pm on 5 January 2007.*

It is my opinion that [T] *does not suffer from any significant, depressive or dementing illness. He has in my opinion the mental capacity to make a new Will and understands the consequence of his actions. I understand that you will arrange to see* [T] *shortly. I await your further instructions on his behalf."*

The new will was subsequently executed by T on 19 January 2007 and benefited D, who was T's carer.

Meanwhile, T's normal solicitor, Mr B, had become aware of T's declining mental state and spoke to T on 29 January 2007. Mr B sought to register an enduring power of attorney that T had previously executed and further examinations of T were carried out, first by T's own GP and then shortly after, on 7 February 2007, by a consultant psychiatrist. The psychiatrist's examination was very thorough and his diagnosis was that T was suffering from dementia with prominent disturbance in his memory: "*His history, current presentation and cognitive profiles are consistent with possible Alzheimer's type dementia.*"

Following T's death, C contested the 2007 will and sought an order granting probate of the 2003 will on the grounds that T lacked capacity to make the 2007 will.

The court decided that it should place great weight on the contemporaneous evidence of T's normal solicitor, Mr B, who had assessed T's capacity, considering it to be of more value than the six-line report provided by a medical professional before the 2007 will was executed. The court said of Mr B he was *"the deceased's very experienced solicitor, who had a long term knowledge of, and relationship with, the deceased and therefore was able to reach a judgment concerning his deterioration over time . . . he was an experienced Private Client solicitor with a particular knowledge and expertise in the question of testamentary capacity in relation to the elderly derived from practical experiences over many years"*.

The court held that, despite the contemporaneous medical evidence obtained prior to the execution of the 2007 will, the medical evidence **overall** was sufficient to show on the balance of probabilities that T did not have capacity when he gave instructions for the preparation of the 2007 will or at the time it was executed. The judge said:

"The evidence which is available to me in the form of the consultant psychiatrist's report and the GP's report suggest inferentially that the deceased would not have

the relevant capacity at the time and that is corroborated by Mr [B]'s evidence concerning his conversation with the deceased on 29 January 2007."

So, the challenge to the 2007 will was successful. Of particular note are the trial judge's comments about the inadequacy of the initial medical report:

"The disturbing aspect of this report at any rate in arriving at a conclusion on the issue I am now considering is that whatever mental state examination was carried out is not described, much less is a sheet attached to the report which sets out the results that were obtained. No indication is given of what the examination entailed which enabled this doctor to arrive at an assessment of capacity. Perhaps most worrying, this doctor concludes that [T], as at the date of his examination, 5 January 2007, did not suffer from any dementing illness at all – a proposition I have difficulty in accepting having regard not merely to the conclusions reached by [T]'s own GP only a few days later and the contents of the report of the consultant psychiatrist who was retained to carry out a detailed examination a few days after that but also the evidence given by Mr [B]."

The case is a reminder to practitioners of the following.

(1) When commissioning a medical report to determine capacity to make a will, it is very important that the expert is properly briefed on the purpose of the report and what is required, and that the contents of the report make it absolutely clear what tests were applied together with their results.

(2) The court can attach weight to the knowledge and observations made by the lawyer in attendance in corroborating the evidence that may be necessary to establish the validity of the will. Hence, the keeping of contemporaneous attendance notes is vital.

This latter point is, of course, in line with what the Court of Appeal said in ***Burgess v Hawes [2013]*** considered in **2.3**.

2.5 Intention to make a will

A testator must also have the *animus testandi*, the general intention to make a will. The testator must intend that their wishes are to be put into effect after their death.

A person making provision for the disposition of their property on their death can be held to have had testamentary intention, even though they do not appreciate that the document they are making is capable of being admitted to probate in the English courts (***Re Berger [1989]***).

Testamentary intention will not be present if the dispositions contained in the document executed by the testator are not intended to operate immediately, as revocable, ambulatory provisions. In ***Corbett v Newey [1996]*** it was held that the only intention that the testatrix had possessed at the time she executed the purported will was to put her signature to a document that would have no effect unless it came to be dated by the solicitors on the happening of an event that might never occur. This did not even amount to a conditional will.

2.6 Knowledge and approval

As well as having the **general intention** to make a will, a testator must also have knowledge and approval of the will they actually sign, that is, **specific intention**.

Suppose a client tells you to write out a will for them and says that the will can be worded to say anything at all and they will sign it without bothering to read it. By signing, the client may have the general intention to make a will, but since they have no idea what it says, they lack specific intention because they cannot be said to have both known and approved the contents of the will. "Approved" means that the testator must understand the document and agree that it says what they meant it to say.

Note the following statements in ***Guardhouse v Blackburn [1866]*** as a guide.

(1) The court must be satisfied that the testator knew and approved the contents.

(2) *Prima facie*, execution by the testator indicates knowledge and approval unless there is evidence of suspicious circumstances.

(3) The testator must intend the document to operate as a will. Even if they knew and approved the contents, the document would be refused probate if it were not intended to take effect on death.

(4) Even if there is knowledge and approval, probate would be denied wholly or in part where there is evidence of fraud.

Before admitting the will to probate, the court has power to call for affidavit evidence from the witnesses and others instrumental in the preparation of the will as to the events surrounding its execution.

The court is unlikely to find that a testator knew and approved of only part of a will (***Fuller v Strum [2002]***). This case also illustrates the willingness of the court to find that a testator did have knowledge and approval of the contents of their will despite the fact that a handwriting expert stated that there was strong evidence that the testator's signature was a forgery.

In ***Re Rowinska [2005]*** the testatrix was aged 87 with poor spoken English. The claimant beneficiary had prepared the will and friends of his witnessed it. She was held not to have known and approved the contents, which left the entire estate to the claimant.

In ***Skillett v Skillett [2022]*** the court had to decide whether the testator, who had died aged 84, had the necessary testamentary capacity and knowledge and approval at the time of executing the will. Evidence was given by a single joint expert, who considered that, although the testator had suffered from some degree of cognitive impairment, he had not lacked capacity to make the will.

Considerable weight was given to many different factors, including that the solicitor who had drawn up the will was an experienced solicitor and had not seen any reason to doubt the testator's capacity; that the medical records tended to show that the hallucinations from which the testator had suffered had reduced with changes in medication, even though that had led to greater mobility issues; and that the testator's GP and others had been able to hold several conversations with him on different matters which the testator had appeared to understand and make valid decisions upon.

The court also considered whether the testator had the appropriate level of knowledge and approval of the will. The claimant (the testator's son) stressed the apparent inequality of the testamentary provisions in the will and argued his father could not have wanted that to happen and, therefore, he could not have understood the provisions of his will sufficiently to be said to have knowledge and approval of them.

The court had to decide whether the testator had known and approved the provisions in his will. He had done. The lack of mathematical equality at the time of death did nothing to undermine the rationality of the provisions which the solicitor had been instructed to incorporate at the time of making the will.

An oversight, or a change in circumstances following the making of a will, would not be enough to invalidate the will. The testator had known what was in his will and had approved it. The fact that its consequences following his death might not have been as he had expected them to be did not undermine that knowledge and approval.

The testator had possessed testamentary capacity and knowledge and approval of the will. Therefore, the will was valid, and probate would be granted.

2.6.1 Time of knowledge and approval

As a general rule, a testator must know and approve the contents of their will at the time of its execution. A will is valid despite lack of knowledge and approval at the time of execution, however, provided that:

- the testator knew and approved the contents of their will when they gave instructions; and

- the will was prepared in accordance with their instructions; and
- at the time of execution the testator understood that they were executing a will for which they had given instructions.

In effect, the rule in ***Parker v Felgate [1883]*** also applies in this context, just as it does to the issue of testamentary capacity, as was confirmed by the Court of Appeal in ***Perrins v Holland and Others [2010]*** (see **2.2.6**).

2.6.2 Burden of proof – suspicious circumstances

A person may have testamentary capacity but at the same time lack testamentary intention, as where the client in **2.6** signs a will that you have written for them without knowing its contents. Similarly, the necessary intention is lacking if a testator knows and understands what the will says but does not genuinely approve of the will in those terms, because, in reality, it reflects the wishes of a third party rather than the testator's own.

In all cases, the burden lies on the propounder of the will to prove intention. In practice, there is a **rebuttable presumption** that a testator who had the necessary capacity and who has duly executed the will did so with the necessary knowledge and approval of its contents. In such cases, those wishing to challenge the will must prove either that the testator lacked the necessary knowledge and approval because of a mistake (see **2.7**) or that they were induced to make the will (or a particular provision in it) by force, fear, fraud or undue influence (see **2.8**). Any part of the will of which the testator did not know and approve cannot be admitted to probate.

There is **no presumption** of knowledge and approval in the following two situations; if one of these is shown to apply by the challenger, the burden of proof is on the propounder.

(1) The testator is **blind or illiterate**, or the **will is signed by someone other than the testator on their behalf** (see **2.6.3**).

(2) There are **circumstances which *"excite the suspicions of the court"*** (***Barry v Butlin [1883]***). So, if the will substantially benefits the person who prepared it or a close relative of such a person, the propounder must remove the suspicion if the will is to be admitted. The degree of suspicion varies according to the circumstances of the case.

In ***Wyniczenko v Plucinska-Surowka [2005]*** the testatrix made a new will, differing from her previous one by excluding charitable bequests and a gift to her niece (the claimant), and leaving all her estate to the defendant. It became apparent that the defendant had drafted the will for the testatrix. The court held that if a beneficiary is involved in the making of the will, the court's suspicions are aroused. The defendant could not satisfy the court that the will reflected the testatrix's true wishes and so the will failed.

A contrasting case is ***Knight v Edonya [2009]***, where the testator made a will two days before he died. The will appointed the claimant as one of the executors and the claimant was given a share of residue along with the defendants in the case. The evidence showed that the claimant initiated the process of drawing up the will but, crucially, she was not present when the testator gave instructions for the will or at the time of its actual execution. The court held that none of the circumstances relied on by the defendants were such as to excite the suspicion and concern of the court as to whether the testator knew and approved of the contents of the will. Furthermore, the court was satisfied that the will truly represented the testator's testamentary intentions, and that he knew and approved its contents.

Sherrington v Sherrington [2005] concerned the will of a solicitor (S) and provisions made for his ex-wife and children as against those made for his current wife. The case deals with several issues. Here, knowledge and approval is considered.

S died in a car accident in October 2001 aged 56, having made a new will in September 2001 leaving all his estate to his second wife and making her the sole executrix of his estate. There was evidence that he still had a very close relationship with his first wife and particularly the three children from his first marriage. There was also evidence that the deceased had been unhappy in his second marriage. The claimants were his three children who claimed it was completely out of character for their father to leave them nothing in his most recent will. They therefore claimed that he lacked knowledge and approval of that will. The defendant was the second wife (D).

D suggested that they both made identical wills in September 2001 as they were due to go on holiday. Despite S being the senior partner of his law firm, there was evidence that the will was prepared by D's daughter. She had no legal qualifications but had worked in a clerical capacity for S.

The 2001 wills were poorly drawn up, with several errors and omissions, and not of the standard expected of an experienced solicitor. The wills were witnessed very shortly before S and D left to go away, so there was an element of urgency.

D bore the burden of proof that S knew and approved the contents of the will. Lightman J did not accept the evidence of D or her daughter. He was not satisfied on the balance of probabilities that S was ever informed of the contents of the will or had even read it. D therefore failed to discharge the burden of proof that S knew and approved of the contents of the will when he signed it.

D appealed and her appeal was granted. The Court of Appeal allowed the appeal reluctantly as they felt that the outcome of the case in the High Court, which held that it was an intestacy, was a much fairer outcome for the family. It was held that it was inconceivable that an experienced solicitor and businessman would sign his own will without reading it and approving it. The court sincerely hoped that the family would be able to put aside their differences and come to a mutually agreeable outcome.

In ***Schrader v Schrader [2013]*** (see **2.2.2.2**) Bill challenged his mother's will. He alleged that she lacked knowledge and approval when she made the will. The claim was largely based on the fact that Nick, the other son, had lived with his mother in her house and had cared for her after she had a fall. Also, Nick had been the one who arranged for a will-writer to attend his mother to make her last will, which gave him the house outright, unlike a previous will which had treated the two brothers equally. These and other matters were, it was claimed, factors which should excite the vigilance of the court, meaning that the burden of proving knowledge and approval was not to be presumed but should be on Nick and discharged only by cogent evidence of actual knowledge and approval on his mother's part.

The judge said there was sufficient evidence on which to find that knowledge and approval was established:

"I find that [the mother] *had the relevant knowledge of this will and approved its contents. I have identified the relevant inquiry – did* [the mother] *understand what she was doing and its effect (that is to say that she was making a will containing certain dispositive provisions) so that the document represented her testamentary intentions? I am quite satisfied that she did. The factors relied on (or at least some of them) are capable of arousing the court's vigilance, but I am satisfied that, that having been done, there is compelling evidence in favour of want of knowledge and approval . . . She gave coherent and rational instructions to the will-writer. She was apparently able to itemise small chattels as well as her house. She knew who her grandchildren were, and even most of their addresses. Her alterations demonstrated an attention to detail. The will was read to her and apparently understood, and it was not a difficult will to understand. All in all I am quite satisfied that the burden on Nick in this respect is fulfilled, and the will cannot be challenged for want of knowledge and approval."*

Having failed on that ground, it left Bill with just one more, which is dealt with in **2.8.3**.

Poole v Everall [2016] is a further example of the distinction between mental capacity and knowledge and approval. In this case, while the testator was in a mental health hospital (shortly after receiving £1,000,000 damages after being involved in an accident), his carer prepared a will for the testator, in which the carer received 95 per cent of the estate. The will was signed. Unsurprisingly, following the testator's death, the beneficiaries under an earlier will challenged this last will on the grounds of lack of capacity and/or lack of knowledge and approval.

Having looked at the medical evidence, the court held that the testator did have sufficient mental capacity to make the will.

With regard to knowledge and approval, the obvious circumstance giving rise to suspicion is that the will was prepared by the carer, who was the principal beneficiary.

Alongside this, the court heard that the carer had deliberately blocked communication between the testator and his solicitor, and between the testator and his family.

The carer was unable to discharge the burden of proof regarding knowledge and approval. He had not read the will over to the testator, or explained its terms. The court found that the will was therefore not valid.

2.6.3 Blind or illiterate testators or the will signed on the testator's behalf

The Registrar or District Judge can call for affidavit evidence to establish that the testator had knowledge of, and approved the contents of, the will. The evidence must show some overt act of acknowledgment or understanding on the part of the testator.

In ***Christian v Intsiful [1954]*** the testator, aged 86 and with eyesight so defective that he was almost blind, handed a document to someone who had been a solicitor's clerk and asked him to type it. He did so, and then gave it back to the testator who afterwards signed it and had it duly attested by two witnesses. The will was then placed in an envelope which was sealed and put into the custody of the court.

The court assumed that the testator was blind and therefore could not have read the will. The court then took account of the elaborate nature of the contents of the will and decided that the solicitor's clerk, who was not acquainted with the testator's life, could not possibly have devised the will. Given these two factors – the testator's poor eyesight and the elaborate nature of the will – the court concluded that the testator must have known what he was doing and declared the will to be valid.

Key Cases

Was the testator illiterate?

Students may assume that whether or not a testator was illiterate would rarely be in doubt. However, in ***Reeves v Drew [2022] EWHC 159 (Ch)*** there was a great deal of conflicting evidence from family and friends on this point which the judge had to consider. This case concerned allegations of undue influence over a self-made millionaire. Students may be interested to read the lurid facts of the case which clearly establish a cast of family members who could be the basis of a TV drama – see https://www.bailii.org/ew/cases/EWHC/Ch/2022/159.html.

2.6.4 Precautions

Where it is doubtful whether a testator knew and approved the contents of a will, it will assist the court in finding that knowledge and approval were present if it can be shown that the will was read over to the testator and that they understood it before signing. In the case of the blind or illiterate testator, the attestation clause in the will (see **3.5**) should be amended to show that this was done.

In a doubtful case, it is insufficient merely to read over the will to the testator. In ***Buckenham v Dickinson [2000]*** the testator was aged 93, nearly blind and totally deaf. The solicitor read the will over to him and asked him a few questions to see if he understood. The testator merely nodded or grunted in response. It was held that this was not sufficient. Open questions should be asked which demand more than the answer "yes" or "no". The grant was revoked and an earlier will admitted to probate.

The "Golden Rule" discussed in **2.4** and the precautions relating to capacity are also relevant to knowledge and approval.

2.7 Mistake

Knowledge and approval may be absent where the testator or the draftsman preparing the will has made a mistake. Mistakes take many forms, from signing the wrong document to clerical errors.

2.7.1 Mistake as to the whole will

In ***Marley v Rawlings [2014]*** a husband and wife each signed the other's will by mistake. The Supreme Court held that the will of Mr Rawlings (the testator) was valid, despite the fact that the document which he had actually signed contained his wife's wishes, not his own.

2.7.2 Mistake as to the words used

The mistake must refer to the words used and not to their legal effect. In ***Collins v Elstone [1893]*** a testatrix left two wills and a codicil to the first will. The second will, which disposed of a life policy, was prepared on a form which contained a printed revocation clause. When the document was read over to her, she objected, saying that she did not want the first will and codicil to be revoked. The person who prepared the will assured her that the clause referred only to the life policy and that to erase a part of the document could invalidate it.

The court refused probate to the first will and codicil in view of the effect of the revocation clause.

The testator is deemed to know and approve technical language used by draftsmen. Such language will be admitted to probate even though the draftsman was mistaken as to its legal effect.

The question to be asked in such cases is "Did the testator intend to use the words which appear in the will?" If so, the words must be admitted to probate with the rest of the will.

2.7.3 Mistake by the testator as to part of the will

Where the testator inadvertently fails to delete a printed clause in a will, they lack knowledge and approval of that particular clause. In ***Re Phelan [1972]*** the testator executed a home-made will dealing with all his property. Subsequently, he executed three printed will forms, each disposing of investments in unit trusts. Each form contained a printed revocation clause. There was no evidence to indicate the order in which the forms were signed, but the court accepted that the testator had never directed his mind to the printed clause in each form and admitted the will together with the three will forms to probate.

2.7.4 Mistake by a draftsman as to part of the will

This can arise through a slip or clerical error in inserting or omitting words; for example, in ***Morrell v Morrell [1882]*** the testator intended to give all his shares but the will stated "40" by mistake.

Courts have the following powers to alter a will:

- to **omit** words where the testator did not know of or approve the inclusion (see **2.7.3**);
- a statutory power to order **rectification** (correction) (see **2.7.5**);
- to **construe** the will as if certain words had been inserted, omitted or changed, if it is clear from the will itself that an error has been made (see **Chapter 14**).

2.7.5 The statutory power to rectify

s20(1) Administration of Justice Act 1982 (**AJA 1982**) gives the court a limited power to rectify wills and codicils.

If the court is satisfied that a will is so expressed that it fails to carry out the testator's intentions, in consequence:

(a) of a clerical error; or

(b) a failure to understand instructions, it may order that the will shall be rectified so as to carry out his intentions.

An application for rectification must be made within six months from the date a grant is first taken out, although the court has discretion to extend the time limit.

The power to rectify was considered in ***Re Segelman [1995]***, where the testator set up a trust by his will and provided that the residue was to be divided among needy members of his family. His secretary was to supply a list of the family members in question. The solicitor drafted the gift in such a way that the issue of any named family member who predeceased them would inherit their parent's share. The list contained the names of six family members and the issue of all but one. The will included the list of names, but provided that the issue of the sixth family member could inherit their share if they predeceased him, contrary to the testator's wishes. The question for the court was whether the error in the will was caused by clerical error.

It was held that the words *clerical error* in **s20(1)** included omissions from the will and a failure by the draftsman to understand the effect of the words used in the will. Chadwick J went on to say that he did not believe that **s20(1)** was confined to cases where *"the intended words of the testator"* could be defined with precision. He said that the jurisdiction extends to cases where the relevant provision of the will has been introduced (or in this case has not been deleted) in circumstances where the draftsman has not applied his mind to its significance or effect.

In ***Sprackling v Sprackling [2008]*** the court ordered rectification of a will in circumstances where the solicitor had incorrectly treated the words "farm" and "farmhouse" as interchangeable. Nonetheless, the testator's intention could be ascertained by the court despite the omissions in the solicitor's attendance note.

In ***Austin v Woodward and Another [2011]*** the court held that a solicitor, who had mistakenly inserted wording from a revised firm's precedent into a will that he was updating with the result that the will no longer reflected the testatrix's intentions, had made a clerical error that could be rectified under **s20(1)**. The solicitor had updated the will by simply inserting his firm's revised precedent wording without realising the effect that the new wording might have on the rest of the will. The outcome was that the testatrix's daughter did not receive an outright gift of the family home as the testatrix had intended.

Is it a clerical error if the draftsman does admit to considering the words used in the will but it then transpires those words do not give effect to what the testator clearly intended? In ***Kell v Jones [2013]*** a solicitor drafted a will which gave the residuary estate to "such of the beneficiaries . . . as shall survive [the testator] . . . in equal shares". Earlier clauses had given monetary legacies to family beneficiaries and to some charity beneficiaries. The solicitor had clearly understood the testator's instructions that she wanted the residue to be shared only by the family members and not by the charities. However, it was pointed out that the wording in the residuary gift entitled both the family and charity beneficiaries to share the estate. A claim by the solicitor to rectify the residuary gift was dismissed. The clause was a fresh clause drafted by the solicitor who therefore had to be taken to have considered the words that he chose to use, rather than just having inserted words in a mechanical way without proper consideration. He clearly knew what his instructions were and his evidence was that he thought he had achieved the testator's intentions by the words that he chose to use. Accordingly, the will's drafting was not attributable to either a clerical error or the draftsman's failure to understand his instructions, and so the court did not have the power to rectify under **s20(1)**.

In ***Marley v Rawlings [2014]*** (see **2.7.1**) Lord Neuberger, giving the unanimous judgment of the Supreme Court, said that **s9 WA 1837** is concerned with formalities for executing a will (see further **3.3.6**). Having established that what Mr Rawlings had signed was a valid will – even if it did not make sense because it contained his **wife's** wishes, rather than his own – the court was then able to consider the claim for rectification.

The fundamental issue was whether the court considered signing the wrong will to be a "clerical error" within **s20 AJA 1982**.

Lord Neuberger initially quoted from ***Bell v Georgiou [2002]***, where it was stated that a clerical error occurs when someone, who may be the testator himself, or his solicitor, or a clerk or a typist, writes something which he did not intend to insert, or omits something which he intended to insert. However, whilst accepting that clerical error could have a narrow meaning, Lord Neuberger said:

"[C]lerical error' is an expression which has to be interpreted in its context, and, in particular on the assumption that section 20 is intended to represent a rational and coherent basis for rectifying wills. While I appreciate that there is an argument for saying that it does nothing to discourage carelessness, it seems to me that the expression 'clerical error' in section 20(1)(a) should be given a wide, rather than a narrow, meaning."

According to Lord Neuberger, if necessary, the **whole** of a will could be rectified to give effect to what was the clear intention of the testator. In this case, the lawyer supervising the execution of the wills had, by his own admission in evidence, made a mistake when he gave the testator the wrong will to sign. He added:

"There was an error, and it can be fairly characterised as clerical, because it arose in connection with office work of a routine nature. Accordingly, given that the present type of case can, as a matter of ordinary language, be said to involve a clerical error, it seems to me to follow that it is susceptible to rectification."

Consequently, the Supreme Court directed that rectification could be made to the will that Mr Rawlings had signed by replacing the typed words that represented his wife's wishes with those contained in the document signed by his wife (and which he thought were in the will he signed). In this way, the will signed by Mr Rawlings would then contain the words which he assumed were there, so as to carry out his wishes.

Interestingly, Lord Neuberger also said that, even if the document that Mr Rawlings had signed was **not** a valid will, because either **s9(b) WA 1837** was not satisfied or he lacked knowledge and approval, the remedy of rectification would still have been available. In effect, rectification would convert an invalid will into a valid one.

While the outcome of ***Marley v Rawlings*** clearly reflects what was the obvious intention of Mr Rawlings and his wife, some commentators have suggested that the more flexible approach taken by the Supreme Court could lead to even more litigation over claims to uphold or amend wills. For example, suppose that the lawyer forgets to ask the testator to sign the will which the testator has previously approved in draft form, but **does** get the witnesses to sign. The unsigned "will" undeniably represents the testator's intentions but does not satisfy **s9 WA 1837**. The lawyer is clearly at fault. Lord Neuberger's judgment appears to suggest that a claim for rectification of the invalid "will" could now be made. If so, how would this work? Would the court be required to order that the "will" be admitted to probate as if it had been signed and thus properly executed? The lawyer has made a "clerical error", if Lord Neuberger's "wide" meaning of this term is correct, but is the statutory remedy of rectification available to ensure the testator's wishes are carried out despite the fact they never signed the "will" in accordance with what is required by **s9**?

Reflective Questions

Do you agree with Lord Neuberger's wide interpretation of "clerical error" in ***Marley v Rawlings***? Do bear in mind that the beneficiaries under the will which Mr Marley **should** have signed would have had a very strong claim against the solicitor for negligence if the Supreme Court had followed the Court of Appeal judgment ruling that the will could **not** be rectified. The solicitor's professional indemnity insurers were, no doubt, delighted by the judgment.

Do you think his flexible approach will encourage more claims to uphold wills which, until now, have been regarded as invalid because they have not been executed in accordance with **s9**? Is this fair to those who would otherwise be entitled under intestacy or under a previous (validly executed) will?

Do you think the law should insist on the requirements of **s9** being complied with in full in **all** cases? Should lawyers (and their insurers) be liable in negligence claims if they fail to ensure that **all** the wills which they draft are executed in accordance with **s9**?

Wills and succession cases rarely progress as far as the Supreme Court. ***Marley v Rawlings [2014]*** is therefore a particularly important case to study in some detail. The judgment is not particularly lengthy and every student should read it in full.

2.7.6 Rectification in preference to other courses of action

Where a will does not reflect the intentions of the testator as a result of a mistake by the solicitor who drafted it, the disappointed beneficiaries may be able to sue in negligence as well as apply for rectification under **s20(1)**. Claimants in negligence cases are expected to mitigate (minimise) their losses, and it was held by the Court of Appeal in ***Walker v Geo H Medlicott & Son [1999]*** that disappointed beneficiaries should first seek the remedy of rectification before suing in negligence. Only if a claim for rectification is not possible or is unlikely to be successful, should the beneficiary sue in negligence.

In ***Horsfall v Haywards (a Firm) [1999]*** rectification was considered to be unlikely to be successful because the proceeds of the estate had been sent to Canada and there was little prospect of recovering them even if the claim were successful.

2.8 Force, fear, fraud and undue influence

Sadly, the wide freedom given to testators to distribute their property to any of their friends and relatives has resulted in some cases where they have been subjected to physical violence or threats. In some instances, forgery of wills has taken place. A less obvious problem that can be harder to identify is that of undue influence. In all these circumstances, the will is treated as invalid if the person making the allegations is able to prove it.

2.8.1 Force or fear

Clearly, evidence of the testator making a will while subject to fear or force will mean that the will is invalid because they will lack genuine knowledge and approval.

2.8.2 Fraud

Examples of fraud include:

- inserting a clause into a will without the testator's knowledge before it is signed;

- forgery;
- deliberately misleading the testator by making false representations about the character of others to induce the testator to make or revoke gifts, or to exclude persons from a proposed will (***Re Edwards [2007]***);
- deliberately misleading the testator as to the content of the will as it is being read to them.

A further example is where a beneficiary has made a false statement to induce a gift in a will. In ***Wilson v Joughlin [1866]*** a woman who was already married pretended to be unmarried. The testator married her and the gift to her was omitted from probate. The remainder of his will continued to apply.

Fraud was alleged in ***Vaughan and Others v Vaughan [2002]*** where a testatrix signed her second will in circumstances which suggested that her signature had been forged. The court held that this allegation was untrue but that the testatrix did not have the required knowledge and approval.

2.8.3 Undue influence

Undue influence is something that overpowers the free will of the testator but does not change their wishes. It can be difficult to distinguish this from powerful persuasion. A person who is weak, mentally or physically, is more likely to be considered by the court to have been subject to undue influence. In ***Hall v Hall [1868]*** Sir J P Wild distinguished "persuasion" which *"appeals to the affections or ties of kindred, to a sentiment of gratitude for past services, or pity for future destitution"* from "pressure" which *"if so exerted as to overcome the volition without convincing the judgment, is a species of restraint under which no valid will can be made"*.

Where gifts are made by a vulnerable person during their lifetime to another person with whom they have a relationship of trust – for example, a patient making gifts to their doctor or a client making gifts to their solicitor – the courts will apply a presumption that there has been undue influence. No such presumption is applied by the courts in relation to gifts in wills. In ***Parfitt v Lawless [1872]*** it was held that there needed to be actual evidence of undue influence before probate could be refused.

In ***Carpeto v Good [2002]*** a claim of undue influence was considered in respect of the will of an elderly testatrix who left her property to her carer and her carer's husband. Although the testatrix was vulnerable, the court held that she had known that she was making a very generous gift to her carers and understood what she was doing. The unsuccessful claimants had to pay the beneficiaries' legal costs on the grounds that the beneficiaries should not have to pay to clear their names.

Undue influence was considered more widely in ***Royal Bank of Scotland v Etridge [2001]***, which dealt with the issue of undue influence inducing a spouse to agree to mortgage her share of the family home. The court held that the person who may be the subject of undue influence must receive independent advice not in the presence of the person applying the pressure. If independent advice is not given, the solicitor should refuse to act.

Killick v Pountney and Another [1999] is an example of a successful claim of undue influence. The court emphasised the importance of a solicitor taking instructions for a will in the absence of any potential beneficiaries.

The facts of ***Gill v Woodall and Others [2010]*** provide a good example of how the courts consider the issue of knowledge and approval as well as providing a situation where undue influence was also a relevant factor.

Mr and Mrs Gill were a Yorkshire farming couple who made mirror wills in 1993 leaving residue to each other, with a default provision if this gift failed to the RSPCA (a charity). Mr Gill died first, so when Mrs Gill died subsequently, the RSPCA stood to benefit. Nothing had been left in either will to the couple's only daughter, Dr Christine Gill, who therefore challenged her mother's will.

Mrs Gill's mental capacity was not in doubt. Instead, Dr Gill first claimed that her mother lacked knowledge and approval of the will's terms. Since the court accepted that it was suspicious that Mrs Gill had disinherited her only child in favour of a charity there could be no presumption of knowledge and approval. Therefore, the burden of proof fell on the RSPCA to establish that she did, in fact, know and approve the contents of her will.

At first instance, the evidence presented was enough to dispel the court's initial suspicion for a number of reasons, including the fact that the correct procedure for the will's preparation had apparently been followed by her solicitor and the will was short and clearly worded. So, the judge found Dr Gill's challenge on this ground failed because Mrs Gill had known and approved the contents of her will by properly understanding its terms.

However, Dr Gill had also challenged the will by alleging undue influence. For her claim to succeed, she would have to show something more than that her mother was advised or persuaded to make the will that she did. Instead, she had to show that her mother had been coerced into making a will that she did not really want to make. Here, the court held that Mr Gill had exerted such pressure on Mrs Gill into making a will that disinherited their only child in favour of the RSPCA that it amounted to coercion on his part. The court based its finding on a number of facts, including the following.

(1) Mrs Gill was a shy and timid lady who suffered from agoraphobia and anxiety disorder, leading to symptoms of extreme anxiety when taken outside her comfort zone (either her home or her car). This disorder meant that she would

have actively done whatever she could to bring the meeting at the solicitor's office to an end as quickly as possible, including executing a will that she did not agree with, in order to return home and feel safe.

(2) Mr and Mrs Gill's relationship was as a "traditional Yorkshire farming couple", where the wife would tend to defer to the husband who, in this case, was said to have had a domineering, bullying personality coupled with outbursts of fury.

(3) Mrs Gill was unusually highly dependent on Mr Gill for support and protection, and was afraid of Mr Gill withdrawing that support.

Accordingly, the court at first instance set aside Mrs Gill's will on the ground of undue influence, amounting to coercion by her husband, notwithstanding that she did not change her will in the 13 years between 1993 and her death in 2006 (not even after her husband died in 1999).

However, the RSPCA disagreed with the court's decision and so the matter was reconsidered by the Court of Appeal. Once again, the will was found to be invalid in favour of Dr Gill, but the Court of Appeal reached its conclusion on different grounds.

In the leading judgment, Lord Neuberger MR stressed that the facts of the case were exceptional (arising from Mrs Gill's unusual mental condition) and that the appeal judges were differing from the first instance decision on an unusual basis. The Court of Appeal agreed that the will was, indeed, invalid but its finding was that Mrs Gill had simply lacked both knowledge and approval when she executed her will. Contrary to the views of the trial judge, the Court of Appeal said that the available evidence could not justify his determination that Mrs Gill had the necessary testamentary intention. While the trial judge had been right to say that a *prima facie* case for knowledge and approval had been made out, he was wrong in concluding that the RSPCA had established it on the balance of probabilities, having regard to the nature and weight of the evidence.

Since the will failed because knowledge and approval had not been established, there was no need for the Court of Appeal to further consider the question of undue influence.

To return to ***Schrader v Schrader [2013]***, Bill has so far failed to have his mother's will declared invalid for lack of capacity (**2.2.2.2**) and in alleging lack of knowledge and approval (**2.6.2**). His claim also cited undue influence, and here the court did find in his favour. The judge set out a number of reasons why he thought the mother had made the will while subject to undue influence, including:

- her vulnerability;
- her dependence on Nick;
- the engagement of a will-writer with no prior contact with the family;
- the reason given to the will-writer for giving the house to Nick had been inaccurate, and its source was likely to have been Nick;

- there was no other reason why the mother would, entirely of her own volition, have wished to change her will in respect of the house;
- Nick's forceful personality;
- Nick's keenly felt view that his parents had not treated him equally with Bill;
- Nick had participated in considering the will but had sought to distance himself from that when giving evidence;
- Nick had not disclosed the latest 2006 will until steps were taken to prove the earlier 1990 will, indicating that he had been aware of, and had misgivings about, the circumstances in which it had been drawn.

"In all those circumstances I find that undue influence has been proved. I think that they require the inference that Nick was instrumental in sowing in his mother's mind the desirability of his having the house, and in doing so he took advantage of her vulnerability. It is not possible to determine any more than that the precise form of the pressure, or its occasion or occasions, but it is not necessary to do so. I am satisfied that this will results from some form of undue influence."

2.8.4 Gifts to CILEX members, solicitors and members of their staff

The **CILEX Code of Conduct** requires CILEX members to comply with nine core principles. The following are particularly relevant to the issue of gifts to CILEX members in wills:

2. Maintain high standards of professional and personal conduct and justify public trust in you, your profession and the provision of legal services.

7. Ensure your independence is not compromised.

Note also Outcome 7.1 – You must:

Not act or continue to act where there is a conflict of interest or a significant risk that a conflict may occur.

Under the **SRA Standards and Regulations 2019**, there are seven mandatory **Principles** which are intended to ensure that solicitors carry out their services for clients in the best possible way and without any form of abuse or malpractice.

The most relevant of the mandatory Principles applicable to the issue of gifts to solicitors and their staff in wills are:

You act:

- in a way that upholds public trust in the solicitors' profession and in legal services provided by authorised persons (**Principle 2**);

- with independence (**Principle 3**);
- with integrity (**Principle 5**);
- in the best interests of each client (**Principle 7**).

The **SRA Standards and Regulations** includes the **SRA Code of Conduct for Solicitors**.

Paragraph 6.1 SRA Code of Conduct for Solicitors deals with conflicts of interest and refers to **own interest conflicts**, which would include drafting wills where solicitors or their staff (or their families) would benefit. There is a prohibition on acting if an own interest conflict is identified.

The Solicitors Regulation Authority (SRA) has issued guidance on the **Drafting and preparation of wills** https://www.sra.org.uk/solicitors/guidance/drafting-preparation-wills/) for solicitors and their staff who are involved in the preparation and drafting of wills. It is not mandatory but the SRA may take it into account when exercising its regulatory functions.

Crucially, it states that where a client wishes to leave a gift "of significant value" to a solicitor or a member of their staff (or to their families), the will- drafter must ensure that the client has first taken independent advice.

Also dealt with are issues arising from:

- the potential appointment of the firm, or those in the firm, as executors;
- the management of the business of will preparation; and
- the storage of wills.

The **SRA Code of Conduct for Solicitors** is concerned with the **professional** (i.e. **ethical**) **issues** involved in solicitors making wills under which they benefit. Breach of the **SRA Code of Conduct for Solicitors** can result in a solicitor facing disciplinary action. However, what about the **legal implications** affecting the validity of the will and, in particular, the requirement that the testator must have knowledge and approval? Suspicious circumstances were alleged in ***Wintle v Nye [1959]***, where the beneficiary of the will was a solicitor.

The litigation was conducted in person by Colonel Wintle, a relative of the testatrix. The testatrix had instructed her solicitors to make a will leaving her large estate to relatives, with the residue to hospitals. The solicitor and a bank were the executors. In April 1937, the testatrix ordered the solicitor to make changes, making him sole executor and leaving the residuary estate to him. The will was drawn up in the solicitor's office. The solicitor had asked her to seek independent advice but she had not done so. Subsequently, a codicil was executed revoking, on the advice of the solicitor, certain annuities. This had the effect of increasing the residue. It was significant that the testatrix was not very bright and was unversed in business matters and that the will was complex, with the solicitor making little effort to ensure that she received independent legal advice.

Colonel Wintle lost at first instance and in the Court of Appeal, but the House of Lords allowed a challenge to the will and codicil on the basis that insufficient direction had been given by the trial judge as to the heavy burden incumbent upon the solicitor taking the benefit.

"It is not the law that in no circumstances can a solicitor or other person who has prepared the will for the testator take a benefit under it. But the fact creates suspicion that must be removed by the person propounding the will. In all cases the court must be vigilant and zealous" (Lord Simmonds).

Despite ***Wintle v Nye*** being such a well-known case, solicitors still run into problems making wills in which they take a benefit. In ***Cushway v Harris [2012]*** a solicitor had drafted wills for his elderly aunts, appointing him as an executor and giving him a one-third share of their residuary estates. However, he had failed to bring any evidence to show that the testators had knowledge and approval of the contents of the wills and they were declared invalid.

2.9 Reform

Link to Practice

Law Commission Consultation Paper ***Making a will*** (Consultation Paper 231)

The Law Commission's Wills consultation has proposed that the ***Banks v Goodfellow [1870]*** test for mental capacity be replaced by the test for mental capacity in the **Mental Capacity Act 2005** (**MCA 2005**). It has recommended that there should be a new Code of Practice which is intended to draw on the benefits of the ***Banks v Goodfellow*** test and subsequent case law. The use of **MCA 2005** would enable greater modern medical knowledge to be applied to the assessment of will-writing capacity.

The rule in ***Parker v Felgate [1883]*** (see **2.2.6**) would, on the face of it, conflict with **MCA 2005** since it allows for execution of a will **after** capacity has been lost if the instructions were made when the testator still had capacity. The Law Commission nonetheless proposes retaining the rule.

2.10 Summary

(1) For a will to be valid, it must be shown that the testator had:

- testamentary capacity;
- knowledge and approval of the contents of the will;
- not been induced to make the will by fraud or undue influence.

(2) Testamentary capacity – the testator must understand:

- they are making a will as opposed to any other document;
- the extent of their property they have to dispose of;
- the moral claims on their generosity (***Banks v Goodfellow [1870]***).

In addition, **s3(1) MCA 2005** states that a person is unable to make a decision, such as making a will, if they cannot understand, retain, use or weigh relevant information or communicate their decision.

(3) The time to apply the test – the testator is regarded as having sufficient capacity if:

- they had capacity at the time they gave instructions to the solicitor;
- the will is prepared in accordance with instructions;
- at the time of executing the will, they were capable of understanding and did understand that they were executing a will for which they had previously given instructions (the rule in ***Parker v Felgate [1883]***).

(4) Presumptions as to capacity:

s1(2) MCA 2005 states that a person is presumed to have capacity unless it is established that they do not.

(5) Knowledge and approval:

- approval means that the testator must understand the will and agree that it says what they meant it to say;
- the court must be satisfied that the testator knew and approved the contents of the will;
- execution by the testator indicates knowledge and approval unless there is evidence of suspicious circumstances;
- the testator must intend the document to operate as a will;
- even if knowledge and approval are proved, the court may deny probate in part or in full where there is evidence of fraud or undue influence;
- the burden of proof is with the person propounding the will, who must establish that the testator knew and approved of its contents. Once it is

established that the testator had capacity and the will is properly executed, there is a rebuttable presumption of knowledge and approval. This means that the evidential burden of establishing lack of knowledge and approval shifts to the person alleging it.

(6) There are three types of mistake:

- mistake as to words;
- mistake by the testator as to part of the will;
- mistake by the draftsman.

There is a statutory power to rectify under **s20 AJA 1982**.

(7) Force, fear, fraud and undue influence:

- force and fear make a will invalid;
- fraud includes forgery, inserting unauthorised material into a will, deliberately misleading the testator and false representations about a will;
- undue influence is more than mere persuasion and overpowers the free will of the testator.

CHAPTER 3

Formalities for Making a Will

Aims of the Chapter:

By the end of this chapter, you should be able to:

- explain the formal requirements for signing and witnessing a will under **s9 Wills Act 1837**;
- describe the acceptable forms of writing and signatures used in a will;
- discuss the role of a witness;
- explain what an attestation clause is; and
- explain the rules relating to beneficiaries who witness a will.

3.1 Introduction

"[Bilbo's will] was unfortunately very clear and correct (according to the legal customs of hobbits, which demanded among other things seven signatures of witnesses in red ink)."

The Lord of the Rings
J R R Tolkien

There are two conflicting principles underlying the rules in England and Wales that deal with signatures and witnesses to wills. First, making a will should be as easy as possible so that testators are less likely to die intestate. Unlike the laws of the hobbits, English law does not require seven witnesses and red ink since this would be a significant deterrent to people making wills at all. On the other hand, the risks of fraud should be kept to a minimum. In order to achieve a fair balance between these objectives, the law provides that a will should be signed by the testator in the presence of two independent witnesses. After the death of the testator, the witnesses can give evidence that the will was actually signed by the testator.

This chapter deals with the precise requirements of this procedure, as set out in **s9 Wills Act 1837** (**WA 1837**) (as amended by **s17 Administration of Justice Act 1982**) and some of the difficulties that have arisen in practice.

3.2 Formalities in s9 Wills Act 1837

s9 sets out succinctly exactly what steps must be taken in order for a will to be validly executed (signed and witnessed). It is important to read this section very carefully. It states:

No will shall be valid unless –

(a) *it is in writing and signed by the testator or by some other person in his presence and by his direction; and*

(b) *it appears that the testator intended by his signature to give effect to the will; and*

(c) *the signature is made or acknowledged by the testator in the presence of two or more witnesses present at the same time; and*

(d) *each witness either –*

 (i) *attests and signs the will; or*

 (ii) *acknowledges his signature, in the presence of the testator (but not necessarily in the presence of any other witness), but no form of attestation shall be necessary.*

s9 does not apply to wills made by testators with privileged status, that is, seamen and members of the armed forces in active service (see **Chapter 4**). Nor does it apply to statutory wills made under powers in the **Mental Capacity Act 2005** on behalf of an adult who lacks capacity (such statutory wills are outside the scope of the course). Subject to these two exceptions, any will that does not comply with the **s9** requirements will be invalid and so cannot be admitted to probate.

Key Cases

Law Commission Consultation Paper *Making a will* (Consultation Paper 231)

The Law Commission's Wills consultation has tentatively proposed that the courts be given a dispensing power to allow records demonstrating testamentary intention which have not complied with the formalities in **s9 WA 1837** to be treated as valid. Such records could include audio and video recordings.

Law Commission Supplementary Consultation Paper – October 2023

This supplementary consultation asked for the views of consultees on the regulation of wholly electronic wills in the light of developing technology, including blockchains. The results of the consultation are being assessed.

See https://lawcom.gov.uk/project/wills/.

3.2.1 Recommended approach to executing a will

Clearly **s9** allows for some variation in the way in which a will can be executed. In practice, though, acknowledgments of signatures and witnesses entering and leaving the room during the process can cause confusion and lead to evidential problems in proving the will. In order to ensure that the requirements of **s9** are met without risking these difficulties the following approach is recommended:

- the testator and two suitable witnesses (see **3.4.2** and **3.6**) need to remain together (i.e. in the same room) and attentive throughout the process, so as to comply with the statutory requirement of *presence*;
- the two witnesses both watch the testator date and sign the will;
- each witness in turn then signs the will, watched by the testator and the other witness; and

- the will contains an attestation clause at the end confirming that the testator signed in the presence of both witnesses who also signed in the presence of the testator.

Following these steps complies with the **s9** procedure and no further evidence should be needed beyond the will itself to show that it was validly executed. In fact, ensuring that the witnesses see each other sign, having already seen the testator sign, goes a little beyond the **s9** requirements for the sake of further evidential proof should anyone decide to dispute what actually took place.

If the recommended approach has not been followed, it is likely that the court will require additional evidence, such as affidavits from the witnesses, confirming that the requirements of **s9** were met.

3.3 Writing and signature

A will must be in writing. The will can be written in the testator's own hand (holograph) or be written by someone else, or typed or word-processed.

The will may be written in ink or pencil or a combination of both. If, however, it is in both and there is a conflict, the court will presume that the points written in pencil are merely deliberative (i.e. not reflecting the testator's final decision) and would therefore be excluded from probate.

In ***In the Goods of Adams [1872]*** the ink writing extended over the pencil; the court ignored the pencil writing, concluding that the intention was to supersede this with ink.

A will may be altered in pencil as, for example, in ***In the Goods of Tonge [1891]*** where a printed revocation clause was struck out in pencil. Such alterations must be shown to be intended as final alterations (***Muir's Trustees [1869]***).

A will may be written on any material: in ***Hodson v Barnes [1926]*** the will was written on an eggshell. Also, the will may be written in any language: in ***Kell v Charmer [1856]*** a will was admitted containing bequests written in a jeweller's code.

3.3.1 Form and manner of the signature

The courts have adopted a wide interpretation of "signature". The signature need not be the testator's name so long as the signing shows an intention to execute the will. For example, in ***Re Cook [1960]*** the testatrix commenced her will in the form of a letter "I Emmie Cook . . ." and signed the paper "Your loving mother". The letter was attested and held to be a valid will because in each case what was done was intended as a signature.

In ***In the Goods of Savory [1851]*** initials were held to be a valid signature and in ***In the Estate of Finn [1935]*** the thumbprint of the testator was accepted as valid execution of the will.

In ***In the Goods of Sperling [1863]*** the deceased signed the will in the presence of a servant. The servant signed as witness, not with his name, but wrote "servant to Mr Sperling". The court accepted that this was intended as a signature.

In ***Re Chalcraft [1948]*** the testatrix signed her will on her deathbed. She was so weak that she could only sign "E Chal" instead of "E Chalcraft". The court accepted this as a valid signature because she had done all she could in the circumstances.

Weatherhill v Pearce [1995] concerned a home-made will on a pre-printed form. The testatrix's name appeared in the middle of the attestation clause (see **3.5**), but nowhere else at the end of the will. One of the questions that arose was whether this constituted a signature for the purposes of **s9**. It was held that the testatrix had intended her name so positioned to constitute signature and, as such, the **s9** requirement of signature had been satisfied.

What about a case where the testator is very weak and has to be assisted in writing a signature? In ***Barrett v Bem [2012]*** the court said that if a testator chooses to sign the will personally, as opposed to directing another person to sign on their behalf, then they can be assisted by another person provided that the testator makes some "*positive and discernible contribution to the signing process*" as opposed to abstaining from preventing the signing. So, if the testator holds the pen but has to have their hand steadied while writing **their** signature, then this would appear to suffice as his signature. However, if they just hold the pen and their hand is guided across the page by a helper, this would probably not suffice because the signature would be that of the helper rather than the testator. This would then raise the question of whether the testator had, in fact, directed another to sign on their behalf (see **3.3.5**).

Witnesses' signatures

As the final requirement for the valid execution of a will, **s9 WA 1837** requires that each witness either attests and "signs" the will or acknowledges his signature in the presence of the testator. In ***Payne and Another v Payne [2018]*** the Court of Appeal had to decide if the mere printing of the witnesses' names in the absence of a traditional "signature" was acceptable.

The witnesses said they had seen the testator add his signature and then filled in details of their name, address and occupation but had not actually signed the will because there was insufficient room to make their signatures.

The **Wills Act 1837** had been amended back in 1982 and the court compared the pre-1982 wording with the substituted wording. The previous requirement that witnesses should "subscribe" had been replaced with a need for them to "sign". This change in wording, the court found, appeared to be designed to get rid of archaic phraseology rather than introduce stricter formality requirements for witnesses. Therefore, the new word "sign" should be interpreted as having the same meaning as "subscribe".

Consequently, the requirement in **s9** means, as it has always done, that the witnesses merely have to write their names with the intention that the act of writing should operate as an attestation. This will was valid even though the witnesses did not "sign" in the traditional sense.

NB This decision is in keeping with what the court has always said if there is an issue of whether the **testator** has signed to meet the **s9** requirements. So, whether it is the testator or the witnesses, it does not really matter what the writer puts on the will as long as the court is satisfied that what was written was intended to either give effect to the will (in the case of the testator) or to attest the will (in the case of a witness).

3.3.2 The position of the signature

s9 states: *the testator intended by his signature to give effect to the will.*

Its effect is that the testator can place a signature anywhere on the will so long as it is apparent from the positioning of the signature that it is intended to give effect to the will.

In ***Wood v Smith [1992]*** a testator wrote in his own handwriting at the top of his will, "My Will by Percy Winterbone", before writing the rest of his will. He did not sign his name at the foot of the will. Evidence from the witnesses suggested that the testator regarded his name at the top to be his signature. The Court of Appeal held that even though the will had, in effect, been signed before its provisions were written down, as the testator's name and the provisions of the will had been written in a single operation, there was clear evidence that the testator's signature was intended to give effect to the will. Consequently, the will had met the requirements of **s9**, although the will was not admissible to probate as the testator did not have testamentary capacity.

Wood v Smith was applied in ***Weatherhill v Pearce [1995]*** (see **3.3.1**) where the signature by the testatrix in the middle of the attestation clause was held to be valid.

In all such cases, the outcome depends on whether the evidence (normally from the witnesses) indicates that the testator intended their name to be a signature or merely a part of the will. In all cases where a will is signed in an unusual place (i.e. other than at the end, opposite the attestation clause), the Registrar or District

Judge will require affidavit evidence of the testator's intention before admitting the will to probate.

3.3.3 Will with more than one page

Where the will is written on more than one piece of paper, the courts look for some connection between the various pages so that the whole document can be validated by the signature. Ideally, the pages will be fastened together, perhaps with a staple or paper clip. Otherwise, the connection may be apparent if the wording "flows on" from page to page.

In ***Re Little [1960]*** the will was written on five sheets of paper which were not fastened together at the time of execution but were placed on top of one another; the fifth page, which the testator signed, was on top. The court admitted all five – the pressing on all sheets by the testator providing sufficient connection.

The flexibility of the court on this point is illustrated by ***In the Goods of Tiernan [1942]*** (an Irish case). The will consisted of three separate sheets of paper, only one of which was signed by the testator and witnesses. The only other writing on this sheet was an attestation clause. There was no evidence to show that the three sheets had been connected and the witnesses could not recall seeing the other two sheets. Probate was granted on the basis of a presumption that the whole will was in the room at the time and under the testator's control at the time of execution.

In any case where the pages are not physically fastened together, it is advisable for the testator to sign every page of the will and to have their signature attested.

3.3.4 The "envelope" cases

The problem here is that there are at least two pieces of paper, the purported will and the envelope containing the will. The will itself may not have been signed, but the testator's name appears on the envelope. It is a question of fact in each case which is the operative signature of the testator. Is the name on the envelope intended to be a signature giving effect to the will inside or does it merely identify the contents of the envelope?

In ***In the Goods of Mann [1942]*** the testatrix wrote on the envelope "Last will and testament of J C Mann", signed the envelope and two witnesses added their signatures. The envelope containing the will was placed in a larger envelope and sealed. This was held to be valid execution because the evidence indicated that the testatrix intended her name to appear as a signature.

3.3.5 Signature on the testator's behalf

s9 permits a will to be valid if it is signed on the testator's behalf, so long as it is in their **presence** (see **3.4.2.1**) and by their **direction**. This means that a testator who is infirm and incapable of writing, or perhaps one who is blind or illiterate, may direct someone to sign the will on their behalf. This is not essential, because the testator could instead "make their mark" (perhaps drawing a cross) on the will, which would be an effective signature. Whatever solution is adopted, the attestation clause should be amended to reflect the procedure which is adopted.

Barrett v Bem [2012] (see **3.3.1**) involved a case where the testator's sister helped him to sign his will some three hours before he died in hospital. Two nurses witnessed the will but there was a great deal of conflicting evidence about exactly how the testator's signature was made, although it was clear that the sister was holding the testator's writing hand.

The Court of Appeal reversed the decision of the trial judge by saying that there was insufficient evidence to support his conclusion that the testator had directed his sister to sign the will.

The President of the Court of Appeal, in the leading judgment, found that although the testator wanted to make a will and had tried but failed to sign it personally, this in itself was not sufficient as a direction to his sister, as required by **s9 WA 1837**. The question was not whether the testator wanted to direct his sister to sign the will but whether, as a matter of fact, he actually did so. There must be some positive communication to amount to a direction and the evidence fell short of establishing that this was the case. So, just as there must be some positive contribution if the testator signs himself, there must also be some positive communication (verbal or non-verbal) for a valid direction under **s9**.

This case, described by the trial judge as extraordinary, contained another unusual feature because the sister who helped the testator to sign was, in fact, the sole beneficiary of the will. This was clearly something, as recognised in this case, which would "*excite the suspicions of the court*" (see **2.6.2**) and raise an issue about the testator's knowledge and approval. Since the will was held to be invalid anyway, the Court of Appeal was not called upon to consider the question of whether a **beneficiary** can sign a will **on the testator's behalf** if directed to do so. However, the President echoed the trial judge's view that it is plainly undesirable that beneficiaries should be permitted to execute a will in their own favour in any capacity and that Parliament should consider changing the law to ensure that this cannot happen in the future. For the situation where a beneficiary signs as a **witness**, see **3.6**.

As a matter of practice and to avoid disputes, it is essential to have an independent person signing on the testator's behalf if this becomes necessary – and, of course, the wording of the attestation clause should always be amended to reflect the circumstances of the will's execution.

Link to Practice

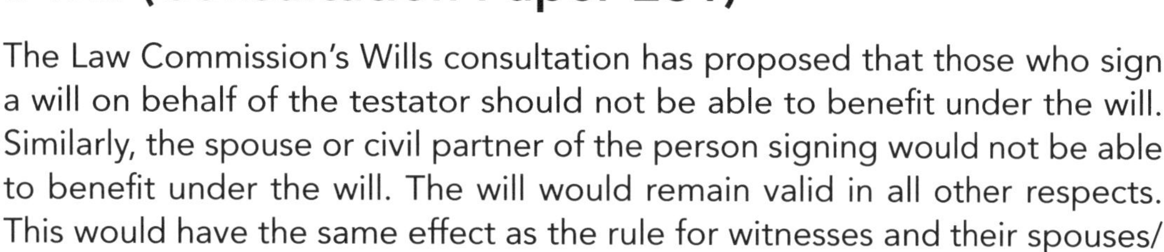

Law Commission Consultation Paper *Making a will* (Consultation Paper 231)

The Law Commission's Wills consultation has proposed that those who sign a will on behalf of the testator should not be able to benefit under the will. Similarly, the spouse or civil partner of the person signing would not be able to benefit under the will. The will would remain valid in all other respects. This would have the same effect as the rule for witnesses and their spouses/civil partners under **s15 WA 1837**.

3.3.6 The interpretation of s9(b)

s9(b) states that no will shall be valid unless it appears that the testator intended by their signature to give effect to the will. The drafting does not make clear from what source the intention must appear. In ***Re Chapman [1999]*** the testator had prepared "outline will provisions" with the assistance of B. P, the major residuary beneficiary under these provisions, sought to prove them as a will. If the provisions were not admitted to probate, then there would be an intestacy and P would receive nothing. The outline will provisions had been signed by the deceased and witnessed by the deceased's two brothers-in-law. They also put their addresses and occupations. At the time of the case, one witness was dead but the other one was still alive. He did not recall signing the document but thought that the signatures were genuine.

The beneficiary on intestacy argued that the will did not comply with **s9(b)** or **s9(c)**. He submitted that the deceased's intentions must appear from the face of the testamentary instrument, but this was rejected. Extrinsic evidence was admissible to confirm intention. In this case, the deceased had told B that the will had been signed by her and witnessed. This was sufficient to demonstrate that the deceased had intended by her signature to give effect to the will.

In ***Marley v Rawlings [2014]*** (see **2.7.1**) Lord Neuberger said that **s9 WA 1837** is concerned with formalities for executing a will.

"It is unchallengeable that Mr Rawlings signed it, and that he did so, both on the face of the document, and as a matter of fact, with the intention of it being his last will and testament. Thus, whatever else may be said about the document, it is, on its face (and was in fact according to the evidence), unambiguously intended to be a formal will, and it was, on its face (and was in fact according to the evidence), signed by Mr Rawlings, in the presence of two witnesses, on the basis that it was indeed his will."

Having established that what Mr Rawlings had signed was a valid will, even though it did not make sense because it contained his **wife's** wishes, not his own, the court then considered the claim for rectification (see **2.7.5**).

In ***Guthrie v Morel and Others [2015]*** the court reviewed a will which was, in fact, a letter written by the testator to his solicitor setting out a list of gifts and stating that this was his full and final expression of wishes regarding his will. The letter was signed, dated and witnessed by two people.

The trial judge followed the reasoning applied by Lord Neuberger in ***Marley v Rawlings*** in holding that the letter was clearly intended to be the deceased's will.

3.4 Function of the witnesses

s9 requires the testator either to sign the will in the presence of the witnesses or to acknowledge their signature in the presence of the witnesses. The testator need not sign the will in the presence of the witnesses. They could sign the document alone or in the presence of only one witness provided that they acknowledge their signature in the presence of two witnesses present at the same time (**s9(c)**).

3.4.1 Meaning of "acknowledged"

An acknowledgment may be express or implied. The testator is saying, in effect, "This is my signature". It would also be sufficient to say, "Please witness this", or to gesture to the will.

The witnesses are attesting to the fact of the testator's signature. It follows that the witnesses must be in a position to see the signature. The acknowledgment is therefore invalid where the signature is covered by paper, as in ***Re Gunstan [1882]***.

The witnesses do not have to see the contents of the will so long as they know that they are witnessing the testator's signature or the acknowledgment of that signature.

A gesture on the part of the testator may be a sufficient acknowledgment – for example, the raising of a hand in response to a question from a witness where the testator is too ill to speak.

In ***Weatherhill v Pearce [1995]*** acknowledgment of signature was said to have taken place where the testatrix simply told the witnesses that she had come to the house to execute her will, which she then showed to the witnesses.

3.4.2 Witnesses' acknowledgment

s9 allows acknowledgment by a witness of their signature. This means that the testator and the witnesses could each sign the will alone and then meet to validate their signatures. The testator would acknowledge their own signature, then the witnesses could each acknowledge theirs. Alternatively, the testator and one witness could sign, then, when a second witness has been obtained, the testator could acknowledge, followed by the first witness. Note that the testator must validly make or acknowledge their signature in the presence of both witnesses before any witness may acknowledge.

In ***Couser v Couser [1996]*** it was held that an allegation by a witness that a signature was invalid may amount to a valid acknowledgment of that signature. The testator acknowledged his signature to the witnesses. One witness then signed while the other witness was absent. When the other witness returned, both witnesses urged the testator to go to the bank to get the will executed. The first witness said the will was invalid because the testator had not signed it in her presence. It was held that, by urging the testator to go to the bank and by alleging that the will was invalid, the witness's words were to be treated as an acknowledgment of her own signature. This is the first case on acknowledgment by a witness.

3.4.2.1 "Presence" of witnesses

"Presence" is referred to three times in **s9**. When someone signs the will on behalf of the testator, it must be in their presence, the testator must sign or acknowledge in the presence of two or more witnesses and the witnesses must sign in the presence of the testator.

"Presence" requires both a mental and a physical element. Mental presence involves understanding what is taking place and physical presence means seeing what is taking place. This means that a person who is unconscious, sleeping, drunk, mentally ill, very young or under the influence of drugs may not be mentally present. A blind person is not capable of physical presence (***Re Gibson [1949]***). These tests are strictly applied in the case of witnesses, because they may need to give evidence as to what took place.

In ***Brown v Skirrow [1902]*** the testatrix took her will to a local shop to execute it. There were two assistants serving from separate counters situated at either end of the shop. The testatrix signed in the presence of the first assistant while the second assistant was busy serving a customer. The first assistant attested, then the testatrix asked the second assistant to attest. The will was invalid, because at the time of the signing by the testatrix, the second assistant did not know what was going on. A more relaxed attitude is taken to the presence of the testator when the witnesses sign – the test here is whether the testator retains some degree of mental alertness. In ***Re Chalcraft [1948]*** (see **3.3.1**), when the testatrix signed "E Chal", she was drugged and dying. When the witnesses signed, she was lapsing into unconsciousness. The court accepted that she was still mentally present.

Casson v Dade [1781] dealt with physical presence (whether he could have seen the witnesses if he had looked, or if he had not been blind). Here, the testatrix signed her will in the presence of two witnesses, then left the office and returned to her carriage. The witnesses brought the will to the window (which was at street level) where the light was better and signed. The window was in line of sight from the carriage and therefore the will had been signed in her presence.

There is no minimum age to be a witness, but a young person should be mature enough to appreciate the act of attestation (i.e. capable of mental presence) and therefore be able to give evidence if called upon to do so. In ***Wilson v Beddard [1841]*** a 14-year-old boy was accepted as a witness, though it is arguable that a much younger witness would not be acceptable.

The witnesses need not sign in the presence of one another (***Re Webb [1855]***). In practice, the standard form attestation clause does require the witnesses to sign in the presence of one another. The Registrar or District Judge will accept such a clause as proof of attestation without calling for affidavit evidence unless some other factor alerts suspicion.

The **Wills Act 1837 (Electronic Communications) (Amendment) (Coronavirus) Order 2020 SI 2020/952** provides for the legalisation of the remote witnessing of wills during the coronavirus (COVID-19) pandemic. The government has stressed that this procedure should be used only as a last resort and every effort should be made to execute wills in the usual manner. This will mean that wills witnessed via video link will be legally recognised, so long as the quality of sound and video is sufficient to see and hear what is happening. The measures will be backdated to 31 January 2020 and, following the **Wills Act 1837 (Electronic Communications) (Amendment) (Coronavirus) Order 2022 (SI 2022/18)**, will remain in place until 31 January 2024. It is considering whether these provisions should be made permanent in the light of the Law Commission consultation on wills.

The government has also provided guidance on making wills via video- conferencing (see https://www.gov.uk/guidance/guidance-on-making-wills-using-video-conferencing).

3.4.2.2 Knowledge required by the witnesses

In ***Sherrington v Sherrington [2005]*** (see **2.6.2**) another issue that had to be decided was whether the witnesses to the execution of the will knew what they were doing. Witnesses do not need to read the will or even know that the document is a will, as long as they know that they are witnessing the testator's signature on a document.

In this case, the testator and his second wife were in a hurry to get their wills signed. The two witnesses were B and T. T was from overseas and had a limited knowledge of English. When giving evidence, both B and T admitted that neither of them had actually seen the testator sign the document or acknowledge his signature. They could not be said to have signed as witnesses to the signature of the testator, hence the will was also invalid for want of due execution.

The Court of Appeal observed that this aspect of the case was very much a matter of conflicting evidence as to whether the witnesses had actually seen the testator sign or acknowledge his signature. The court held that there was insufficient evidence to state categorically that the will had not been correctly witnessed, so on this point the defendant was successful in overturning the High Court judgment (see **3.5** for comment on the presence of an attestation clause).

3.5 Attestation clauses

Clearly, most testators would be horrified at the thought that arguments over the arrangements for signing their wills would hold up the granting of probate and the administration of their estates. In order to avoid such uncertainty and to reassure the court that the requirements of **s9** were met, a properly drafted will should always contain an attestation clause at the end. Note the following example of such a clause.

Signed by the above named [testator's name] *as his last will in the presence of us present at the same time who at his request and in his presence and in the presence of each other have hereunto subscribed our names as witnesses.*

Attestation clauses can be varied in the light of the circumstances of the execution of the will, reflecting, for example, a person signing on behalf of a blind testator. An attestation clause raises a presumption that the will has been properly executed and is therefore valid unless there is evidence raised to show otherwise.

In ***Sherrington v Sherrington [2005]*** (see **2.6.2** and **3.4.2.2**) the Court of Appeal held that the strongest evidence is necessary to rebut the presumption of due execution if a will containing an attestation clause has the appearance of being properly executed.

However, in ***Ahluwalia v Singh and Others [2011]*** the will was held to be invalid after the claimant had successfully alleged that the will was not, in fact, signed by the testator in the presence of both witnesses when present at the same time despite there being an attestation clause which recited that this was the case. Having heard evidence from the two witnesses, and finding one more credible than the other, the judge said the claimant had satisfied the burden of producing the strongest evidence. The evidential force of the presumption in favour of due execution did not outweigh the judge's finding that one of the witnesses had signed in the testator's presence when the other witness was not there.

Note that **s9(d)(ii)** specifically states that no attestation is necessary. If it was, most home-made wills would probably be invalid. If there is no attestation clause, **r12(2) Non-Contentious Probate Rules 1987** states that the Registrar or District Judge may require an affidavit of due execution from a witness or another person present at the signing of the will confirming that the requirements of **s9** were met. If no such evidence is available and there is no evidence raising doubts about the execution, the court may grant probate using the legal maxim that all the necessary formalities are presumed to have been complied with.

This legal maxim was applied in ***Channon v Perkins [2005]***, where the witnesses admitted that the signatures on the will were theirs although they could not recall having signed the will. Applying the maxim, the Court of Appeal held that the will was valid.

3.6 The witness as beneficiary

In order to prevent fraud, **s15 WA 1837** prevents a beneficiary from taking a benefit under a will which they or their spouse or civil partner attested. The will remains valid in respect of all other gifts. **s15** does not apply if a beneficiary signs the will on behalf of the testator at their direction but it is clearly inadvisable that a beneficiary should do so (see ***Barrett v Bem [2012]*** in **3.3.5**).

s1 Wills Act 1968 states that, where a will has more than two witnesses, the attestation of excess witnesses may be disregarded if the will would still be valid if their signatures were removed.

There are a number of situations in which **s15** will not apply to deprive a beneficiary of his benefit.

(1) If the beneficiary had not yet married or entered into a civil partnership with the witness at the date of the will.

    In ***Thorpe v Beswick [1881]*** the testator made a will leaving property to a spinster, X. After the execution of the will but before the death of the testator, a witness to the will married X. The gift was effective.

(2) The courts will uphold a gift if it can be said to have arisen under any testamentary instrument that the witness did not attest. If the beneficiary attests the will and the will is subsequently confirmed by a codicil the witness does not attest, then the witness can take the gift, for they do so by reference to the codicil (***Anderson v Anderson [1872]***).

(3) If the witness inherits the gift only as a trustee.

In ***Re Ray's Will Trusts [1936]*** a gift in a will was made to the person who was the abbess of a particular convent when the testator died. At the death, a nun (who had witnessed the will) had become abbess. The gift was effective because it was not a gift to the nun in her personal capacity.

s28(4) Trustee Act 2000 provides that payment to an executor is to be regarded as remuneration rather than a gift or legacy. So, the right to payment is not lost if the executor witnesses the will.

Note the effect of **s15** on joint gifts:

- in a legacy given to A and B jointly, if A witnesses the will, B would take the entire property;
- in a gift to A and B as tenants in common, if A witnesses, their share would lapse.

Link to Practice

Law Commission Consultation Paper *Making a will* (Consultation Paper 231)

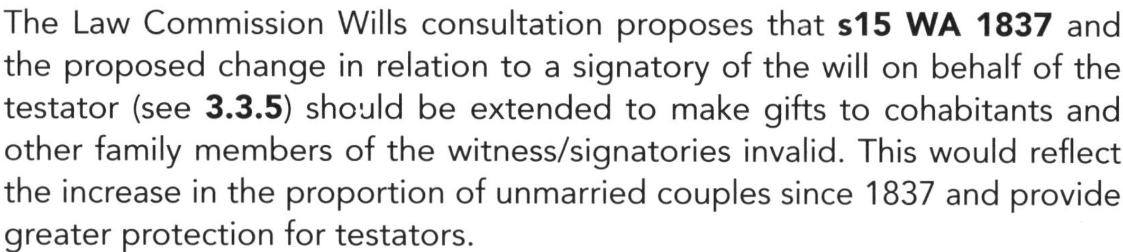

The Law Commission Wills consultation proposes that **s15 WA 1837** and the proposed change in relation to a signatory of the will on behalf of the testator (see **3.3.5**) should be extended to make gifts to cohabitants and other family members of the witness/signatories invalid. This would reflect the increase in the proportion of unmarried couples since 1837 and provide greater protection for testators.

3.7 Summary

(1) The formal requirements for the making of a valid will are found in **s9 WA 1837**. The essential features are:

- a will must be in writing;
- the will must be signed by the testator or signed on their behalf and by their direction;
- the signature must be witnessed by a minimum of two witnesses;
- the testator must sign or acknowledge their signature on the will in the presence of both the witnesses;
- the witnesses must sign or acknowledge their signatures in the presence of the testator but not necessarily in the presence of each other.

(2) It is desirable to include an attestation clause, as it gives rise to the presumption of due execution of the will, so facilitates the obtaining of the grant of probate.

(3) **s15 WA 1837** prevents a beneficiary from taking a benefit under a will which they or their spouse or civil partner witnessed.

CHAPTER 4

Privileged Wills

Aims of the Chapter:

By the end of this chapter, you should be able to:

- explain how a privileged will does not need to be completed with the formalities under **s9 Wills Act 1837**;
- discuss the requirement of actual military service for soldiers, members of the Royal Navy and the RAF;
- describe the circumstances when merchant seafarers can make wills;
- explain the requirement of testamentary intention; and
- identify how a will may be revoked under privileged status.

4.1 Introduction

Sadly, we are all too familiar with the tragic deaths of soldiers and other UK military personnel in recent wars in Iraq and Afghanistan. British military personnel have been dying in wars for several centuries. **s11 Wills Act 1837** (**WA 1837**) grants them the right to make oral or informal wills without requiring the normal formalities, including witnesses, while *in actual military service*. These informal wills are known as **privileged wills**.

s11 has extended this right to any *mariner at sea* merchant seamen. This inclusion reflects the higher risks of sudden death facing merchant seamen. Privileged wills may be made by service personnel and merchant seamen under 18 years as an exception to the normal rule in **s7**, which requires all testators to be 18 years or older.

It is crucial to note that a privileged will remains valid even after the military service or time at sea has ended. Wartime wills will be valid even after many years of peace.

4.2 Soldier

s11 refers to *Any soldier* and, for obvious reasons given the nature of warfare in 1837, makes no mention of RAF personnel. **s5(2) Wills (Soldiers and Sailors) Act 1918** stated that RAF personnel were included in the definition. Women as well as men are covered, together with civilian support staff such as nurses or stretcher-bearers (***In the Estate of Stanley [1916]***).

4.2.1 Actual military service

Actual military service is a question of fact in each case. In ***Re Wingham [1949]*** the testator made an informal disposition while at a training camp for airmen in Canada during the Second World War. Although Wingham was some 3,000 miles from the theatre of war when he made the disposition, the Court of Appeal was unanimous in declaring the will privileged.

Bucknell LJ said: *"Actual military service means active military service, that is, such service directly concerned with operations of war which is/has been in progress or is imminent."* Here, Wingham was liable at any time to be posted to the operational area.

4.2.2 Application of Re Wingham

In ***In the Estate of Spark [1941]*** Private Spark was a member of the territorial services that were mobilised on 1 September 1939. Later, at a camp in the UK, he told a friend that he wanted his wife to have all his property should he be killed. He died two days later during an air raid on the camp. The oral statement was held to be a valid will because war was imminent.

In ***Re Colman [1958]*** Colman executed a formal will in 1955 while on leave in England from service in the British army of occupation of the Rhine. He was under age. The will was admitted as privileged. This may appear nowadays to be a strange decision. Two factors should be borne in mind. The armed services in the Rhineland in the 1950s were an army of occupation in a defeated country, and, on a technical point, no formal peace treaty had been fully concluded at the time the disposition was made.

So, in wartime, a soldier may be in actual military service as soon as he receives orders in connection with the war, and may remain in actual military service after the war has ended, as a member of an army of occupation. The soldier does not have to be in a war zone when making a privileged will.

In peacetime, a soldier will be in actual military service only if military operations are imminent. The test is rather narrower.

Re Anderson [1958] is a good example of the application of **s11** to the role of the modern army. The deceased was a member of the Australian forces during the Malayan Emergency of the 1950s. He was killed in operations against guerrilla forces. In admitting his informal disposition, the court said that a formal state of war need not exist; it was sufficient for there to be warlike operations.

s11 and the role of the army in Northern Ireland was considered in ***Re Jones (Deceased) [1981]***. Jones, a serving soldier in Northern Ireland in 1978, was mortally wounded. En route to hospital he told his warrant officer "If I don't make it, make sure Anne [his fiancée] gets all my stuff." In an earlier formal will he had left everything to his mother.

The oral will was held to be valid. The court should look at the nature of the activities and the unit or force to which the deceased was attached and not the character of the opposition: *"one looks at the totality of the environment."* Any doubt should be resolved in favour of validation.

4.3 Mariner

This means members of the Royal Navy or the merchant navy or anyone else who is employed on board a ship. In ***In the Goods of Hale [1915]*** Sarah Hale was a typist employed by the Cunard line. She wrote a letter home from her lodgings in Southampton prior to embarking on the last voyage of The "*Lusitania*". The letter contained testamentary wishes and was admitted as privileged, for she was at sea.

4.3.1 At sea

This phrase has been widely interpreted and can include anyone attached to a ship.

It follows that a mariner on shore can make a privileged will so long as they have not been paid off but are under orders to return to their ship (***In the Goods of McMurdo [1868]***).

In ***In the Estate of Rapley (Deceased) [1983]*** the seaman had made an informal disposition after he was discharged from one ship of the company but before posting to a new ship. The court held that he was not at sea, because he did not receive his orders to join his new ship until some time after making the disposition. To hold the will privileged in these circumstances would deprive the words "at sea" of any meaning in this context.

In ***Ayling v Summers and Others [2009]*** the High Court held that a British merchant seaman had made a privileged will when he said: "What I told you before still applies. If anything happens to me, if I snuff it, I want everything to go to Auntie Anne."

The court found that his oral statement was intended to be a privileged will because it was made at a time when he was under orders to join his ship and technically at sea. The court also held that it did not matter that the ship in question was not registered in the UK.

4.4 Testamentary intention

To establish the exceptional circumstances of privileged status, it is not sufficient simply to prove that the testator came within one of the categories. The court must be satisfied that the words used conveyed testamentary intent.

The testator need not be conscious of making a will so long as the words indicate testamentary intention, that is, clear evidence of disposition on death.

In ***Re Stable [1919]*** a young officer stated while in military service: "If I stop a bullet, everything of mine shall be yours." The words were held to be a privileged will.

Contrast the decision in ***Stable*** with ***In the Estate of Knibbs [1962]***, where a barman on a passenger liner remarked on several occasions in the course of casual general conversation to his fellow barman that, should anything happen to him, "Iris [his sister] would get everything I have got." The court concluded that the words did not convey testamentary intent, but rather conveyed information about steps which had already been taken.

In ***Re Spicer [1949]*** the words used were similar to Knibbs' but at the time the soldier was holding his army pay book. The pay book could not be found at death, but the words were taken as evidence of the contents of the pay book and admissible as a privileged will. (The army pay book contained a section at the back where a soldier could write out his last wishes.)

4.5 Revocation

WA 1837 states that revocation can be informal while the testator enjoys privileged status.

A privileged will can be made by a minor. **s3(3) Family Law Reform Act 1969** provides that where a minor has made a privileged will and leaves privileged status, they may revoke the will informally. To make a new will, the person must regain privileged status or attain 18 and make a formal will.

In ***Re Gossage's Estate [1921]*** a soldier, while privileged, made a formal will. While still privileged, he wrote an unattested letter from South Africa to his sister in England asking her to burn his will "for I have already cancelled it". She did burn the will and, following his death, a copy of the will was found. This will was not admissible; it had been revoked by the direction given while in privileged status.

When the person has left privileged status (***Re Booth [1926]***), revocation must comply with **s18** or **s20 WA 1837** (see **Chapter 6**).

s15 WA 1837 (see **3.6**) has no application to the privileged will because it does not need to be witnessed to be declared valid (***Re Limond [1915]***). Similarly, alterations to a privileged will are presumed to have been made during privileged status. Note that the courts adopt the reverse presumption in the case of unattested alterations in a formal will (see **8.3**).

4.6 Are privileged wills still needed?

The British armed forces have changed enormously since 1837. Most soldiers, sailors and RAF personnel can read, and all have access to military lawyers for legal advice. Members of the armed forces have easy access to simple will forms and are encouraged to make conventional wills. Although the army still recruits teenagers under 18 years (who cannot make conventional wills), there are far fewer of them than in the days when large numbers of drummer boys were needed. Merchant seamen are far better educated than in the days of sailing ships and can print simple will forms from the internet.

These changes all mean that potential testators using privileged wills arguably do have the same opportunities to make conventional wills as do ordinary members of the public. A more serious criticism, however, is that a privileged will continues to be valid even after the testator has lost privileged status, for example, when the war is over. Their family may suffer many years later from the effects of a badly drafted or worded informal will when a much fairer outcome would have been achieved if the testator had died intestate.

Link to Practice

Law Commission Consultation Paper *Making a will* (Consultation Paper 231)

The Law Commission's Wills consultation has reviewed this area of law in the light of modern military practice. It notes various concerns about the use of privileged wills (including whether drone operators thousands of miles away from the battlefield should be treated as being on active service) but concludes that they should be retained for members of the armed forces on active service as part of the so-called "military covenant" between the country and its armed forces. It proposes that they should also be extended to cover civilian contractors working with military personnel on active service. The right of merchant seamen to make privileged wills would be removed.

4.7 Summary

(1) **s11 WA 1837**, as amended by the **Wills (Soldiers and Sailors) Act 1918**, removes all will-making formalities for those who can prove that, at the time at which the disposition is made, they fall within one of two privileged categories:

- a soldier or aircrew being in actual military service; or
- any mariner at sea.

Actual military service is a question of fact.

(2) There must be clear evidence that the testator's instructions, particularly if they are verbal, indicated testamentary intent.

(3) Privileged wills can be revoked informally.

(4) A privileged will remains effective even after the testator has lost their privileged status.

CHAPTER 5

Incorporation by Reference

Aims of the Chapter:

By the end of this chapter, you should be able to:

- identify why a testator may wish to incorporate a separate documentinto a will;
- describe the requirements for a document to be effectively incorporated; and
- describe the effect of incorporation.

5.1 Introduction

A testator may have numerous individual items that they wish to leave to different people. Rather than fill the will with long lists, the testator may prefer to include the items in a separate document. For the document to have testamentary effect, it must be validly incorporated into the will itself. This means that the document becomes legally part of the will. It is not sufficient, for example, for the prospective testatrix to go around pasting the names of relatives on the underside of various objects saying "I want our Henry to have this", and "I want our Olive to have this vase"!

A document will not be admissible to probate if it is not attested and valid within **s9 Wills Act 1837** (**WA 1837**). It is possible, however, for a testator to include the terms of another unattested document as part of the will which has been duly executed. The doctrine of incorporation by reference will permit the admission of such documents, provided that three conditions are met. The document must:

- be in existence at the date on which the will was executed;
- be referred to in the will as being in existence; and
- be clearly identified in the will.

These conditions are strictly applied if incorporation of an unexecuted document is to be allowed.

5.2 In existence at the date of execution of the will

If a document is not in existence at the date on which the will is executed, but the will is republished (executed again) or a codicil is made to the will, provided that the document is in existence at the date of republication or the date of the codicil, it is validly incorporated so long as the other requirements are satisfied (***In the Goods of Lady Truro [1866]***).

NB Once the will has been executed, the document cannot be changed.

5.3 Referred to as in existence at the date of the will

The will must also **refer** to it as being in existence. This condition was not satisfied in ***University College of North Wales v Taylor [1908]***. On the facts of the case, a testator left a gift by will which was conditional on compliance with "any memorandum found in my papers". The court held that the reference to "any memorandum" could refer to a document not in existence at the date of the will so the document had not been validly incorporated. Similarly, the incorporation of a document was held to be invalid in ***Re Bateman's Will Trusts [1970]*** where the executors of a will were directed to pay the income from the fund to "such persons as shall be stated by me in a sealed letter in my handwriting and addressed to my trustee". "Shall be stated" suggested that the letter had not necessarily been written at the date of the execution of the will.

5.4 Clear identification of the document

The document to be incorporated must be identified in the will. If the identification is vague, it will be invalid. In ***In the Goods of Garnett [1894]*** the testator referred in his will to documents numbered one to six, but there were so many papers in his desk at death that it was impossible to identify with certainty the documents in question.

5.5 The effect of incorporation

The incorporated document is admitted to probate as part of the will, although this may be dispensed with if impracticable, as with a large library catalogue in ***In the Goods of Balme [1897]***.

Where a will is invalid, a subsequent valid codicil that refers to the will as being in existence may incorporate the will. In ***Re Berger [1989]*** a Jewish will, known as a *zavah*, met the requirements of **s9 WA 1837** and was held to have incorporated an earlier will.

Since the incorporated document is admitted to probate as part of the will:

- if a witness to the will itself is named in the incorporated document as a beneficiary (or the witness is the beneficiary's spouse/civil partner), then **s15 WA 1837** will apply to deprive the beneficiary of the benefit (see **3.6**);
- the terms of the incorporated document will be open to public scrutiny, like the will itself, once probate has been granted. The grant of probate will therefore include a copy of the incorporated document as well as the will. As a result, incorporation by reference is not a means of keeping provisions of a will secret (if secrecy is required, then it is possible to create a secret trust in a will, but this type of trust, recognised in equity, is beyond the scope of this textbook).

Reflective Questions

Testators sometimes want to include separate documents with their wills for two main reasons. First, they wish to have a separate list of gifts of individual items which they want to be able to change without making a new will. Second, they want to include gifts which will be kept secret on death.

The current rules do not permit changes to the incorporated document after execution and require all incorporated documents to be made public on death. Do you think these rules are too restrictive? If you think they should be changed, what do you think the implications might be for the requirements of **s9 WA 1837**?

5.6 Summary

(1) For a separate document (e.g. one containing a long list of beneficiaries) to have testamentary effect, it must be validly incorporated into the will itself.

(2) For effective incorporation, a document must:

- be in existence at the date on which the will was executed;
- be referred to in the will as being in existence; and
- be clearly identified in the will itself.

(3) The incorporated document is then admitted to probate as part of the will.

CHAPTER 6

Revocation of Wills

Aims of the Chapter:

By the end of this chapter, you should be able to:

- explain how to expressly revoke a will;
- describe revocation by implication and destruction;
- describe the significance of a conditional revocation; and
- explain the implications of marriage, civil partnerships and divorce in relation to existing wills.

6.1 Introduction

Making a will is an important decision that should be made in the light of the testator's personal circumstances and financial resources at the time. So far as possible, a professionally drafted will should try to anticipate the likely changes that may affect how a testator wishes their property to be disposed of on death. Nonetheless, testators have a right to revoke (cancel) their wills until death intervenes. Indeed, some testators take great pleasure in changing, or threatening to change, their wills.

Given the importance that English law attaches to the correct formalities for making a will, it is logical that revoking a will should also meet certain requirements. Essentially, there must be an intention to revoke (*animus revocandi*, pronounced "rev-oh-can-die") accompanying either:

- an express or implied revocation by a subsequent will, codicil or other document executed as if it were a will; or
- destruction of the will.

English law also provides that an existing will is revoked, regardless of the testator's intention, where the testator marries or enters into a civil partnership. Entering into one of these legal relationships is treated as being such a life- transforming event that it would be inappropriate for an earlier will to continue to be valid.

6.2 Express revocation

No will or codicil, or any part thereof, shall be revoked otherwise than as aforesaid, or by some writing declaring an intention to revoke the same, and executed in the manner in which a will is hereinbefore required to be executed (**s20 Wills Act 1837** (**WA 1837**)).

A common form is the phrase "I hereby revoke all former testamentary instruments made by me."

Merely describing a document as the last will does not constitute express revocation (***Kitcat v King [1930]***). There may, however, have been implied revocation as to a part or the whole of the will (see **6.3.1**).

The revocation need not be contained in a will so long as the document is executed in accordance with **s9**. In ***Re Durance [1872]*** the testator wrote from Canada to his brother in England requesting him to collect and destroy his will. Although the destruction in isolation would have been ineffective (see **6.4.1**), the letter was signed in accordance with **s9** and was admitted as a testamentary direction.

6.2.1 Lack of knowledge and approval

An express revocation clause may be rejected for want of knowledge and approval by the testator, but the clause will be effective if it was included as a result of the testator's mistake as to its legal effect.

In ***Re Wayland [1951]*** a British subject domiciled in England made a will in Brussels in accordance with English law expressed to deal only with his Belgian property. Two years later, he executed a will dealing with his English property. This later will contained an express revocation clause.

The court held that it was clear from his actions that the testator did not intend to revoke the earlier will but rather wished to have two wills dealing with the separate properties.

Note, however, that a revocation clause is not to be lightly disregarded. Langton J in ***Lowthorpe-Lutwidge v Lowthorpe-Lutwidge [1935]*** emphasised that there is a heavy burden of proof on someone who claims that an express clause is not intended to revoke previous dispositions.

6.3 Revocation by implication

In ***Pepper v Pepper [1870]*** the testator made a will in 1864 leaving certain specific gifts. In 1865, he executed a will containing general bequests and leaving the residue to X.

It was held that since the later will disposed of the entire estate, it impliedly revoked the will of 1864.

Re Howard [1944] is a strange case. The testator executed a will in 1933 disposing of all his property. In 1940, he executed two wills, both on the same day, one leaving all his property to his wife, the other leaving all his property to his son. All three died in an air raid. The wills of 1940 were not admitted to probate as they were wholly inconsistent and there was nothing to indicate which was executed first. They were effective as an intention to revoke the will of 1933, however, so the testator died intestate.

Henn-Collins J said *"since the testator contemplated that one or other would be operative and both revoked all earlier dispositions one is on safe ground in supposing that he intended that no earlier dispositions should have effect"*.

Re Howard underlines the importance of the date of the instrument. Where there is doubt as to the correct date or the document is not dated at all, the Registrar or District Judge will call for affidavit evidence by way of search to try to determine the date.

While a later will that deals with the whole estate by including a residuary gift would usually revoke the whole of an earlier will by implication, this is not always the case. Two or more testamentary documents can be read together to constitute the will of the deceased. There is a presumption against implied revocation, which will be found only to the extent that there are logical inconsistencies between the two documents, or the later simply repeats what is in the former, in which case, the later revokes the earlier, either wholly or in part. It is, therefore, a question of construction of the clauses.

In ***Curati v Perdoni [2012]*** a will made in 1994 repeated a gift to W made in an earlier will made in 1980 but, unlike the earlier will, it did not contain a substitution provision in favour of X if W predeceased. W did predecease and so the gift failed. The Court of Appeal held that while the gift to W in the earlier will had been revoked by the later one (repetition), the substitution provision in the earlier will had not and so that part of the earlier will could be read in conjunction with the later one to determine that X was entitled to the gift.

6.3.1 Failure of the revoking gift

Suppose the testator gives Blackacre to X by will and by a later will gives Blackacre to Y; this impliedly revokes the gift to X (***Re Hawksley's Settlement [1934]***). What happens, however, if the gift to Y is not legally valid? Has the testator shown an intention to revoke the gift to X in any event or only on condition that the gift to Y takes effect? In this latter case, X would still be entitled to Blackacre.

In ***Re Robinson [1930]*** the testatrix by her will gave her estate on trust to pay an annuity to her son, H, and after his death to divide the capital between her grandchildren at 21. By a later will she gave her whole estate to H absolutely. This gift failed because H's wife was an attesting witness.

The court held that the testatrix had not shown an intention to revoke her earlier will in any event. Instead, her intention to revoke was conditional on the absolute gift to H taking effect.

6.3.2 Intention to revoke must be unambiguous

Re Freeman [1910] shows that the intention to revoke must be unambiguous. Here, the testator by his will appointed A to be one of his executors and gave him a legacy of £1,000 if he should prove the will; it also gave him a share of the residue. By a codicil, the testator revoked the appointment of A as executor and the gift of £1,000 and appointed B. The testator declared, using imprecise language, that his will should be construed as if the name B were inserted throughout instead of A. The Court of Appeal held that the declaration did not revoke the gift of the share of residue to A.

6.4 Revocation by destruction

Given the importance attached to the physical document of a will by English law, a non-lawyer might well think that simply destroying it would automatically revoke it. In fact, a rule as straightforward as this would inevitably result in unfairness, particularly where the destruction is accidental or beyond the intentions of the testator. Although houses in England and Wales have far fewer open fires and candles than their equivalents had in 1837, accidental fires do still happen. Wills can be damaged or torn accidentally, or even put through shredders.

s20 WA 1837 provides:

No will or codicil, or any part thereof, shall be revoked otherwise than as aforesaid . . . or by burning, tearing or otherwise destroying the same by the testator, or by some person in his presence and by his direction, with the intention of revoking the same.

The section refers to two elements: the act of destruction and the intention to revoke, the *animus revocandi*. These two elements must be present at the same time to effect a valid revocation by destruction.

6.4.1 The act of destruction

s20 WA 1837 refers to *burning, tearing or otherwise destroying*. Do the words *or otherwise destroying the same* include symbolic destruction?

The court held that they did not in ***Cheese v Lovejoy [1877]***. The testator put a line across the will and wrote "all these are revoked", crumpled the paper and threw it into the corner of the room. A housekeeper found the will and retained it until the death of the testator.

The court held that there was no revocation, for there was insufficient destruction. The words *or otherwise destroying the same* were treated as requiring physical destruction of the will.

The meaning of "destruction" in relation to the signature of the testator was considered in ***In the Estate of Adams [1990]***, where the testatrix telephoned her solicitor instructing him to destroy her will. Her solicitor wrote to her enclosing the will and saying that it would be better if she destroyed it. When the testatrix died five years later, the will was found among her possessions. The typescript had been scribbled over in several places with a blue-black ball- point pen, and the signatures of the attesting witnesses and the testatrix had been particularly heavily scored out.

The court concluded that the will had been revoked. The court used by analogy the rules on unattested alterations in **s21 WA 1837**, namely, were the original signatures apparent? Since they were not, applying that test, the will was revoked.

If the entire will is not destroyed, a sufficiently large or vital part (e.g. the signature) must be destroyed (***Hobbs v Knight [1838]***).

In ***In the Estate of Nunn [1936]*** the testatrix gave a number of legacies to different persons. Some time later, she literally cut the gifts out of the will and stitched the remainder together. The will would have stood because the remainder made sense. Subsequently, she cut out her signature – this was held to be revocation of the entire will. In ***In the Estate of Morton [1887]*** where the testator scratched out his signature with a knife, the will was revoked with *animus revocandi*.

The question is whether the testator has done all they could to destroy the will. It is a question of construction whether parts of the will can stand.

In ***In the Goods of Gullan [1858]*** the will originally comprised several pages but, at death, only the middle pages had been preserved. The whole will was revoked. Although each page had been signed and attested, the key operative part, the final page with the signatures of the testator and witnesses, was missing.

The testator need not destroy the will personally. **s20** is satisfied if someone else destroys the will, provided that the act is carried out in the presence of the testator and by their direction. The testator must be in a position to see the act of destruction. In ***In the Goods of Dadds [1857]***, for example, a codicil that was burned in an adjoining room was not a valid revocation.

Another good example is ***Re De Kremer [1965]***, where the testator's solicitor destroyed the will after being instructed to do so by a telephone call from the testator. Not surprisingly, the revocation was invalid.

The direction to destroy must be given prior to the destruction.

6.4.2 Intention

The intention to revoke must be present when destruction takes place, although intention will be presumed if there is no evidence of the testator's actual intention. A later agreement to the revocation will not suffice. So, in ***Gill v Gill [1909]***, where the testator's will was torn up by his wife during the course of a row between them, there was no revocation. This is so even though the testator did nothing subsequently about his will and probably acquiesced in the action. The intention was not present when the act of destruction took place.

The testator may intend to revoke only part of the will. If only a non-vital part is destroyed, such a limited intention will be inferred by the court (***Re Everest [1975]***).

The testator must have the same mental capacity when revoking their will as when first making it. In ***Brunt v Brunt [1873]*** the testator suffered from *delirium tremens* (mental disturbance caused by alcohol withdrawal symptoms), causing him to lapse into a state of automatism. Whilst he was suffering from this, he took his will from a safe and tore it up. His wife preserved the pieces. The court held that there was no revocation.

Similarly, in ***Re Booth [1926]*** there was no revocation where the will was accidentally destroyed by fire.

A clear intention is crucial to effect revocation under **s20**. Where a will was torn up as the result of a mistaken belief, there was no valid revocation (***Re Southerden [1925]***). Before going to America, the deceased made a will leaving all his property to his wife. On his return, he threw the will in the fire saying to his wife: "This is no good now. We have safely returned and it is all yours. We might as well burn it." The testator believed that his wife would take all the estate on his intestacy, but this was not the case.

The court held that there was no revocation – the action of burning was done on the basis of a mistaken belief.

Was this a mistake of fact or a mistake of law? The intention to destroy the document is not the same as the intention to revoke the will.

Perkes v Perkes [1820] shows that the intention must be present throughout the act of destruction. During a quarrel with a beneficiary, the testator tore his will into four pieces. He was then restrained by a bystander and, after apologies from the beneficiary, the testator calmed down and put the will in his pocket. Later he took the will out again and said, "It is a good job it is no worse." The will was not revoked.

6.5 Presumption as to revocation

Where the original will was in the possession of the testator at death and is found in a mutilated condition, there is a presumption that the testator carried out the act with *animus revocandi* (***Lambell v Lambell [1831]***).

Where a will, known to be in the possession of the testator, cannot be found at death after reasonable searches and enquiries, the presumption arises that he has destroyed it with the intention of revoking it (***Welch v Philips [1836]***). The presumption can be rebutted by evidence to the contrary.

In ***Sugden v Lord St Leonards [1876]*** a former Lord Chancellor kept his will, a lengthy document, together with codicils, in a box to which he had the key. After his death, the will (but not the codicils) was found to be missing from the box. Evidence showed that it was possible for a number of people to have had access to the key.

Evidence was admitted to show that Lord St Leonards made numerous references to his will, and his daughter, who had acted as his secretary, was able to give a full account of the contents of the will that was fully consistent with the codicils. The court was impressed with her evidence and, further, considered that a Chancery lawyer was extremely unlikely to destroy his will without also destroying the codicils. Given his attitude to the will and the fact that the box could have been interfered with, the court concluded that the presumption of revocation with *animus revocandi* had been rebutted. ***Sugden*** shows the importance of evidence of the testator's attitude in rebutting the presumption.

6.5.1 Proof of lost or destroyed wills

It must be proved by affidavit evidence that a lost or destroyed will was validly executed and that it was not validly revoked. Also, the contents of the will must be proved. This may be done by producing a completed draft, or a copy, or the will may be reconstructed from the evidence of anyone who has knowledge of its contents, for example, a solicitor, witnesses or beneficiaries.

If a will is lost or destroyed, the court may need to determine whether it revoked an earlier will. The issue is whether the court is satisfied on the evidence that the earlier will was expressly or impliedly revoked.

In ***Re Wyatt [1952]*** the court declined to accept the evidence of the solicitor who prepared the will that it was his usual practice to insert a revocation clause. Contrast this decision with ***In the Estate of Hampshire [1951]***, where Karminski J thought it unlikely that a will prepared by a solicitor would not contain a revocation clause and therefore concluded that the later missing will, on the balance of probabilities, revoked the earlier will.

6.6 Dependent relative (conditional) revocation

If the testator makes a new will that purports to revoke an existing one, but the **new** will turns out **not** to be valid, then the old will remains valid.

The courts apply a presumption that the testator intended the old will to be revoked only on condition that the new will was valid.

In ***Re Jones [1976]*** the court laid down a series of questions to be asked to determine whether the revocation is conditional. The testatrix made a will in 1965 in which she left a smallholding to two nieces. In a conversation with her bank manager in 1970, shortly before her death, she complained about the attitude of the nieces and said that she intended to leave the property to the children of a nephew. A few days later, she told another nephew that she had not made a will. She arranged to see her solicitor to make another will but died before she could do so. After her death, the 1965 will was found with the signatures of the testatrix and witnesses scratched out. Evidence indicated that this action was done soon after the conversation with the bank manager.

The Court of Appeal posed a series of questions to be asked where a testator destroys their will.

- Did they do so with the intention of revoking it? If not, there is no revocation.
- If there was an intention to revoke, is the intention absolute or qualified?
- If qualified, what is the nature of the qualification?
- If the qualification is in the form of a condition or contingency, has that condition or contingency been fulfilled? If not, the revocation is ineffective.

Here, the court accepted the evidence that the revocation was unconditional, therefore she died intestate.

Conditional revocation was considered in some detail in ***Re Finnemore (Deceased) [1992]***. The testator made a will leaving a house, contents and three-quarters of the residuary estate to X and the remaining quarter to Y and Z. Two years later, in 1986, the testator executed two further wills. Both these wills of 1986 contained express revocation clauses. The first 1986 will repeated the gift to X and gave the remaining quarter to two charities. The second will was identical save that the quarter share of residue was now divided between three charities. Unfortunately, the two wills of 1986 were attested by X's husband, thereby avoiding the gifts to X by virtue of **s15 WA 1837**.

The court was asked to give directions as to whether, the gift to X having failed, the property should be held on trust for X on the basis that the express revocation clause in the last two wills was conditional, in that the intention of the testator all along was to benefit X, or whether the property passed on intestacy. The court held that the express revocation clauses could be given a distributive meaning, confirming some gifts and varying others. In adopting such an approach, the court was then able to hold that the revocation clause could apply absolutely in respect of the gift of one-quarter of the residue, but only conditionally to the gifts to X, thereby allowing an application of conditional revocation to save the gifts to her.

Conditional revocation will also apply to revocation by **destruction** if the testator intentionally revokes their will under a mistaken belief or where the testator revokes subject to a condition which is never fulfilled. ***Re Southerden [1925]*** (see **6.4.2**) is a good example of the application of the doctrine where a will is destroyed.

6.7 Revocation by marriage and civil partnership

English law regards entering into a marriage or a civil partnership as a highly significant change in personal circumstances. Once two people marry, they acquire rights and obligations in law including the right to inherit when one of them dies intestate. A same-sex couple who choose to enter into a civil partnership also transform their legal status and acquire equivalent rights to married people. In the light of this, English law assumes that existing wills will no longer be appropriate and simply provides that any existing will or codicil is revoked on marriage or civil partnership.

s18(1) WA 1837, as amended by **s18 Administration of Justice Act 1982** (**AJA 1982**), provides that a will *shall be revoked by the testator's marriage*. Marriage includes a voidable marriage. **s18B WA 1837** states that a will is revoked by entry into a civil partnership.

6.7.1 Wills made in expectation of marriage or civil partnership

Most people, once they have signed the marriage certificate, do not immediately reach for the pen to sign a new will. Weddings are expected to be happy occasions and an anticipation of death is generally felt to diminish the party spirit. Immediately after the wedding, most people go on a honeymoon, often flying abroad and travelling long distances. It may be several weeks before even the most organised of couples return home to normal life and the opportunity to make new wills. During this period, there is a risk that one or both of the couple may die leaving their property subject to the intestacy rules.

To deal with this situation, **WA 1837** (as amended by **AJA 1982**) provides a mechanism for an organised person who is about to marry to make a will that will continue to be valid after marriage.

s18(3) states:

Where it appears from a will that at the time it was made the testator was expecting to be married to a particular person and that he intended that the will should not be revoked by the marriage, the will shall not be revoked by his marriage to that person.

Under **s18(3)**, the will must show two things:

- that the testator was expecting to marry a particular person; and
- an intention that it would not be revoked by the marriage.

s18(4) provides:

Where it appears from a will at the time it was made the testator was expecting to be married to a particular person and that he intended that a disposition in the will should not be revoked by his marriage to that person:

(a) *that disposition shall take effect notwithstanding the marriage; and*

(b) *any other disposition in the will shall take effect also unless it appears from the will that the testator intended the disposition to be revoked by the marriage.*

If the testator should marry someone other than the person expressed in the contemplation, then the will will be revoked.

ss18B(3) and **(4)** apply similar rules in respect of wills made in expectation of a civil partnership to a particular person.

In ***Court and Others v Despallieres [2009]*** the court considered a will where the testator had subsequently entered into a civil partnership.

Clause 2 of the will stated that the will "shall not be revoked by neither subsequent marriage, civil union partnership nor adoption" and clause 4 gave the whole estate to X with whom the testator later entered into a civil partnership.

The court held that **s18B(3)** had not been complied with to save the will from revocation because the language of the will did not show that the testator expected to form a civil partnership specifically with X. The court found that clause 2 was merely a general statement that the will was intended to survive any marriage, civil partnership or adoption.

It did not show that the testator expected to form a civil partnership, let alone a civil partnership with a particular person. Nor was the court prepared to find that **s18B(3)** had been satisfied just because clause 4 made X the sole beneficiary, since there was nothing in the wording of the will itself to connect clause 2 with clause 4.

Same-sex marriages

The **Marriage (Same Sex Couples) Act 2013** (**M(SSC)A 2013**) came into force on 13 March 2014, permitting same-sex marriages.

As a consequence of **M(SSC)A 2013**, a will is automatically revoked by a same- sex marriage in the same way as if it was an opposite-sex marriage.

Under **M(SSC)A 2013** an existing civil partnership may be converted into a marriage; the marriage will be treated as having existed since the date on which the civil partnership was formed.

s18D WA 1837 provides that such a conversion of a civil partnership into a marriage will not revoke an existing will made by one of the parties to the marriage. In addition, where a will was made in expectation of a civil partnership with a particular person which was subsequently converted to a marriage, it will **not** be revoked by the subsequent conversion of the civil partnership to a marriage. Similarly, where the will was made in expectation of a civil partnership with a particular person and the parties chose, instead, to get married, the marriage will **not** revoke the will.

Predatory marriages

Private client lawyers may encounter situations where an elderly and vulnerable person establishes a relationship with a younger person who persuades them to marry. Other relatives, typically the children of the vulnerable spouse, are often anxious that they will be disinherited as a result. The following *Guardian* article discussing the case of Joan Blass illustrates how such a marriage can arise https://www.theguardian.com/society/2021/sep/15/daphne-franks-the-woman-who-lost-her-much-loved-mother-to-a-predatory-marriage.

Test for capacity to marry

The test for capacity to marry is much lower than the test for capacity to make a will. In ***NB v MI [2021] EWHC 224 (Fam)*** it was held that a prospective spouse *"must have the capacity to understand, in broad terms, that marriage confers on the couple the status of a recognised union which gives right to the expectation to share each other's society, comfort and assistance"*.

Available remedies

Where family members become aware of an intended predatory marriage, they can enter into a caveat under **s29 Marriage Act 1949** which will delay the marriage until the superintendent registrar has considered the circumstances. Alternatively, it may be possible to apply for a forced marriage protection order under **s63A Family Law Act 1996**.

Once a predatory marriage has taken place (which is often the first point family members become aware of it), they can apply to the Court of Protection for a statutory will to be made to ensure that they retain at least some of their expected share of the inheritance.

After the vulnerable person has died, following a predatory marriage, other relatives may be able to make a claim under the **Inheritance (Provision for Family and Dependants) Act 1975**.

Reform

The Law Commission's supplementary consultation paper in its *Making a Will* project is reviewing the law of wills in the round. The consultation included questions about whether the automatic revocation of wills on marriage should be reformed. For further details see https://www.lawcom.gov.uk/project/wills/.

6.7.2 Divorce, nullity and dissolution of a civil partnership

Unlike in the cases of marriage or civil partnership, English law does not consider it appropriate to revoke automatically an existing will when the testator gets divorced, has their marriage annulled or civil partnership dissolved. Clearly, though, the relationship with the ex-spouse or ex-civil partner will have changed. In most such cases, the testator will not want their ex-spouse or ex- civil partner to receive any more assets from their estate than were ordered to be paid by the courts. It is also unlikely that the testator will want the ex-spouse or ex-civil partner to be their executor. In other respects, however, the testator may be happy to leave the will unchanged.

Reflecting these assumptions, **s18A WA 1837**, until it was amended by the **Law Reform (Succession) Act 1995** (**LR(S)A 1995**), provided that a gift to a spouse in a will would fail if the testator subsequently divorced. In ***Re Sinclair [1985]*** such a gift was treated as simply lapsing when the testator died, despite the fact that the will had provided that the gift should pass to a charity if the wife predeceased the testator. So, the gift passed under the intestacy rules because the wife had not, in fact, predeceased and the gift did not pass to the charity. This result was considered by legal commentators to be unsatisfactory, given that the testator was assumed to have been more likely to have preferred that the charity should receive the legacy.

The revised **s18A**, which now applies, states that any appointment of a spouse as an executor will be invalid after divorce or nullity. **s18A** also provides that where an ex-spouse receives a gift under the will after divorce or nullity, they are to be **treated as having predeceased** the testator. The effect of the revised section on the facts of ***Re Sinclair*** would be that the gift would pass to the charity. **s18C** provides similar rules in relation to the appointment of ex-civil partners as executors and to gifts to ex-civil partners.

s6 Children Act 1989 provides that any appointment of an ex-spouse or ex- civil partner as a guardian of a child will be revoked by the subsequent divorce or dissolution of a civil partnership. This applies only where the ex-spouse or ex-civil partner is **not** the natural parent of the child.

6.8 Summary

(1) Wills are revocable until death – a will can be revoked only:

- expressly or impliedly by a subsequent testamentary instrument;
- by destruction with the necessary intention;
- by subsequent marriage or civil partnership.

Where a new will purports to revoke an existing one, but the new will turns out not to be valid, then the old one remains valid.

(2) Revocation by implication: two or more testamentary instruments can together constitute the will of the deceased to the extent to which they are not inconsistent. If they are inconsistent, the later one revokes the earlier one wholly or partly. It is a question of construction of the clauses.

(3) Revocation by destruction is governed by **s20 WA 1837**. There must be:

- an act of destruction; and
- an intention to revoke.

(4) Where the original will was in the possession of the testator at death and is found in a mutilated condition, there is a presumption that the testator carried out the act of destruction with the intention of destroying the will.

(5) **s18 WA 1837** provides that a will shall be revoked by the testator's marriage; **s18B** makes similar provision if the testator enters into a civil partnership. A will is not revoked if made in expectation of marriage to or civil partnership with a particular person.

(6) Divorce does not revoke a will, but under **s18A WA 1837** the will is construed as if the spouse had died on the date of the divorce. **s18C** similarly provides that, in the absence of any contrary intention expressed in the will, dissolution of a civil partnership shall cause a will to be construed as if a civil partner named in the will had died on the date of the dissolution.

CHAPTER 7
Mutual Wills

Aims of the Chapter:

By the end of this chapter, you should be able to:

- describe what is meant by a mutual will;
- detail how to prove the agreement, when the trust arises and what property the trust applies to; and
- discuss the problems that can arise from mutual wills.

7.1 Introduction

As discussed in **Chapter 1**, one of the key principles of English law is that every adult has a right to make a will leaving their property to anyone they choose. Tied into this principle is the right to revoke your will and make a new one. This freedom to change your mind is a right which an individual can exercise without regard to the wishes of anyone else.

Where two individuals are married or in a civil partnership or simply have closely tied their lives and finances together in a family, this freedom to revoke a will and replace it can become a source of worry. Consider the following example.

Scenario

Connie and Jim are a married couple in their 60s. They have four children. Connie is convinced, despite the disbelief of all her friends and family that, as soon as she dies, Jim will find another woman and leave everything he owns to her in his will. Nonetheless, Connie still wants to leave all her property to Jim with a proviso that if he predeceases her, her property will pass to their four children. Jim, who always leaves financial affairs to Connie anyway, is quite happy to make a will giving all his property to Connie or to their children if she has predeceased him. How can Connie be reassured that her wishes will be followed after her death if she predeceases Jim?

In order to deal with this sort of situation where there is a measure of distrust affecting the relationship, the concept of mutual wills has been devised. Essentially, it applies where the testators have **agreed** to make wills leaving their property in the same way on the understanding that, on the death of the first one to die, the surviving testator will not make a new will changing the beneficiaries. In these circumstances, the law will impose a **constructive trust** on the second of the couple to die which will take away their freedom to make a new will breaking the agreed provisions.

7.2 The principle of the mutual will

The principle is described in the headnote to ***Stone v Hoskins [1905]***: *"Where two persons have made an arrangement as to the disposal of their property and then executed mutual wills in pursuance of that arrangement, the one of them who predeceases the other dies with the implied promise of the survivor that the arrangement shall hold good; and if the survivor, after taking a benefit under the arrangement, alters his will, his personal representative takes the property upon trust to perform the contract, for the will of the one who has died first has, by the death, become irrevocable. But, on the contrary, where the one who dies first has departed from the bargain by executing a fresh will revoking the former one, the survivor, who has, on the death of the other party to the arrangement, notice of the alteration, cannot claim to have the later will of the deceased set aside or modified, either by way of declaration of trust or otherwise."*

In ***Re Dale (Deceased) [1993]*** Morritt J held that the doctrine of mutual wills was not confined to cases where the second testator benefited under the will of the testator who was the first to die. The aim of the principle was to prevent the latter from being defrauded.

In ***Re Dale*** a husband and wife each made wills in 1988 on the same terms, whereby they left their property to the husband's (H's) daughter and the wife's (W's) son. H died two months later. In 1990, W made a new will revoking her 1988 will and, after a bequest to H's daughter, left the bulk of the estate to her son. H's daughter commenced proceedings, claiming that the 1988 wills were made in pursuance of an agreement and that W was bound in equity to adhere to the terms of the 1988 wills.

Morritt J applied ***Dufour v Pereira [1769]***: there must be a legally binding contract to make and not to revoke mutual wills and the first testator must have died having performed their part of the agreement. He cited Lord Camden LC who said that the basis of the doctrine is: *"if the other then refuses, he is guilty of a fraud, can never unbind himself, and becomes a trustee of course. For no man shall deceive another to his prejudice. By engaging to do something that is in his power, he is made trustee for the performance, and transmits that trust to those that claim under him."*

The doctrine applied when the second testator benefited under the will of the first testator; however, Morritt J said that it should not be any less fraud on the first testator if the agreement was that each testator should leave their property to particular beneficiaries (e.g. their children) rather than to each other. It should be assumed that they had good reason for doing so and, in any event, that was what the parties bargained for. In each case, there was a binding contract. In each case, it had been performed by the first testator on the faith of the promise of the second testator. A fraud on the first testator would include cases where the second testator benefited, but there was no reason why the principle should not be confined to such cases. It was therefore held to be consistent with the authorities and was in furtherance of equity's original jurisdiction to intervene in cases of fraud.

In ***Fry v Densham-Smith [2010]*** the Court of Appeal reviewed previous authorities and said that in order to prove the existence of mutual wills, the evidence has to establish:

- a prior agreement by the testators to make mutual wills intending their agreement to become irrevocable on the death of the first to die; and
- the making of mutual wills pursuant to that agreement.

If the testators failed to execute mutual wills pursuant to their agreement, that agreement did not become irrevocable on the death of the first to die.

The evidence required for an express agreement not to revoke the wills had to be:

- certain; and
- unequivocal or clear; and
- satisfactory;

so as to satisfy the court that, on the balance of probabilities, such an agreement had been made.

An agreement would not be implied simply from the fact that the testators had made similar reciprocal (mirror) wills.

In this case, the Court of Appeal found that the trial judge had been entitled to find on the evidence that there had been an oral mutual wills agreement so as to entitle the defendant to one-half of the survivor's estate, despite the survivor having changed her will three times after the first party to the agreement had died. In effect, a constructive trust had been imposed when the first party died and this was binding on the survivor's estate. Under the trust, the defendant was entitled to half of the survivor's net estate with the other half going to the claimant who had tried to establish that the defendant had no interest in it.

The main questions to consider are:

- How do you prove the agreement?
- When does the trust arise?
- What property does the trust affect?

7.2.1 The agreement

"To enforce a mutual will there has to be clear evidence on the balance of probabilities that there has been agreement between the two parties to dispose of their property in a similar way in mutual wills" (per Nourse J in ***Re Cleaver [1981]***).

The fact that the wills are executed simultaneously and are similar in form are relevant circumstances to be taken into account, but not enough, by themselves, to establish the necessary agreement.

In ***Re Oldham [1925]*** Astbury J stated that *"the fact that the two wills were made in identical terms does not necessarily connote any agreement beyond that of so making them"*. The agreement required is generally an agreement not to revoke the mutual wills unilaterally.

In ***Re Goodchild [1996]*** it was suggested that nothing would suffice short of a contract not to revoke one will without the consent of the other testator. A high standard of proof is not required as in secret or constructive trust cases, because there is no fraud involved – only the trustee's own property is affected. The court went on to say that even if it was not correct to say that a binding contract was required, more was required than a mere understanding between the testators that the agreed beneficiary should benefit. It must also be agreed that neither testator could change their will without the consent of the other, and be understood that the surviving testator could not prevent the agreed beneficiary from inheriting.

In ***Birmingham v Renfrew [1937]*** the court allowed extrinsic evidence to establish whether or not there was an enforceable agreement.

In ***Re Cleaver*** the parties were married in October 1967 when the testator was aged 78 and the testatrix 74. The testator had three children from a previous marriage; the testatrix had none. They each had their own assets and kept their finances separate. In December 1967 and June 1970, each made successive wills in similar terms – all property to the survivor and thereafter to the testator's children in equal shares. In 1974, the testator decided to restrict the share of his daughter to a life interest; the testatrix either shared his views or at least was prepared to go along with the limited interest and both executed similar wills in February 1974, giving a life interest to the daughter with a gift over in favour of the other children.

The testator died a year later. The same evening the testatrix had a conversation with a son of the testator recognising her obligation to the testator. In May 1975, another will was executed, virtually identical to the 1974 will. In November 1975, another will left all the property to the three children in equal shares. In June 1977, the last will left all the property to the daughter and her husband, excluding the other children (the claimants).

On the death of the testatrix a year later, the claimants sought a declaration that the estate of the testatrix was to be distributed in accordance with the 1974 will on the basis of an enforceable agreement to execute mutual wills. The court granted the declaration.

Charles and Others v Fraser [2010] involved reciprocal wills made in 1991 by two sisters. The issue was whether the evidence justified a finding that both sisters had committed themselves to testamentary dispositions which were to be irrevocable on the part of the survivor. The surviving sister had changed her will after the first sister's death.

The deputy judge was satisfied that there had been such agreement between the two sisters through mutual promises made to each other, but what is perhaps most important in this case are the *per curiam* remarks made by the deputy judge. He was critical about those involved in the drafting of the mutual wills for apparently not establishing the sisters' intentions as to revocation, nor advising on the effect of making mutual wills and then failing to ensure that the agreement was clearly and accurately recorded. He said that it was the "*plain duty*" of a solicitor, so instructed, to have done these things.

Practitioners should ensure that each testator considers whether the survivor is free to revoke their will. Above all is the need to record carefully any agreement, both in the will and in a separate attendance note. Indeed, if reciprocal or mirror wills are not intended to be mutual, then it is also worth recording this fact in each will so as to avoid allegations to the contrary being made after the survivor's death.

Healey v Brown [2002] held that if a mutual wills agreement affects land, then it is subject to **s2 Law of Property (Miscellaneous Provisions) Act 1989** as a contract for the disposition of an interest in land. As such, the agreement must not only be in writing but must be signed by both parties. In this case, the court found that both wills did form a contract intended to deal with the devolution of property, formerly held jointly, on the survivor's death. However, since neither will contained **both** signatures of the two parties, it could not be enforceable as a contract for the disposal of an interest in land. Therefore, if a mutual wills agreement is likely to deal with land or an interest in land, there needs to be a separate written agreement signed by both parties.

7.2.2 When does the trust arise?

The survivor of the parties to the agreement cannot, after the death of the first party, be allowed to depart from the arrangement. Any new will is admitted to probate, but equity imposes a constructive trust on the PRs to give effect to the terms of the agreement. The trust becomes binding once the first testator dies while the mutual wills are still in force. This is known as the **crystallisation** of the trust.

While both parties are alive, the relationship is founded upon contract and the arrangement can be ended unilaterally, with or without notice to the other, for example, by revocation of the will as in ***Stone v Hoskins [1905]***. Further, if one testator alters their will while both testators are alive, then unless the other is known to have agreed, this will revoke the mutual will. It was argued in ***Re Hobley [1997]*** that an insignificant alteration should not invalidate the agreement for mutual wills. This argument was rejected on the ground that what was important was the views of the other testator on the alteration – what is significant to one party may not be so to the other. Further, it was held to be irrelevant that the alteration did not disadvantage the other testator. In short, any alteration without the consent of the other testator will invalidate the mutual will.

In ***Re Hagger [1930]*** spouses executed a joint mutual will whereby all property was to go to the survivor for life and thereafter on trust for nine named beneficiaries, including P. P died after the death of the wife but before the death of the husband. It was held that P's share did not lapse. P obtained a vested interest on the death of the wife in respect of her property and was protected as regards the trust that arose on the death of the wife on the basis of the mutual will.

It was thought in the past that revocation of a mutual will by remarriage of the surviving testator would not be a breach of the mutual will arrangement. In ***Re Goodchild [1996]***, however, it was held that revocation of a mutual will by marriage would give rise to the trust to give effect to the terms of the mutual will.

7.2.3 What property does the trust affect?

Does the trust cover all the property of the party who dies first? Does the trust extend to all the property of the survivor?

In ***Re Green [1951]*** a husband and wife executed wills leaving their property to one another with the proviso that the survivor was to leave half of the property to certain specified charities. The wife died first and the husband remarried, executing a will in favour of his second wife.

It was held that the later will was effective to deal only with half the property of the husband, the other half being subject to the trusts of the mutual will.

It is clear from ***Re Green*** that the survivor's entire estate is not subject to the trust and the trust generally applies only to the estate inherited from the other testator. There is some doubt about which property is subject to the trust. In principle, the trust applies to all the property owned when the first testator died, because that is when the trust arose. On this basis, the trust would apply to the property inherited from the first testator, which was subject to the agreement, and also to the survivor's property that they owned at that time. On the other hand, it does not apply to property acquired by the survivor after that date. In practice, the trust can apply only to the assets owned by the survivor on death, which appears to fly in the face of normal trust principles. The trust will not, in practice, prevent the survivor from disposing of what they reasonably believe to be their assets.

A solution is suggested in the Australian case of ***Birmingham v Renfrew [1937]*** – the survivor is to be treated as the absolute owner of the property during their lifetime (subject to any stipulation in the will) but, on death, the property must devolve in the agreed manner.

Per Dixon J: "[T]*he object of the transaction is to put the survivor in a position to enjoy for his own benefit the full ownership so that, for instance, he may convert it and expend the proceeds as he chooses. But when he dies he is to bequeath what is left in the manner agreed upon.*" Dixon J went on to describe the requirements of the mutual wills as a *"floating obligation"* which will, on the death of the survivor, *"crystallise into a trust"*.

7.2.4 What is the nature of the trust?

Cases on mutual wills are only one example of a wider category of cases in which a court of equity will intervene to impose a constructive trust. It follows, therefore, that there must be, in addition to proof of agreement, certainty of subject matter and objects.

7.3 Criticisms of mutual wills

Although English judges subsequently used the concept of the constructive trust to justify the doctrine, Lord Camden in ***Dufour v Pereira [1769]*** was (unusually) influenced by French law, which had a concept of shared mutual family property. This was probably as a result of the parties in this case being French.

The key problem is that the doctrine of mutual wills undermines the clear-cut concept of testamentary freedom. When one member of a couple dies, the survivor may live for many years and have legitimate reasons for changing their will to reflect radically different circumstances. Setting up express trusts under the wills of each party is a much more practical alternative because the assets affected are clearly defined at the outset and are subject to detailed rules on the powers of trustees.

Key Concepts

Law Commission Consultation Paper *Making a will* (Consultation Paper 231)

The Law Commission's consultation reviewed the problems with mutual wills, including the difficulties created by the rigidity of arrangements made many years earlier applying to the changed circumstances of the last testator to die. Despite these difficulties, it considers that full abolition would be too great an attack on contractual freedom.

Self-assessment Question

In the light of the difficulties with the case law on mutual wills, do you think that the doctrine should be retained? If it should be retained, how do you think it should be reformed?

7.4 Summary

(1) A mutual will arises when there has been an agreement between two people to make wills in similar terms to achieve agreed results. This creates a constructive trust.

(2) The trust created by the agreement arises when the first person dies. Until that date, each person retains complete freedom to make a new will outside the terms of the agreement.

(3) The property covered by the mutual wills is generally considered to be the property inherited by the second party to die from the first party to die, although there is some uncertainty in the case law.

CHAPTER 8

Alterations to Wills

Aims of the Chapter:

By the end of this chapter, you should be able to:

- identify the effects of alterations and obliterations on a will;
- distinguish between alterations made before and after the execution of a will;
- explain how a codicil can republish an altered will.

8.1 Introduction

A professionally drafted will should be executed only after it has been carefully checked by the testator, as well as the lawyer. The testator should sign only after they are happy that they understand the effects of the will and that all the details of beneficiaries, legacies and gifts are correct. Changes and amendments to the will should have been dealt with during the drafting stages.

Unfortunately, real life is not always so tidy. Sometimes, the client will identify an error with a will only after taking it home. In other cases, the lawyer may identify small errors only when checking the executed will. While it might generally be better simply to execute a new will, the testator may be dying and there may be insufficient time.

In addition, lawyers may be asked to administer wills where there are hand- written amendments and there is no indication as to when the amendments were made or even whether they were, in fact, made by the testator.

In order to deal with these issues and to minimise the risk of fraud, English law has devised rules setting out when alterations will be effective. The key distinction in these rules lies in whether they were made before or after the will was executed.

8.2 Alterations and obliterations

Before considering the detailed rules, first look at the following examples of the changes that might be found in a will.

(1) **Obliteration**

"I give [illegible] to Georgina Harris."

The original words have been made completely indecipherable.

(2) **Alterations**

£3,000

(a) "I give to Ellen Chang ~~£2,500~~."

(b) "I give to Peter Chekhov a legacy of £500,000"

A stick-on label has covered up the original text.

(c) "I give to Deirdre McBride the sum of *£20,000* free of tax." A gap in the typed text has been filled in by handwriting.

(d) "I give to Morwenna Alys Jones the sum of ~~£45,000~~ free of tax."

£4,500

The amendment is in pencil.

(e) "I give to Abigail Lewis ~~£100~~ free of tax."
£1,000 AL FRC PRC

The testator and the two witnesses have added their initials.

There are two questions when considering the effect of any alteration:

(1) Is it valid so that effect can be given to it?

(2) If it is not valid, how does this affect the relevant provision in the will?

8.3 Alterations made before the execution of the will

When a court is considering a will on which an alteration has been marked but not attested by the testator's and witnesses' signatures or initials, it will apply a legal presumption that the alteration was made after execution and so is invalid. The presumption does not apply if the alteration was simply completing a blank space on the original document (as in **8.2**(2)(c)) (***Cooper v Bockett [1846]***).

Where the alteration is in pencil (as in **8.2**(2)(d)), it is presumed to be merely deliberative, that is, the testator was still mulling over their decision (***In the Goods of Bellamy [1886]***). The alteration will not be valid.

If there is evidence, such as affidavits from the witnesses to the will, that shows that the alteration was present at the time the will was executed, the Registrar or District Judge will be able to overturn the presumption that the alteration was made after execution (**r14 Non-Contentious Probate Rules 1987**). The alteration will be treated as having been made before execution and will therefore be valid.

8.4 Alterations and obliterations made after the execution of the will

Where an alteration has been made to a will or part of the text has been obliterated after the will was executed, **s21 Wills Act 1837** (**WA 1837**) states:

No obliteration, interlineation [insertion between the lines of the will] or other alteration in any will after the execution thereof shall be valid or have any effect, except so far as the words or the effect of the will before such alteration shall not be apparent, unless such alteration shall be executed in like manner as hereinbefore is required for the execution of the will.

This dense paragraph has a number of important effects.

(1) **Alterations and obliterations which have been executed by the testator and witnesses**

Although a will should be signed by the testator and witnesses writing their full signatures, alterations need only be executed by the initials of the testator and witnesses (***In the Goods of Blewitt [1880]***). An example is given at **8.2**(2)(e), where the alteration is valid because it has been initialled.

(2) **Alterations or interlineations where the original text is still apparent and which have not been executed**

An example of this would be where the sum given as a legacy has a line through it and the replacement sum is written above it. Under **s21**, the will is to be construed (interpreted) as if the ruled-through text had not been deleted. The example at **8.2**(2)(a) would be interpreted as:

"I give to Ellen Chang £2,500."

(3) **Unexecuted obliterations of the original text – the original text is not apparent**

Under **s21**, an obliteration applies where the original wording is not **apparent**. An example of such an obliteration is at **8.2**(1). The original wording will not have been obliterated if it can be read by natural means, for example, by using a magnifying glass or holding the paper up to the light. Where strips of paper have been stuck over the original text (see **8.2**(2)(b)), the original wording has been held to have been obliterated (***Re Itter [1950]***). Other scientific methods of finding the original wording, such as infra-red photography, are not permitted since they are not applied using natural means.

The effect of an obliteration will be that probate will be granted with a blank space instead of the obliterated words (***In the Estate of Hamer [1943]***). The example at **8.2**(1) would read:

"I give to Georgina Harris."

In effect, Georgina would receive nothing because the obliteration amounts to a partial revocation of that part of the will.

There are two exceptions to the above rule about obliterations.

(a) Unintentional obliteration

If the testator did not intend to obliterate the words – for example, they spilled ink on the will or a third party obliterated the words without the testator's knowledge – the original wording will still apply because they lacked intention to revoke. Evidence for this wording may be found from a copy will.

(b) Conditional revocation

Where the testator intended the original wording to be obliterated only if replacement wording was valid and the replacement wording was **not** valid – for example, because it was not executed – the doctrine of conditional revocation will apply. In these circumstances, non-natural means or extrinsic evidence such as a copy of the original may be used to identify the original obliterated wording. This doctrine was applied in ***Re Itter*** and the strips of paper were removed to find the original wording. Probate is granted with the original wording. So, in **8.2**(2)(b), because £500,000 has been written on the sticky label with the intention of replacing the original figure, the label can be removed to reveal the original amount, which is then admitted to probate. However, if no replacement figure had been written on the label (or elsewhere on the will), then it is treated as a partial revocation of that part of the will and so Peter would receive nothing.

8.5 Codicil republishing an altered will

Where a will has been altered after execution and the alteration is unexecuted, a codicil to the will will republish (see **9.2**) the will as valid at the date of the codicil. If the codicil refers to the alteration to the will in some way, the alteration will be valid (***In the Goods of Heath [1892]***). Alternatively, the alteration will be valid if there is other evidence that it was made before the codicil was executed.

8.6 Summary

(1) The rules dealing with alterations and obliterations to wills are found in **s21 WA 1837**.

(2) Alterations made before the execution of a will are valid unless they are merely deliberative, but there is a legal presumption that an alteration is made after execution.

(3) Alterations and obliterations made after the execution of the will but which have been executed are valid if they have been executed by the initials of the testator and witnesses.

(4) Unexecuted alterations after the execution of the will, where the original wording is decipherable, are not valid. Probate is granted to the original wording.

(5) Unexecuted obliterations after the will has been executed are valid and treated as a partial revocation if the original wording is not decipherable by natural means. Probate is granted with a blank space. The original wording can be discovered using non-natural means where the obliteration was accidental or where the doctrine of conditional revocation applies.

CHAPTER 9
Republication and Revival

Aims of the Chapter:

By the end of this chapter, you should be able to:

- describe how an existing will may be republished"; and
- explain when a revoked will can be revived.

9.1 Introduction

Where a codicil is made to a will, it has the effect of confirming the will. The confirmed will is treated as operating from the date of the codicil. This process of confirming an unrevoked will is known as **republication**.

A codicil may also be used to revive a revoked will that has not been destroyed. Again, the revoked will becomes valid and operates from the date of the codicil.

9.2 Republication

s34 Wills Act 1837 (**WA 1837**) provides for republication of a will by re- execution or by a codicil to the will. For a codicil to republish the will, it must contain some reference to the will, however slight. This is usually present in professionally drawn codicils.

In ***Re Harvey [1947]*** a codicil made in 1927 which merely recorded that a former codicil had been revoked described itself as "a codicil to my will of 7th November 1912". Vaisey J held that this was sufficient to effect republication.

The doctrine of republication is important in a number of areas, particularly in construing references in the will to persons or property – for example, the rule on ademption (see **13.2**).

The doctrine of republication will not be applied so as to defeat the intention of the testator by, for instance, invalidating a gift which was valid at the date of the will. Per Barton J in ***Re Moore [1907]***: "[R]*epublication is not a rigid or technical rule, but a useful and flexible instrument for effectuating the testator's intentions by ascertaining them down to the latest date at which they have been expressed."*

Although republication updates a will, it does not do so for all purposes. Republication does not revive a legacy that has been revoked or adeemed (failed), nor does it revive a gift that has lapsed.

In ***Re Galway's Will Trusts [1949]*** a codicil dated 1927 contained a specific gift of mines and minerals. The codicil was republished after the **Coal Act 1938** had vested the mines in the Coal Commission. The question arose as to who was entitled to the government compensation money – the specific devisee or the residuary legatee. The court held that the **Coal Act 1938** had caused the devise to adeem and the money fell into residue.

In ***Re Hardyman [1925]*** the testatrix made a will in 1893 by which she bequeathed a legacy of £5,000 "in trust for my cousin, his children and his wife". The cousin was at that time married to X, who died in January 1901. In November 1901, the testatrix, aware of the death of X, made a codicil to her will. The codicil made no mention of the legacy. Later, in 1903, the cousin married Y. Did the reference to "wife" in the will mean X or Y? What was the effect of the codicil?

The court held that the will and the codicil had to be read together. It appeared after republication that the reference was to any lady the cousin might marry and not to the first wife. Y was therefore entitled.

The importance of republication in saving a gift is seen in ***Re Reeves [1928]***. By his will, made in 1921, the testator gave to his daughter "any interest in my present lease of . . .". At the date of the will, the lease of the property had three years to run and, following the expiry of the term, the testator renewed the lease for 12 years. In 1925, after the renewal, he executed a codicil confirming his will. If the legacy had referred more specifically to the lease which ran out, for example, giving the date it was created, the gift would have been adeemed and could not have been saved by the codicil.

The court held that the new lease passed to the daughter because the codicil had republished the will and "present lease" meant the lease at the date of the codicil.

A beneficiary, the testator's spouse or civil partner who witnesses a will cannot take a benefit by **s15 WA 1837** (see **3.6**); however, if a later codicil republishes the will, provided that the beneficiary, spouse or civil partner is not a witness to the **codicil**, the later codicil validates the earlier gift which would not otherwise have passed by virtue of **s15** (***Anderson v Anderson [1872]***).

9.3 Revival

A will that has been revoked other than by destruction can be revived, that is, brought back into effect, by the re-execution of the will or by a codicil properly executed showing an intention to revive it (**s22 WA 1837**). It follows, therefore, that a will revoked by destruction cannot be revived. The court looks for clear evidence of the intention to revive. Following the *dictum* of Sir James Wilde in ***In the Goods of Steele [1868]***, in order to effect revival by a codicil, the intention to revive must appear in the codicil in one of three ways:

- express words showing an intention to revive;
- by some disposition clearly inconsistent with any other intention; or
- by any other form of expression which conveys the intention with reasonable certainty.

In ***Marsh v Marsh [1860]*** merely attaching a codicil to a revoked will by means of a tape did not effect revival.

In ***Re Dear [1975]*** the testatrix made her first will in 1942 and expressly revoked it by a will in 1950. In 1962, she executed a codicil which referred to the previously revoked will of 1942. The court held that the reference in the codicil was insufficient to effect revival (following ***In the Goods of Steele***). The reference merely created an ambiguity, but as there was no evidence to resolve the ambiguity, there was no revival.

Revival can be effected only in the ways set out above. Revocation of a later will that has revoked an earlier will cannot, simply by the act of revocation, revive the earlier will (***In the Goods of Hodgkinson [1893]***). A will may be revoked without the testator realising – for example, revocation by subsequent marriage. There is no English authority as to whether a testator could revive a will which they are unaware of having revoked, though the Malaysian case, ***Re Wan Kee Cheong [1975]***, suggests that they could.

In the Estate of Davis [1952] is the nearest English example. The testator made a will in 1931 leaving all his estate to Ethel Phoebe Horsley; the next year he married the beneficiary, which had the effect of revoking the will, because it had not been made in contemplation of marriage. In 1943, the testator wrote on the will "Ethel Phoebe Horsley is now my lawful wedded wife" and this statement was executed in accordance with **s9**. There was evidence to suggest that the testator had realised that his marriage had revoked the will and so the court held that this was evidence of an intention to revive the will.

The revived will is valid as at the date of the revival. Unattested alterations may then be effective through the revival if made before the revival.

9.4 Summary

(1) An unrevoked will may be confirmed (republished) under **s34 WA 1837** by a later codicil. The will operates from the date of the codicil in most respects although it does not revive a legacy that has been adeemed or revoked (e.g. by an earlier codicil).

(2) The codicil republishing the will must contain some reference to the will, however slight.

(3) A will revoked other than by destruction may be revived by a codicil. The effect is that the will becomes valid as at the date of the codicil. Intention to revive must be indicated in the codicil either by express words or a disposition inconsistent with any other intention.

CHAPTER 10

Intestacy

Aims of the Chapter:

By the end of this chapter, you should be able to:

- describe when an intestacy arises;
- explain when a partial intestacy arises;
- explain how an intestate's estate is distributed by reference to the size of their estate and their family tree;
- describe the rights of legitimate, illegitimate and adopted children under an intestacy; and
- summarise the rules that applied to intestate deaths prior to 1 October 2014.

10.1 Introduction

In the News

The following article in the *Standard* describes how two brothers of a wealthy ex-model inherited huge sums from their sister, Janet Baird, who had died without a will https://www.standard.co.uk/hp/front/found-longlost-brother-of-exmodel-who-left-ps4m-7205018.html.

The majority of the population of England and Wales die, like Janet Baird, intestate, that is, without having made a will. Sometimes, this is a result of a deliberate decision, often based on the assumption that they do not own enough to make one worthwhile. In other cases, they have simply not got round to what can seem a depressing and morbid exercise. On death, their estates are distributed in accordance with fixed rules.

The law of England and Wales that deals with the distribution of assets on intestacy is based on a number of assumptions about what a typical person who has died intestate would have put in any will they might have made.

(1) All their property would have been given to relatives.

(2) Spouses or civil partners would be given priority.

(3) Where the value of the estate is larger, children would share the assets with a spouse or civil partner.

(4) If there is no spouse or civil partner, the estate would be distributed to other relatives, with closer blood relatives taking priority over more distant relatives.

(5) Where there are no relatives at all, the Crown would receive the estate.

The law dealing with intestacy (the intestacy rules) is found in the **Administration of Estates Act 1925** (**AEA 1925**), as amended, and the **Intestates' Estates Act 1952** (**IEA 1952**).

NB The **Inheritance and Trustees' Powers Act 2014** (**ITPA 2014**), which came into force on 1 October 2014, has made significant changes which are covered in this chapter.

10.2 Partial intestacies

A partial intestacy occurs where there is a valid will but one of the following circumstances applies.

(1) The will does not dispose of all of the estate, typically, where a will has no residuary clause.

(2) The will contains provisions that would dispose of all of the estate but a gift of the residuary estate fails – for example, the residuary beneficiary predeceases the testator and there is no clause substituting an alternative beneficiary.

If a partial intestacy occurs, valid legacies under the will must be paid in the normal way. The property that is not disposed of under the will is then distributed under the testator's partial intestacy by applying the intestacy rules.

One consequence of a partial intestacy might be that the rules will favour a relative the testator would not have wanted to benefit, that is, someone who was not mentioned in the testator's will. In practice, a well-drafted will should always avoid the possibility of a partial intestacy arising by making additional provision if the main gifts fail for some reason.

10.3 The s33 statutory trust

When a person dies wholly or partially intestate, all their assets become subject to a statutory trust under **s33 AEA 1925**. The PRs, under **s33**, hold all of the undisposed-of estate on trust with the power to sell. The PRs are required to pay funeral expenses and debts from the intestate's cash and the proceeds of sale of other assets. They must also pay any valid legacies arising under the will in the case of a partial intestacy.

The PRs must then hold the remaining estate to be distributed under the strict order of entitlement in **s46 AEA 1925** (see **10.4**).

NB Do not confuse this **s33** statutory trust of the intestate's property with the **s47** statutory trusts also arising under **AEA 1925**, which set out how the intestate's issue and other relatives take the property when they are entitled. **s47** statutory trusts are explained in **10.4**.

10.4 Distribution on intestacy

Applying the distribution rules in **s46** to a particular individual's estate requires knowledge of the intestate's relatives and the approximate size and nature of their estate. It is usually helpful to draw up a family tree so that you are aware of the various relationships. It is also helpful to show the ages of individuals, particularly those under full age and also whether anyone is married or in a civil partnership.

Your tree must also show the issue (i.e. children, grandchildren, etc.) of any relative who may have predeceased the deceased.

When presented with an intestacy distribution, the best approach is as follows.

(1) Start by asking whether the deceased left a surviving spouse or civil partner.

(2) If the answer is "yes", then you also need to find out what other relatives survived because that will determine how much of the estate will be taken by the surviving spouse or civil partner. Our search for other relatives in this case need not take us beyond the deceased's children (or their issue).

(3) If the answer is that there is no surviving spouse or civil partner, then you need to find out what other relatives survived but, in this case (for reasons that will become apparent later), your enquiries may lead you to classes of more distant relatives (and ultimately to the Crown if there are none).

In the text that follows we will look at a family tree to see how the rules are applied in various situations. There is also a flow chart at **10.4.6** which you will find helpful.

So, first let us have a look at Deirdre's family tree.

Case Study

Deirdre's family tree

When Deirdre dies, she leaves behind her a large and complex family. Her surviving relatives who potentially could inherit her estate are as follows.

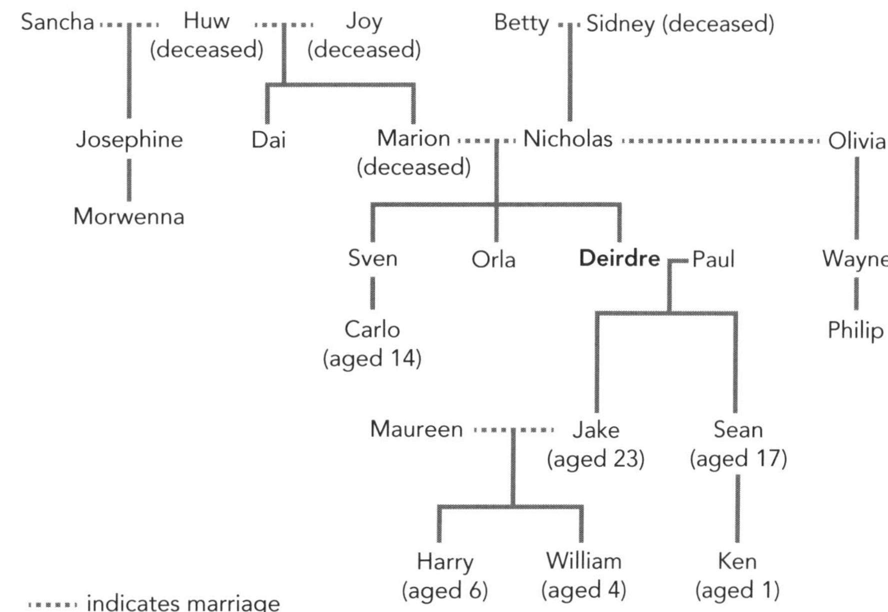

Paul	–	husband
Jake	–	son (Jake's wife, Maureen, is expecting a child in three months)
Sean	–	son (not married or in a civil partnership)
Harry and William	–	Jake's children
Ken	–	Sean's child
Nicholas	–	father
Sven	–	brother (of the whole blood, i.e. with the same mother and father)
Orla	–	sister (of the whole blood, i.e. with the same mother and father)
Wayne	–	brother (of the half blood, i.e. with only one parent (Nicholas) who is the same)
Philip	–	nephew of the half blood (Wayne's issue)
Betty	–	grandparent
Dai	–	uncle (of the whole blood, i.e. brother of the whole blood of Deirdre's mother)
Josephine	–	aunt (of the half blood, i.e. sister of the half blood of Deirdre's mother)

10.4.1 The s46 order of entitlement

The basic order of priority in which relatives are entitled under **s46 AEA 1925** is as follows:

- spouse (this includes spouses in same-sex marriages following the **Marriage (Same Sex Couples) Act 2013**) or civil partner;
- issue (i.e. deceased's children and direct descendants) on the statutory trusts;
- parents;
- brothers and sisters of the whole blood on the statutory trusts;
- brothers and sisters of the half blood on the statutory trusts;
- grandparents;
- uncles and aunts of the whole blood on the statutory trusts;

- uncles and aunts of the half blood on the statutory trusts;
- the Crown (i.e. the state).

Apart from the spouse or civil partner, all the relationships here must be linked by blood, so someone who may be referred to by the family as the intestate's "Auntie Seetha", because they are married to the intestate's uncle, does not qualify to take. However, there are special rules applicable to adopted persons etc. (see **10.5**).

We will consider in **10.4.3** and **10.4.5** how this order is applied but note that some of the relatives in the **s46** order are described as taking "on the statutory trusts"; we will now consider what this term means.

10.4.2 The s47 statutory trusts

Taking on the statutory trusts is defined in **s47 AEA 1925** as including the class of relative to whom it applies together with the issue (i.e. children or other direct descendants) of the relative in question if that relative has **predeceased** the intestate (but see below for a minor exception to this rule).

It is easiest to explain the workings of the statutory trusts in the context of one arising in favour of the children of the deceased. We will do this **but** keep in mind that the operation of the statutory trusts will be exactly the same where it applies to other classes of relatives, such as brothers and sisters or uncles and aunts.

If the deceased has several children who are entitled under the intestacy, the property available for distribution is divided up *per stirpes* [Latin: pronounced "per stirpays"], that is, in equal shares. Included in the definition of a child is a child *en ventre sa mère* [French: "in its mother's womb"] that is, unborn at the date of death but later born alive.

There are two important qualifications to the way in which the statutory trusts in **s47** work.

(1) If a child has **predeceased** the intestate leaving a child of his own (i.e. intestate's grandchild), then that child will "step into his deceased parent's shoes" and inherit the parent's share of the estate. If the intestate has more than one child of their own, those children share equally their parent's share of the estate.

(2) The shares due to children (or their issue) are **contingent** on them attaining the age of **18 years** or **marrying** (or **forming a civil partnership**) **earlier**. So, if a child survives the intestate but dies before attaining 18 years or earlier marriage/civil partnership, their share will devolve as if they had not existed. Note, however, that **s1 Marriage and Civil Partnership (Minimum Age) Act 2022** has increased the minimum age at which a person can marry to 18 years. This applies to all marriages from 27 February 2023 onwards.

Case Study (continued)

Consider Deirdre's family tree. If her children are entitled on the statutory trusts, the available property will be divided equally between Jake and Sean.

Jake has already reached 18 and so has attained a vested interest in the half share. Sean is only 17 and so has a contingent entitlement. It will become vested when he attains 18.

If Jake had predeceased Deirdre, his own children, Harry, William, and also his expected child, if later born alive, would have the same potential rights to inherit as Jake would have had if he had not predeceased. So, Jake's half share will be further divided into three. Harry, William and the new-born child will need to satisfy the **s47** contingency before attaining a vested interest.

If, in this scenario, Harry later died aged 10, then Jake's half share would now be held equally for William and the new- born child. In other words, it would be as if Harry had never existed at the time of Deirdre's death.

Finally, as was said above, there is a minor exception to the rule that the issue of a member of the class can take only if the original class member has predeceased. Ordinarily, if a potential beneficiary identified at the date of the intestate's death dies later and before attaining a vested interest (i.e. before reaching 18 years), then the estate is dealt with as though that person had never existed. There is now an exceptional case if the intestate died on or after 1 February 2012 and **s3 Estates of Deceased Persons (Forfeiture Rule and Law of Succession) Act 2011** applies.

The position under **s3** is that if the beneficiary in question actually dies after the intestate without having attained a vested interest but leaves issue, then the beneficiary is nonetheless treated as if they had predeceased. This means that their issue can take their share under the statutory trusts in just the same way that they would have done if the beneficiary had actually predeceased the intestate.

Case Study (continued)

Go back to the previous example and the distribution of Deirdre's estate. In that example, we saw what happened if Jake **predeceased** Deirdre and how his children would then take his share on the statutory trusts.

What would have happened if Jake had died soon **after** Deirdre while her estate was still being administered? Since Jake is 23, he would already have had a vested interest in Deirdre's estate and so his later death would have meant that his share would simply devolve as an asset of his own will (or intestacy, if he did not have one).

Let's now consider his brother, Sean, who is equally entitled under the statutory trusts. The difference, remember, is that being only 17, his share is **contingent**.

If Sean **predeceased** Deirdre, then his son, Ken, would be able to take his share as long as he reaches 18. The fact that Ken is Sean's illegitimate child is no bar to him inheriting (see **10.5**). So, in this respect, Sean's position and the entitlement of his issue if he predeceases, is the same as Jake's.

However, what if **Sean dies after Deirdre**, still aged 17? Can Ken still inherit under the statutory trusts? If Deirdre had died before 1 February 2012, the answer would have been "no", because the substitution of a dead class member's issue could apply only if the class member actually predeceased. Consequently, it would be Jake who would take Sean's potential share as the only one of Deirdre's issue to have obtained a vested interest.

However, if Deirdre died on or after 1 February 2012, Sean is treated in this case **as if** he had predeceased, so allowing Ken to take in the same way as he would have done had Sean actually died before Deirdre.

Remember that everything we have said regarding the statutory trusts, if they are applied to the deceased's own children, will apply in the same way when applied to the other classes of relative for which **s47** is relevant.

Having considered the meaning of statutory trusts, we can now consider the rules that determine which classes of relative are entitled. The first question is to see whether or not there is a surviving spouse or civil partner.

10.4.3 Distribution if there is a surviving spouse or civil partner and no issue

A surviving spouse or civil partner, where there is no issue, will inherit the entire estate. The priority given to spouses and civil partners reflects the continuing assumption by the law that most testators give priority in their wills to protecting the financial interests of their spouses or civil partners.

Divorced or judicially separated spouses and ex-civil partners where the civil partnership has been dissolved are not entitled to share in the estate.

s46(2A) AEA 1925 states that a spouse or civil partner must survive the intestate by at least 28 days before they can inherit. This statutory survivorship period mirrors the effects of the normal survivorship clause in most professionally drafted wills for couples. (Note that this statutory survivorship period applies only to spouses and civil partners and not when other relatives inherit on intestacy.)

In ***Official Solicitor v Yemoh and Others [2010]*** the deceased was domiciled in Ghana and was believed to have been a party to at least six polygamous marriages contracted in accordance with Ghanaian customary law. Since he died intestate and owned land in England, the issue was whether these marriages would be recognised for the purpose of succession to his land in England. The court also had to determine whether two or more persons could fall within the category of surviving spouse for the purpose of **s46 AEA 1925**. The court held that a spouse who had been lawfully married, in accordance with the law of their domicile, to an intestate was entitled to be recognised in England as the surviving spouse for the purposes of **s46**. In this case, relying on **s6 Interpretation Act 1978** that words expressed in the singular are to be interpreted as including the plural, the surviving wives of a valid polygamous marriage could succeed to the husband's property on his dying intestate.

10.4.4 The entitlement of the spouse/civil partner where there is issue

The spouse or civil partner inherits:

- personal chattels (personal possessions) as defined in **s55(1)(x) AEA 1925** (see **10.4.4.2**);
- a statutory legacy of £322,000 plus interest at the Bank of England base rate effective at the end of the day on which the intestate died, from the date of death until payment. Details of the current and historic Bank of England rates are available at https://www.bankofengland.co.uk/monetary-policy/the-interest-rate-bank-rate.

Sch 1 ITPA 2014 requires the Lord Chancellor to reset the statutory legacy every five years, starting within five years of the Act coming into force. The Lord Chancellor must increase the statutory legacy between these five-year review dates if the consumer prices index (CPI) measure of inflation rises to 15 per cent or more, in any month, over its base amount. The rate of increase at this point is at the discretion of the Lord Chancellor. When this mechanism is triggered, the five-year period is reset to begin again from that date. The **Administration of Estates Act 1925**

(Fixed Net Sum) Order 2023 increased the statutory legacy to £322,000 from £270,000 for deaths from 26 July 2023 onwards.

Unless the Lord Chancellor determines otherwise, the statutory legacy will increase in line with the (index-linked) CPI;

- a half share of the residue.

The other half of the residue passes to the issue on the statutory trusts (see **10.4.2**).

Case Study (continued)

Suppose Deirdre dies leaving a surviving spouse, Paul, and issue, her sons, Jake and Sean. Paul, Jake and Sean will receive different amounts depending on the size of her estate. In all the scenarios below, her estate consists of personal chattels, cash and some investments.

Scenario 1

Personal chattels: £4,000

Cash and investments: £150,000

Here, Paul will receive the personal chattels and a statutory legacy consisting of all her other assets. Since the cash and investments are valued at less than £322,000, nothing remains for Jake and Sean, who therefore receive nothing.

Scenario 2

Personal chattels: £4,000

Cash and investments: £370,000

Paul will receive the personal chattels and a statutory legacy of £322,000 together with interest from the date of death (in accordance with the relevant Bank of England base rate). The balance of the estate (£100,000 less interest) will be split in half.

Paul will receive a half share of the residue (£50,000).

The other half of the balance will pass to Jake and Sean on the statutory trusts. Jake has a vested interest while Sean's is contingent until he reaches 18.

10.4.4.1 The family home

Often, the most pressing priority of a surviving spouse/civil partner is to ensure that he or she can continue to live in the family home. In many estates, the family home is the biggest asset, and it may represent much of the intestate's wealth. There is often a lot of sentimental attachment to the home where the couple may have brought up their children.

The first issue to consider is the beneficial ownership of the family home. If the home is owned by the couple as joint tenants, the survivor will take the intestate's share by survivorship, so it does not pass on intestacy anyway. If the property is owned by the couple as tenants in common, the intestate's share will form part of their estate and pass under the intestacy rules. Alternatively, the family home may have been owned by the intestate alone. The spouse/civil partner will be anxious in these circumstances to ensure that the family home (or the intestate's share in it) is appropriated (transferred from the estate) to them.

s41 AEA 1925 gives PRs a general power to appropriate all types of asset, including houses, to individual beneficiaries instead of their cash equivalent. The PRs can therefore choose to appropriate the family home to the spouse/ civil partner, but only if its value does not exceed the spouse/civil partner's entitlement under the intestacy rules.

If the PRs are uncooperative, or the value of the house is greater than the surviving spouse/civil partner's entitlement, it may be possible for the surviving spouse/civil partner to require the PRs to appropriate the family home to them under **Sch 2 IEA 1952**. In order to exercise this right, the following requirements must be met.

(1) The right must be exercised within 12 months of the date of the grant. During this period, the PRs may not sell the property without the written consent of the spouse/civil partner unless the sale is required to pay off debts of the estate and no other assets are available.

(2) Written notice must be given to the PRs. If the spouse/civil partner is the sole PR, they must give written notice to the court, appoint a second PR, or obtain the consent of the beneficiaries if they are all adult. The importance of these additional steps was emphasised in ***Kane v Radley-Kane and Others [1998]***.

(3) The family home must be valued at the date of the appropriation, not the date of death (***Re Collins [1975]***). This has important practical implications if house prices are falling – the spouse/civil partner is likely to benefit from a lower valuation if they postpone the valuation to the end of the 12-month period for election.

(4) If the value of the family home exceeds the share of the estate which is due to the spouse or civil partner, they will be required to pay the difference (equality money) from their own money to the PRs so that the other beneficiaries do not lose out.

The consent of the court to the appropriation under **Sch 2** must be obtained in certain circumstances where it might diminish the value of the whole estate. These circumstances are where:

- the home forms part of a larger building, the rest of which is included in the residuary estate;
- the home forms part of agricultural land that is included in the agricultural estate;
- the home or part of it was used as a hotel or lodging house;
- part of the home was used for non-domestic purposes, for example, where an antiques business was run from the home.

10.4.4.2 Personal chattels

The definition of "personal chattels" at **s55(1)(x) AEA 1925** (as amended by **s3 ITPA 2014**) is: *tangible movable property, other than any such property which:*

- *consists of money or securities for money; or*
- *was used at the death of the intestate solely or mainly for business purposes; or*
- *was held at the death of the intestate solely as an investment.*

Usually, identifying the intestate's personal possessions is straightforward. The courts have, nonetheless, been required to consider the distinction between articles for personal use and those used for business or investment purposes. In ***Re Reynolds [1966]*** a stamp collection was held to be an article of personal use. In ***Re Crispin's Will Trusts [1974]*** the argument related to whether chattels held largely for investment purposes were personal chattels or excluded because they were for business purposes. The Court of Appeal stated that the key question was whether the articles themselves were of their very nature for personal use. The collection of watches and clocks was held to be personal chattels despite forming a very large proportion of the value of the estate.

If articles are used for mixed business and personal use, it was held in ***Re MacCulloch [1981]*** that the dominant purpose of their use must be determined. Here, a yacht was used partly for pleasure and part of the time was hired out. The dominant purpose was held to be for business and it was not a personal chattel.

10.4.5 Distribution on intestacy where there is no surviving spouse/ civil partner

This is a straight application of the order in **s46**. The main point to bear in mind is that those at the top of the order have priority over those lower down, and, once it is established that there is at least one member of the relevant class of relative who is entitled (that is, by obtaining a vested interest under the statutory trusts, where applicable), that excludes any possibility of any class lower down the order taking.

In other words, in an estate where there is no spouse or civil partner to take a share, it is never possible for the estate to be shared between relatives in a different class in the **s46** order – all the beneficiaries, if more than one, must come from the same class.

So, the first class to consider at the top of the order is the deceased's issue.

(1) **Issue**

If there is no spouse or civil partner surviving, the issue will inherit the entire estate on the statutory trusts regardless of value and regardless of whether there are any other relatives.

Case Study (continued)

In Deirdre's estate, Jake and Sean would inherit all of Deirdre's estate, regardless of its size, if Paul predeceased her (or failed to survive 28 days).

(2) **No issue, but parents**

If there is no spouse/civil partner or issue surviving, the parents will inherit the entire estate in equal shares.

So, on the death of a child, who has not married or entered into a civil partnership or made a privileged will (see **Chapter 4**), the parents will normally inherit the entire estate (unless the child already has a child of their own).

(3) **No issue, no parents, but brothers and sisters of the whole blood**

In these circumstances, the brothers and sisters who share both parents with the intestate, or their issue if they have predeceased, will inherit the entire estate on the statutory trusts.

(4) **No issue, no parents, no brothers and sisters of the whole blood or their issue, but brothers and sisters of the half blood**

In these circumstances, brothers and sisters who share one parent with the intestate, or their issue, will inherit the entire estate on the statutory trusts.

In our example, Wayne is Deirdre's half-brother. If Wayne had predeceased, his son, Philip (Wayne's issue), would take his entitlement under the statutory trusts.

(5) **No issue, no parents, no brothers and sisters of the whole blood or their issue, no brothers and sisters of the half blood or their issue, but grandparents**

Here, the grandparents inherit the entire estate in equal shares.

(6) **No issue, no parents, no brothers and sisters of the whole blood or their issue, no brothers and sisters of the half blood or their issue, no grandparents, but uncles and aunts of the whole blood or their issue**

Here, the uncles or aunts who shared the same parents as the intestate's own mother or father (or their issue) inherit the estate in equal shares on the statutory trusts. Each uncle or aunt receives an equal share regardless of whether the relationship is through the intestate's mother or father. If an intestate had three aunts who were sisters of their mother and one uncle who was a brother of their father, each aunt and the uncle would receive one-quarter of the estate.

Case Study (continued)

Consider Deirdre's estate again. Dai is Deirdre's only uncle of the whole blood because his parents, Huw and Joy, were the same as Marion's who was Deirdre's mother.

(7) **No issue, no parents, no brothers and sisters of the whole blood or their issue, no brothers and sisters of the half blood or their issue, no grandparents, no uncles and aunts of the whole blood or their issue, but uncles and aunts of the half blood or their issue**

In these circumstances, the uncles and aunts of the half blood or their issue inherit the entire estate in equal shares on the statutory trusts.

Case Study (continued)

In Deirdre's estate, Josephine is Deirdre's aunt of the half blood because she shared only one parent, Huw, with Marion who was Deirdre's mother. Josephine's daughter, Morwenna (Josephine's issue), would inherit her share if Josephine had predeceased Deirdre.

(8) **None of the above relatives**

The entire estate will pass to the Crown, unless the intestate died in Cornwall or in the Duchy of Lancaster (an area covering Lancashire and parts of Cumbria) in which cases it will pass to the Duke of Cornwall or Duchy of Lancaster, respectively. The estate is described as *bona vacantia*.

Under **s46(1)(vi) AEA 1925**, the Crown (or the Duke of Cornwall or Duchy of Lancaster) has a discretion to provide for persons who were dependent on the intestate at the date of death or for whom the intestate should have provided in a will.

It is, in practice, extremely rare for someone to die intestate without any surviving relatives entitled to their estate at all. Where the estate is treated as *bona vacantia* it will pass to the Crown or the Duchy of Cornwall or the Duchy of Lancaster (depending on where the intestate died). Following the death of Queen Elizabeth in September 2022, Prince William is now the Duke of Cornwall and King Charles also has the title of Duke of Lancaster.

The website of Farrer & Co which represents both Duchies has a very helpful description of the procedures involved where the deceased died within the boundaries of the Duchies, including a postcode checker – see https://www.farrer.co.uk/campaigns/bona-vacantia/.

The Treasury Solicitor deals with *bona vacantia* estates in the rest of England and Wales. Further details of its procedures are available at https://www.gov.uk/government/organisations/bona-vacantia.

Note that there has been some criticism by the campaign group *Republic* of the different treatment of estates which are *bona vacantia* in the Duchies of Cornwall and Lancaster from the rest of England and Wales – see https://www.republic.org.uk/the_duchy_s_powers_and_privileges. Further criticisms are set out in the following *Guardian* article https://www.theguardian.com/uk-news/2023/nov/23/revealed-king-charles-secretly-profiting-from-the-assets-of-dead-citizens.

10.4.6 Disclaimers and forfeiture

Sometimes, a beneficiary will not wish to take their share of the estate, for example, because they feel that they have no need of the intestate's money. Such a beneficiary may disclaim their entitlement. Very occasionally, a person entitled may be disqualified from inheriting as a result of having been convicted of killing the intestate.

The effect of a disclaimer has always been that if a beneficiary under a will or intestacy disclaims, then the property passes as if the gift or entitlement had failed (***Re Scott [1975]***). The application of this seemingly straightforward rule has given rise to some uncertainties in the past so, for deaths on or after 1 February 2012, it has been given statutory effect by the **Estates of Deceased Persons (Forfeiture Rule and Law of Succession) Act 2011** (**EDP(FRLS)A 2011**).

s1 EDP(FRLS)A 2011 provides that if a person entitled on intestacy disclaims, then the property will devolve under the intestacy rules as if that person had died immediately before the intestate. Therefore, if that person leaves issue capable of taking under the statutory trusts, then they will do so.

Otherwise, the entitlement will devolve as though the beneficiary had never existed. So, the property will pass to the other members of the beneficiary's class of relatives who are entitled (e.g. other brothers and sisters of the whole blood) and so increase the size of their shares; if the disclaiming beneficiary was the only member of the class, then it will pass to the next class of relatives in the intestacy order of entitlement.

s1 also provides for the same consequences if, instead of disclaiming, a person entitled on intestacy is disqualified from taking their potential inheritance as a result of killing the intestate. They become subject to the forfeiture rule, which is considered at **13.5**.

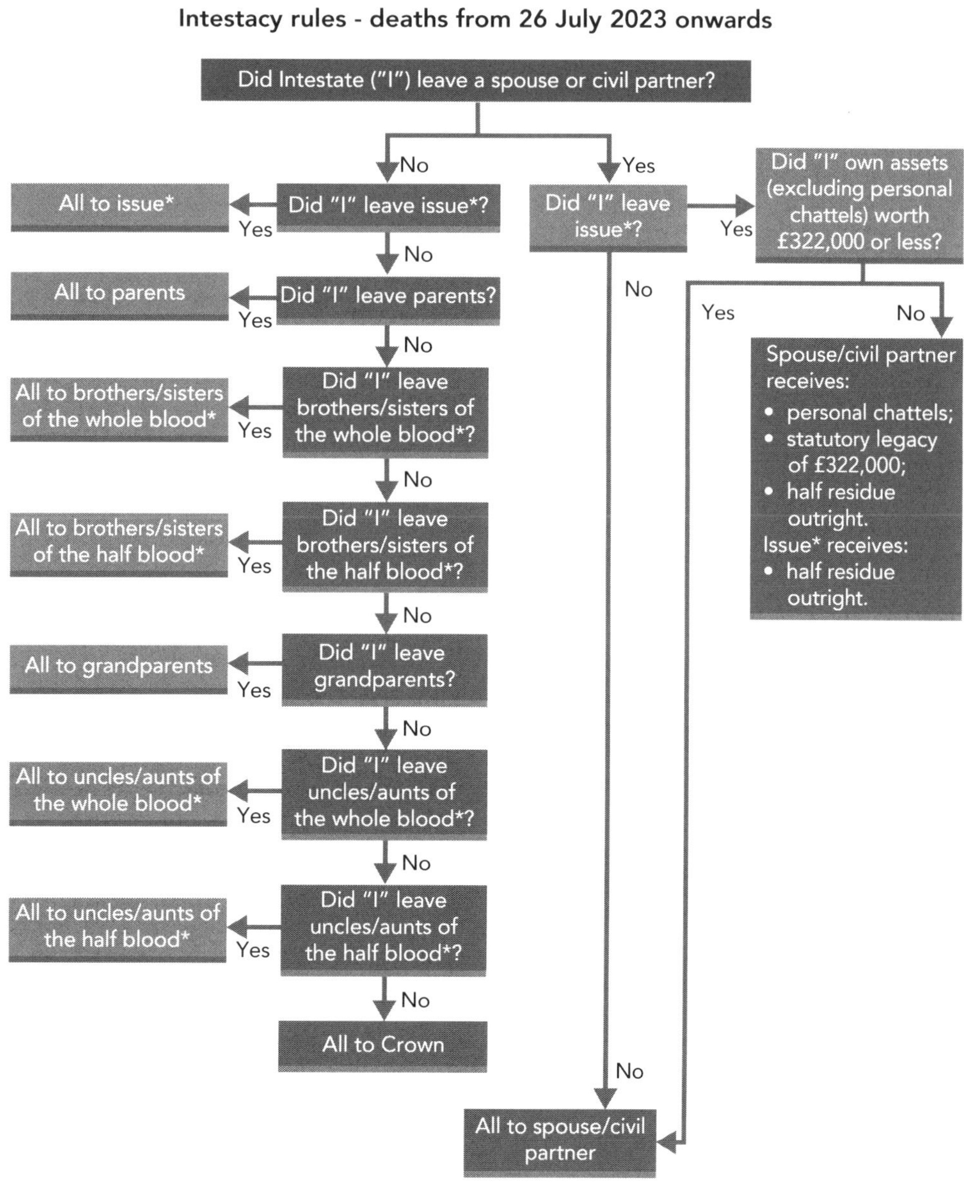

10.5 Legitimacy, illegitimacy, adoption

AEA 1925 originally applied only to legitimate children of the deceased and their legitimate issue. Changes have subsequently been made by statute to recognise the rights of illegitimate beneficiaries and their issue.

(1) **Legitimate and legitimated children**

Children are legitimate if born of parents married at the time of conception or of birth. A child can be said to be legitimated if born to parents who were not married but who later did marry.

If, under the **Human Fertilisation and Embryology Act 2008**, a woman is a child's other parent as a result of a written consent and subsequently forms a civil partnership with the child's mother, the child will be legitimated.

(a) Voidable marriage

A voidable marriage has a flaw (e.g. it has not been consummated – no sex between the parties) which entitles one or both of the parties to choose to annul it. If a voidable marriage is dissolved, this annuls the marriage from the date of the decree. Any children born before annulment will be legitimate (**s16 Matrimonial Causes Act 1973**).

(b) Void marriage

A void marriage has a more fundamental flaw (e.g. one of the parties was already married) and is treated as effectively not being a marriage at all. A child of a void marriage can be regarded as legitimate if, at the time of conception, or at the time of the marriage if later, both or either of the parties to the marriage reasonably believed the marriage to be valid.

(2) **Illegitimate children**

An illegitimate child is treated in the same way as a legitimate child as regards beneficial distribution.

s18(1) Family Law Reform Act 1987 (**FLRA 1987**) provides that references to any relationship between two persons are to be construed without regard to whether the father or mother of either of them (or of any person through whom the relationship is deduced) were married to each other at any time. The effect is to remove illegitimacy as a bar to sharing in intestate succession. In the intestacy rules, a child *en ventre sa mère* at the deceased's death is entitled to benefit in the same way as one already alive at the intestate's death.

There may be practical problems for the PRs, who may be unaware of the existence of illegitimate family members or have difficulty in finding them. There is no special rule to protect the PRs, who must rely, if they can, on **s27 Trustee Act 1925** or such other means of protection as may be appropriate in the circumstances (see **16.3.3.1** and **17.7.1**).

On the death of an illegitimate person, there can be a problem regarding the identity of the deceased's father whose name, unlike that of the mother, may not be on the death certificate. By **s18(2) FLRA 1987**, there is a presumption that the intestate child is not survived by their father or any other person related to them through their father, unless the contrary is shown. This rule, of course, would be relevant only if the illegitimate person died intestate in circumstances where their parents had an entitlement under the intestacy.

(3) **Adopted children**

Under **s67 Adoption and Children Act 2002** (**ACA 2002**), as from the date of the adoption order, an adopted child is treated as the child of the adoptive parents and not of any other person, such as the natural parents.

The child becomes a full member of the family of the people who adopted them, and so could, for example, inherit on the intestacy of their adoptive brothers and sisters.

Inheritance and Trustees' Powers Act 2014

The effect of **s67 ACA 2002** was that, following an adoption, the adopted child lost entitlement to interests held **contingently** on the statutory trusts arising on intestacy (and also on a similar trust created by will).

s4 ITPA 2014 has amended the effect of **s67 ACA 2002** so that where, immediately before adoption, the child's legal parent has already died and some or all of that parent's estate is held on contingent trusts – whether created by will or arising on intestacy – for the child, the interest of the child will not be affected by the adoption.

Francis dies in June 2023 leaving his daughter Lisa, who is aged three months at the date of his death. Lisa's mother, Hilary, died in May 2023.

Lisa is now an orphan and, following Francis's death, Deirdre and Paul have agreed to adopt her.

Under the statutory trusts (see **10.4.2**) Lisa has a contingent interest in Francis's estate. She will inherit Francis's entire estate if she attains 18 years.

Lisa will retain her contingent interest in Francis's estate after the adoption and will inherit if she subsequently attains 18 years.

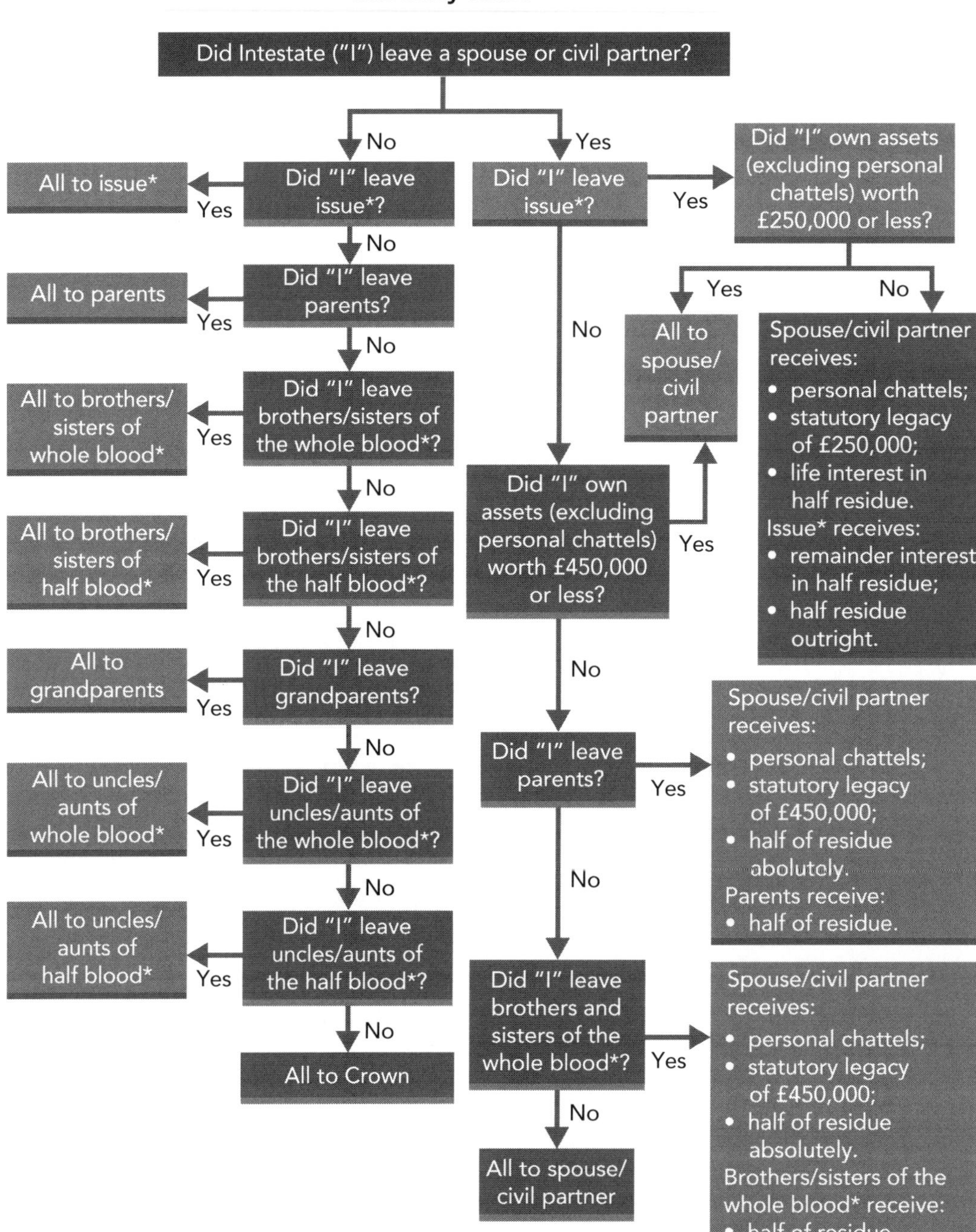

NB If Lisa had been adopted **before** Francis's death, she would not acquire a contingent interest in his estate under the intestacy rules.

NB Lisa will be treated as a child of Deirdre and Paul from the date of the adoption under the intestacy rules.

(4) **Children born as a result of fertilisation techniques or surrogacy arrangements**

At common law, a child's legal parents are their genetic parents. However, the **Human Fertilisation and Embryology Acts 1990** and **2008** now contain complex provisions to determine parentage in cases of assisted reproduction and the making of parental orders if a child is born through a surrogacy arrangement. These provisions are outside the scope of this course.

10.6 Intestacy rules – deaths from 1 October 2014 until 25 July 2023

The same order of distribution applied as has been described for deaths from 26 July 2023, except that the statutory legacy payable to the spouse/civil partner was **£250,000** between 1 October 2014 and 5 February 2020 and **£270,000** between 6 February 2020 and 25 July 2023.

10.7 Intestacy rules – deaths before 1 October 2014

Until **ITPA 2014** came into force on 1 October 2014, the rights under the intestacy rules of spouses and civil partners, in particular, were more limited. The rules which apply to deaths prior to 1 October 2014, are summarised in the following diagram:

10.8 Reform of the intestacy rules

The Law Commission recommended significant changes to the intestacy rules in its 2011 report *Intestacy and Family Provision: Claims on Death*. Many of the proposed changes were enacted in **ITPA 2014**.

Part 8 of the report https://lawcom.gov.uk/project/intestacy-and-family-provision-claims-on-death/ dealt with the rights of unmarried cohabitants under the intestacy rules. Part 8 was not accepted by the government. The report included a draft **Inheritance (Cohabitants) Bill** which was introduced in the House of Lords but was not enacted.

Part 8 discussed the background to the issue and highlighted the following points.

(1) Approximately 15 per cent of all couples are living as cohabitants and the percentage is expected to increase.

(2) Cohabitants are less likely to have made wills than married couples (though they do tend to be younger and younger people are generally less likely to have made wills).

(3) Although cohabitants can claim a share of the estate through **I(PFD)A 1975**, the requirement to go to court is onerous and causes unnecessary difficulties and legal costs when the underage children of the couple have to have separate representation as the defendants.

(4) Many unmarried couples are unaware that they do not have any rights under the intestacy rules against each other's estates.

(5) As with married couples, the finances of unmarried couples are often intertwined and interdependent.

(6) Other jurisdictions in Australia, Canada and New Zealand have been able to provide for cohabitants under intestacy without significant difficulties.

A particularly controversial area is the issue of choice and commitment. The report noted the arguments that all unmarried couples had the choice as to whether or not to get married (or form a civil partnership in the case of same-sex couples). It also noted that they had the opportunity to make wills. Nonetheless, it argued that simply relying on choice could lead to injustice – **both** parties had to agree to a marriage or civil partnership and the reluctance of one party to agree to a marriage or civil partnership could be unfair on the other. Similarly, one party could not compel the other to make a will.

In relation to commitment similar arguments apply. The Law Commission did not accept the argument that the value of a public commitment to each other in a marriage or civil partnership ceremony had to be reinforced through the intestacy rules.

The Law Commission proposed in its draft Bill to give unmarried cohabitants who have lived together for **five years** or more the same rights on intestacy as a spouse or civil partner.

If the couple had had a child together, the period would be reduced to **two years**.

Self-assessment Questions

Do you think that the proposed changes would be an improvement on the current intestacy rules? Do you think they would undermine the importance of marriage/civil partnership?

10.9 Summary

(1) Intestate succession applies when a person dies without a will. A partial intestacy occurs when the will does not dispose of the entire estate.

(2) Property is held on the statutory trust, pending distribution (**s33 AEA 1925**). This means that the administrators must first pay debts, funeral and administrative expenses before distributing in accordance with **s46**.

(3) The order of entitlement for the distribution on intestacy is set out in **s46 AEA 1925**. The key issues that are taken into account are the size and nature of the assets, and the surviving family members. Note the meaning and operation of the statutory trusts arising under **s47**.

(4) Spouses and civil partners are given priority under the rules. All other beneficiaries must be blood relatives (i.e. not related only by marriage). Ultimately, the Crown (or Duke of Cornwall or Duchy of Lancaster) receives the estates of those with absolutely no surviving relatives.

(5) Spouses and civil partners have the right to take the family home as their share of the estate.

(6) Adopted children are treated as if they were the natural children of their adoptive parents. If their natural parent dies intestate **before** their adoption, their contingent rights to inherit under the intestacy rules are preserved, even after they are adopted. Illegitimate children are treated in the same way as legitimate children under the intestacy rules.

CHAPTER 11

Family Provision

Aims of the Chapter:

By the end of this chapter, you should be able to:

- explain why the **Inheritance (Provision for Family and Dependants) Act 1975** breaches the principle of testamentary freedom;
- describe the significance of domicile and *locus standi;*
- describe the requirement of reasonable financial provision;
- explain the categories of applicants and the particular guidelines for their claims;
- identify what is the "net estate"; and
- list the powers of the court to make orders.

11.1 Introduction

The principle of testamentary freedom in the law of England and Wales has led to a number of problems. Some testators have disinherited members of their family or others financially dependent on them for reasons that seem unfair and even perverse. Surviving members of unmarried couples have lost out in favour of spouses who abandoned the deceased many years earlier. Again, the application of the intestacy rules can be unfair to some family members.

The **Inheritance (Provisions for Family and Dependants Act 1975** (**I(PFD)A 1975**) is designed to enable the courts to change the effects of a testator's will or the effects of the intestacy rules if certain requirements are met. The court's powers are partly discretionary and often require a judgment to be made between the competing claims of several beneficiaries.

In this chapter, we will first consider the nature of the right to bring an application, including whether or not it continues after the **applicant's** death. We will also look at the tricky issue of attempts to discourage future applications using clauses in the will.

Next, we will review the requirement that the deceased was domiciled in England and Wales. (Domicile is a legal status normally based on a person's place of permanent residence.)

We will then consider the *locus standi* (pronounced "lock-us stan-die") (right to make a claim) of potential applicants who fall into the six categories in **s1(1) I(PFD) A 1975**.

The key test which is applied in considering whether or not **I(PFD)A 1975** should be used to alter the distribution of an estate is whether or not the will or the intestacy rules made **reasonable financial provision**. We will consider this test and the common guidelines set out in **I(PFD)A 1975**, as well as the particular guidelines for the different categories of applicants.

Finally, we will consider other practical issues, including time limits for applications, the property which can be subject to an application under **I(PFD)A 1975**, anti-avoidance provisions and the range of orders which the court can make.

11.2 The nature of the right to bring an application

The right is a personal one which does not continue after the death of the **applicant**. In ***Whyte v Ticehurst [1986]*** a husband died in February 1984. In July 1984, his widow made a claim under **I(PFD)A 1975** but died in December 1984 before the claim had been heard. Her PRs were refused permission to continue the claim on behalf of the estate.

Where a child of the deceased has been adopted into another family before a claim is made, the child loses the right to make a claim under **I(PFD)A 1975**. In ***Re Collins (Deceased) [1990]*** the deceased died intestate and her husband inherited the entire estate. Her son, who had been adopted into another family after the death but before the application, was unsuccessful because he no longer qualified as the deceased's child.

It is not uncommon to see clauses in wills which attempt to discourage beneficiaries from bringing an action against the estate. They are normally coupled with a legacy just large enough to make the beneficiary think twice about risking its loss. In ***Nathan (Deceased), Nathan v Leonard [2003]*** the court considered whether such a clause is repugnant to public policy.

The condition was, in effect, that a beneficiary who chose to challenge the will would lose the benefits given to them by the will. The court found that, although this might well have a strong deterrent effect on the beneficiary making a claim under **I(PFD)A 1975**, such a condition was not repugnant or contrary to public policy.

Self-assessment Question

It's not fair!

When individuals die, they leave behind them a wide variety of family situations. They may have left a will or may simply have left the distribution of their estate to the intestacy rules. In either case, their past behaviour and the circumstances of their family lives may leave surviving family members with a strong sense of injustice when they learn what, if anything, they will receive from the estate.

Attempting to address this sense of injustice was a challenging task for those drafting **I(PFD)A 1975**. A big responsibility was given to judges who were required to make a *"value judgment"* taking account of the common and particular guidelines in *"the Act and the Act alone"* (***Ilott v Mitson [2011]***).

As you study the way in which **I(PFD)A 1975** works, consider the following question.

Does the **I(PFD)A 1975** reflect what most people would consider a fair and just approach in 2024?

11.3 Domicile

In order for a claim to be made under **I(PFD)A 1975** the **deceased** must have been domiciled in England and Wales. Domicile is a complex area of law which is often an issue in taxation cases. In recent years it has become a more common area of dispute in succession cases, reflecting greater mobility by individuals moving from one country to another.

Everyone is treated, by the law, as having a **domicile of origin** at birth – normally the country in which they were born. A person may acquire a **domicile of choice** instead if they can be shown to intend to make their home in a new country to the end of their days, unless and until something happens to make them change their minds. In order to lose a domicile of choice, a person must have ceased to reside in the new country and have no intention of returning there.

In ***Cyganik v Agulian [2005]*** the Court of Appeal considered whether the deceased had been domiciled in Cyprus or England. It held that he had been domiciled in Cyprus and emphasised the "*adhesiveness*" (stickiness) of the domicile of origin. "*Cogent and convincing*" evidence is required to prove a change in domicile and the burden of proof is on the person alleging that there had been such a change.

NB It is not necessary for the **applicant** to be domiciled in England and Wales.

11.4 Locus standi

s1(1) I(PFD)A 1975, as amended, allows six categories of applicant to apply on the grounds that the deceased's will or the rules of intestacy or a combination of both fail to *make reasonable financial provision* for the applicant.

11.4.1 s1(1)(a) – the wife or husband or civil partner of the deceased

The applicant must prove that they were validly married to, or in a civil partnership with, the deceased and that the marriage or civil partnership was subsisting at the death of the deceased. A marriage or civil partnership certificate is *prima facie* evidence of a valid marriage or civil partnership unless challenged, when further proof will be necessary.

As an example, suppose that the husband deserts and he is not seen or heard of for many years and the wife remarries. The second husband dies and the wife is making application in the estate of the second husband. The validity of the second marriage is challenged.

In ***Watkins v Watkins [1953]*** the husband deserted the wife in 1922 and was never heard of again. The wife remarried in 1948. On the death of her new husband, the wife made a claim under **s1(1)(a)** against his estate. In view of the length of time that had elapsed, and the fact that the wife had kept in contact with the family of the first husband and nothing had been heard of him, the court presumed that he had died and therefore the wife had *locus standi*. Compare ***Re Peete [1952]***, where the wife had not kept in contact with the family of the first husband and the court did not accept that she had *locus standi*.

11.4.1.1 Polygamous marriages

In ***Re Sehota [1978]*** the deceased contracted two marriages under Indian law but, at his death in 1976, he had acquired an English domicile of choice. By his will, he left all his property to his second wife. The court accepted that the first wife could make an application on the basis that the marriage was validly contracted under an Indian law which permitted polygamy. Further, there was no difficulty in regard to two or more persons claiming relief under **I(PFD)A 1975** as this could often be the case.

11.4.1.2 s25(4) – void marriages

A party to a void marriage (see **10.5**) with the deceased will be treated as a spouse for the purposes of application if they can prove that:

- the applicant entered into the marriage in good faith;
- the marriage was not dissolved or annulled during the lifetime of the deceased; and
- the applicant had not entered into a later marriage during the lifetime of the deceased.

The purpose of this section is to give relief where an English court may not recognise a divorce decree from a foreign court.

In ***Gandhi v Patel [2002]*** a Hindu ceremony of marriage which did not comply with the **Marriage Acts** was held not to give rise even to a void marriage. Even if it had been treated as a void marriage, the applicant did not enter into it in good faith.

11.4.1.3 Judicially separated spouses and separated civil partners

Despite a decree of judicial separation, spouses remain spouses and are therefore *prima facie* entitled to apply; however, at or after the time of the decree, the court may order that, on the death of one spouse, the other shall not be entitled to apply under **s15 I(PFD)A 1975** (as amended by **s8 Matrimonial and Family**

Proceedings Act 1984). The consent of the spouse against whom the order is made is not needed, but the court must think it just to make an order.

Even if an order is made by the court, it will be effective to prevent an application only if:

- the decree is in force at the date of death of the deceased; and
- the separation, in fact, continued until the death of the deceased.

Where there is a decree of separation in force for civil partners, similar rules apply if the court made an order under **s15ZA** preventing an application under **I(PFD)A 1975**.

11.4.2 s1(1)(b) – a former wife or former husband or former civil partner of the deceased who has not yet remarried or entered into a further civil partnership

Application can be made if:

- the applicant has been validly married to the deceased;
- during the lifetime of the deceased, the marriage was dissolved or annulled; and
- the applicant has not remarried either before or after the death of the deceased. (The applicant is treated as having remarried even if that marriage is void or voidable (**s25(5)**).)

As with the judicially separated spouse, the court that dealt with the dissolution of the marriage may order that no application can be made.

Traditionally, courts were reluctant to award provisions under **I(PFD)A 1975** to former spouses (in most cases, wives) as the view was that the former spouse would have received provision for the future under the matrimonial ancillary relief legislation. Former spouses can use **I(PFD)A 1975** where the parties have obtained decree absolute and are thus divorced but one spouse dies before negotiations or court proceedings relating to ancillary relief have been finalised.

An example of the traditional approach taken by the courts was illustrated in ***Barrass v Harding and Newman [2001]***. The deceased and his former wife (the claimant) divorced in 1964 and, as part of the divorce settlement, he provided the claimant with a flat to live in. Eventually, the claimant went to live with the couple's son and received a modest sum in lieu of the accommodation. The deceased had remarried but his second wife predeceased him and he left all his assets to his second wife's sister, having left lifetime gifts to his son.

The claimant applied for financial provision from the deceased's estate under **I(PFD) A 1975**. The Court of Appeal held that, despite the claimant's poor financial circumstances, the deceased's failure to provide for the applicant was not unreasonable under the circumstances even though in today's terms the 1964 divorce settlement was unsatisfactory for the claimant.

In ***Chekov v Fryer and Another [2015]*** the High Court held that a court order preventing the former spouse or civil partner of the deceased from making a claim under **I(PFD)A 1975** does not prevent such a person from making a claim as a cohabitee of the deceased under **s1(1)(ba)** (see **11.4.2.1**) if that person is otherwise entitled to claim in that capacity.

Presumably, the remarriage of a former spouse would similarly not prevent that former spouse from making a claim in the capacity of cohabitee if they otherwise satisfied the two-year qualification for bringing a claim in that capacity.

Note the inclusion in this section of former civil partners under the **Civil Partnership Act 2004** (**CPA 2004**).

11.4.2.1 s1(1)(ba) – a person living in the same household as husband or wife or civil partner

Where the deceased died after 1 January 1996, a claim may be made by a person who does not fall within **s1(1)(a)** or **(b)** but who, throughout the period of two years immediately prior to the deceased's death, was living in the same household as the deceased as a spouse or civil partner of the deceased.

It should be noted that for a successful claim the applicant must have been living with the deceased at the date of death, there must have been no break in cohabitation during the two-year period before death, and the parties must have been openly living together as spouses or civil partners, so platonic relationships (relationships without sex) will not qualify to justify a claim under this category.

In ***Re John Watson (Deceased) [1999]*** the parties had lived together for some years. Before cohabiting, the parties had enjoyed a sexual relationship but during the period they lived together they were not intimate. It was held that they had lived together as husband and wife and that the absence of sexual relations was not conclusive – it was not unusual for a happily married couple to abstain from sexual relations in their later years.

If the parties are unable to cohabit immediately before the death (perhaps because of the deceased's last illness), it is likely the court will follow ***Jelley v Iliffe [1981]***, where the Court of Appeal asked whether the arrangement for cohabitation was subsisting at the date of death.

In ***Gully v Dix [2004]*** the claimant and deceased had lived together since 1974. The deceased became addicted to alcohol and the claimant, fearing for her safety, left the deceased in August 2001. The deceased died in October 2001. The claimant sought provision from the deceased's estate. Her application was opposed by the defendant, the deceased's brother, on the basis that the claimant and the deceased had not been living together in the same household *immediately before* (see **11.4.5.1**) the deceased's death and the claimant had not therefore been maintained by the deceased immediately before his death.

The Court of Appeal held that, but for the deceased's alcohol problem, the couple would have lived together until the deceased's death. There had been a "*settled state of affairs*" between the parties during a long period of cohabitation, and the claimant was successful.

Gully v Dix was followed in ***Kaur v Singh Dhaliwal [2014]*** where the parties had cohabited for one year and 49 weeks immediately before the deceased's death and so there was an apparent shortfall of about three weeks to satisfy the two-year period of cohabitation required by **s1(1)(ba) I(PFD)A 1975**. In ***Kaur*** the parties had spent time apart and had admittedly not lived together all the time because of a combination of accommodation and family problems. Their temporary separation, even though lengthy, was not relevant because it was clear their relationship had openly subsisted throughout the necessary two years immediately before the deceased's death. Consequently, the judge held that there was a *"settled state of affairs"* and the claimant was entitled to make her claim under **s1(1)(ba)**.

In ***Banfield v Campbell [2018]*** Mrs Campbell, a widow who had not remarried, died at the age of 63. In her will, which she made in 2001, she left:

- a legacy of £5,000 to Mr Banfield, whom in her will she described as her friend;
- the rest of her estate to her only child, who was her son (then aged 25).

In 1993 – about a year after Mrs Campbell's husband died – Mrs Campbell and Mr Banfield entered into a relationship described by various witnesses as "romantic". Mr Banfield started to stay at Mrs Campbell's house for a few nights every week. For the rest of the week, Mr Banfield stayed at the house of his elderly mother, until her death in 2010, when he moved in to Mrs Campbell's house permanently.

In 1999, Mr Banfield and Mrs Campbell became unofficially "engaged" – he bought her a ring, which she wore, but there were never any plans for them to marry.

From 2008 onwards, Mr Banfield's health deteriorated. He had difficulty coping with stairs, so slept separately in a room on the ground floor. He needed a lot of care, and witnesses gave evidence to the effect that he became bad- tempered and that Mrs Campbell found the relationship a burden. However, she continued to look after him, saying that she "needed to be needed".

Mrs Campbell died in 2015, while on holiday with Mr Banfield.

Mr Banfield then made a claim under **I(PFD)A 1975** for further provision out of her estate.

The court considered whether Mr Banfield could bring a claim under:

- **s1(1)(ba) I(PFD)A 1975**, as a person who was living with the deceased "as husband and wife" for the two years prior to the death; or
- **s1(1)(e)**, as a person being maintained by the deceased immediately before the death.

The son argued that the **s1(1)(ba)** criteria were not met. From 2011 onwards, Mr Banfield had slept downstairs, so the couple cannot have been living as husband and wife.

The court did not accept this argument. Quoting ***Re Watson [1999]***, the court said that, in considering this question, *"one should not ignore the multifarious nature of marital relationships"*. It was also noted that:

- an element of mutual support still existed in the relationship;
- shortly before the death, they had booked a holiday together;
- Mr Banfield's will left 50 per cent of his estate to Mrs Campbell.

The court allowed a claim under **s1(1)(ba)**. It was therefore not necessary to consider whether a claim could be brought under **s1(1)(e)**. It was ordered that the deceased's house should be sold, and a trust fund be set up with 50 per cent of the proceeds, in which Mr Banfield would be given a life interest. This could be used to buy a property for him to live in for the rest of his life. On his death, the property (or whatever other assets the fund was held in) would pass to the son.

The case illustrates the flexibility of the court in defining *living as husband and wife*, and the way in which the parties' conduct is taken into account in assessing a complex situation. The use of a life interest trust fund, as a way of providing for a claimant without, in the long term, depriving the original beneficiary, is a popular and practical solution in **I(PFD)A 1975** cases.

In ***Thompson v Raggett [2018]*** the option of awarding a life interest was rejected by the court, in contrast with ***Banfield v Campbell [2018]***. In ***Thompson*** the deceased had lived with the claimant for 42 years but left his entire estate of £1.5 m to two of his young tenants. He expected the claimant (aged 79 years) to go into local authority care and the last thing he wanted was for his money to end up with the claimant's children. Nonetheless, the court awarded her the home outright, £169,000 for her care and £29,000 to renovate the house.

The complexity of human relationships was also highlighted in ***Swetenham v Walkley [2014]*** where an 80-year-old woman had maintained a close relationship with the deceased for 30 years which included attending family events as his partner. Despite the claimant's help with his washing and mutual support for medical problems, the deceased did not inform the claimant that he had retired and maintained a separate home. Nonetheless, the court held that the couple had lived together as husband and wife for the purposes of **s1(1)(ba)**.

Civil partners are included in the provisions of **s1(1)(ba)** under **CPA 2004**.

11.4.3 s1(1)(c) – a child of the deceased

"Child" includes an illegitimate or adopted child and children *en ventre sa mère* (**s25(1)**). It does not include a stepchild.

There is no age limit for children seeking an award under **I(PFD)A 1975**, but where the child is able-bodied and able to earn a living, it is possible for no provision by a testator for that child to be considered reasonable. Formerly, the court would look for a special circumstance, such as a moral obligation owed by the deceased parent. This would be classified as one of the *obligations and responsibilities* referred to in **s3(1)(d) I(PFD)A 1975** as one of the considerations to which the court should have regard.

Oliver J, the judge at first instance in ***Re Coventry [1979]***, said: "*There must . . . be established some sort of moral claim by the applicant to be maintained by the deceased or at the expense of his estate beyond the mere fact of a blood relationship, some reason why it can be said that, in the circumstances, it is unreasonable that no or no greater provision was in fact made.*" This statement was approved by the Court of Appeal, although it clearly stated that such a moral obligation was **not** a prerequisite of an application under **s1(1)(c)**.

A moral claim would readily be found where, say, the child was disabled, or had worked in the family business on a low wage, perhaps in the expectation of being provided for on death (***Re Abram (Deceased) [1996]***). In the absence of such an obligation, the courts generally took the view that a testator was not under any moral duty to provide for the maintenance of an adult child. In ***Re Jennings [1994]*** Nourse LJ stated: "[i]*t was established . . . in Re Coventry (Deceased) that on an application by an adult son of the deceased who is able to earn, and earns, his own living, there must be some special circumstance, typically a moral obligation of the deceased towards him, before the question* [whether the deceased failed to make reasonable financial provision for this applicant] *can be determined in his favour.*"

This line of reasoning was followed until ***Re Hancock (Deceased) [1998]***, which concerned an application by a daughter aged 58 at the date of the deceased's death and 69 at the date of the hearing. The Court of Appeal restated the true position as follows:

"[T]he 1975 Act does not require, in an application under section 1(1)(c), that an adult child . . . has in all cases to show obligation or other special circumstance. But on facts similar to those in Re Coventry and even more so with the comparatively affluent applicant in Re Jennings, if the facts disclose that the adult child is in employment, with an earning capacity for the foreseeable future, it is unlikely that he will succeed in his application without some special circumstance, such as a moral obligation."

In ***Espinosa v Bourke [1999]*** the Court of Appeal held definitively that the 57-year-old daughter did not have to show any kind of special circumstance:

"An adult child is, consequently, in no different position from any other applicant who has to prove his case. The court has to have regard to section 3(1)(a)–(g) and assess the relevance and the weight to be given to each factor in the list. If the applicant is of working age, with a job or capable of obtaining a job which would be available, the factors in favour of his claim for financial provision may not be of much weight in the scales."

In ***Re Nahajec (Deceased) [2017]*** the deceased left his entire estate of £265,000 to a friend, and made no provision for his three children. His daughter made a claim under **I(PFD)A 1975**.

The claimant was the child of the deceased's first marriage, which ended 20 years prior to the death, when she was 11 years old. Since then, the claimant had tried several times to resume her relationship with her father, but he had avoided all such contact.

The claimant had a part-time job, but wanted to train to become a veterinary nurse (she worked a few hours a week as an unpaid assistant for a local vet). However, she could not afford the course fees, and in fact had significant debts.

Her claim was allowed, and she was awarded £30,000 out of the estate. The court explained that:

- no reasonable financial provision had been made for the claimant in the will;
- as a child of the deceased, she was entitled to bring a claim under **s1(1)(c) I(PFD)A 1975**;
- although she was an adult, and was independent of the deceased, she had a moral claim for provision out of the estate;

- it was not her fault that the relationship between herself and the deceased had broken down;
- there was nothing to suggest she would waste any award;
- she had a *"genuine and not fanciful"* desire to improve her circumstances by qualifying as a veterinary nurse;
- she had shown commitment to her ambitions by working unpaid for a vet;
- the size of the estate was sufficient to justify her claim, even when the claims of the residuary beneficiary were taken into account.

It is useful to see the reasoning behind the award. The claimant did not have to show any financial dependence on the deceased, and in making the award the court paid great attention to how she was likely to use the money and the beneficial impact it would have on her life.

11.4.4 s1(1)(d) – a person treated as a child of the family

s1(1)(d) deals with *any person (not being a child of the deceased) who in relation to any marriage or civil partnership to which the deceased was at any time a party, or otherwise in relation to any family in which the deceased at any time stood in the role of a parent, was treated by the deceased as a child of the family.*

This category includes:

- a stepchild, provided that there is proof that the step-parent treated the child as a *child of the family*; and
- a child of the deceased's family, such as an orphaned nephew.

Note that the sub-section includes children in unmarried families where the deceased acted in a parental role and treated the applicant as a child of that family. Other family members who formed part of the deceased's unmarried family, but in relation to whom the deceased did not stand in a parental role, will not be covered by this sub-section.

This category is not confined to infant children (***Re Callaghan [1984]***).

A *child of the family* means something more than a display of mere affection. In the case of an infant, some indication of treatment of that child as *"an unfledged person"* (*dictum* of Slade LJ in ***Leach v Lindeman [1985]***).

In ***Leach v Lindeman*** the Court of Appeal allowed an application by a 55-year- old stepdaughter in the estate of her stepmother. Although the stepdaughter had not lived in the same house as the deceased, nor had she been maintained by her, the court found that the deceased had assumed responsibility for the applicant and treated her as a daughter. A key factor here was the closeness of the relationship.

Gora v Treasury Solicitor [2003] is somewhat unusual on its facts. The deceased died intestate without statutory next of kin. The claimant was the deceased's step-daughter. The net estate of the deceased was worth approximately £110,000 and had been inherited by the deceased on the death of the claimant's mother contrary to her intention as her will had been invalid for lack of formality. The deceased's estate passed to the Crown as *bona vacantia*. The Crown did not object to the application but felt that the matter should be resolved by the court.

The claimant was married to a much older man. Their only income was from his business and he was due to retire shortly. They had an autistic son who needed constant care. The application was granted, particularly in view of the fact that, had the claimant's mother's will been valid, the bulk of her estate would have passed to her daughter. In addition, the deceased had promised his wife that he would leave her portfolio of shares to the claimant.

11.4.5 s1(1)(e) – a person maintained by the deceased

s1(1)(e) deals with *any person (not being a person included in the foregoing paragraphs of this subsection) who immediately before the death of the deceased was being maintained, either wholly or partly, by the deceased.*

This category widened considerably the class of potential applicants, in particular, giving some cohabitants a right of application. The category is not confined to cohabitants, who may now be able to claim under **s1(1)(ba)** (see **11.4.2.1**), but would include, for example, brothers and sisters living together, perhaps later in life, to look after one another.

In order to have *locus standi* under this heading, the applicant must show that:

- they do not come within any other category;
- the deceased was wholly maintaining the applicant or making a **substantial** contribution, in money or money's worth, towards their reasonable needs;
- they were being maintained by the deceased **immediately before** the death of the deceased;
- the deceased was not making a contribution *for full valuable consideration pursuant to an arrangement of a commercial nature* (**s1(3)** as amended by **ITPA 2014**). Note that the amended version of **s1(3)** is designed to ensure

that contributions made between people in a domestic context should not be weighed against each other; and

- the arrangement for maintenance was in place when the deceased died.

NB The deceased and the applicant need not be related nor have lived under the same roof. The maintenance requirement within **s1(1)(e)** will be satisfied if the deceased provided accommodation for the applicant even if the accommodation was shared with the deceased and the parties were otherwise financially independent.

The Law Commission rejected the idea of a minimum period of dependence to establish a claim, although the period of dependence is clearly relevant in assessing an award.

11.4.5.1 Immediately before death

Although there is no minimum period, the concept of maintenance denotes recurrence or continuance. Also, the agreement for maintenance must have been in existence when the deceased died.

In ***Re Beaumont [1980]*** Megarry VC said that the court must not look simply at the facts immediately before the death, but the normal, habitual state. He gave the example of the dependant who nurses the deceased through a terminal illness but in the final period the deceased is hospitalised. During the period of nursing, the value of attention given could greatly exceed the value of maintenance given.

Megarry VC did envisage difficulties where, for example, A and B live together for many years as husband and wife but the relationship breaks down and they part company, say, two or three weeks before the husband's death, and no provision is made for the wife's maintenance. The applicant could be in difficulty if she could not establish that there had been a chance of reconciliation. In ***Jelley v Iliffe [1981]*** the court said that the test was satisfied if the deceased was making a substantial contribution on a settled basis that was either in force immediately before the death or would have lasted until the death but for the approach of death and the inability through incapacity of either party to carry out the arrangement.

It follows that if the settled state of affairs had come to an end for other reasons before the deceased had died, the deceased would not have been maintaining the applicant immediately before the death.

In ***Kourkey v Lusher [1982]*** the deceased married W in 1939. There were no children of the marriage. The deceased started a chiropody practice in 1946 and W joined him in 1951 as his secretary, working full-time at first and then three days a week until his death in 1979. The marriage was happy and contented and the deceased was well-liked by patients, although he was not endowed with strength of character.

The deceased met X, the applicant, in 1963 when she attended as a patient. In 1969, the deceased left the family home and went to live with X. He left clothes at his home, and the practice continued as if nothing had happened, W deciding to make the best of the situation. In 1972, there was some deterioration in the relationship between the deceased and X and, in 1979, the deceased asked W if she would go on holiday with him. After the holiday in July 1979, the deceased did not rejoin X and he died in August 1979.

The court held that the evidence pointed to the deceased having abandoned financial responsibility for X prior to July 1979, and the application failed.

In ***Re Beaumont*** Megarry VC construed **s1(1)(e)** as if there were an implied condition that the deceased had assumed responsibility for the applicant. He referred to a demonstrable act of assumption, rather than mere maintenance. The parties were held to have chosen to pool their resources, neither assuming responsibility for the other. In ***Jelley v Iliffe*** the court said that the bare fact of maintenance generally raised a presumption of assumption of responsibility. In ***Bishop v Plumley [1991]*** the Court of Appeal referred to a commonsense approach: one should look at the situation in the round.

11.5 Reasonable financial provision

The legislation sets out a two-stage process.

(1) Has the will or intestacy or a combination of both had the effect of failing to make reasonable financial provision for the applicant?

(2) If so, what would amount to reasonable financial provision for that applicant?

It will be noted that the test of reasonableness must be applied at two stages in the application – first, to decide whether the provision made for the applicant was reasonable and, second, to decide whether it is reasonable to make an order now. Both questions must be answered in the applicant's favour if they are to succeed. The Supreme Court in ***Ilott v The Blue Cross [2017]*** reversed the Court of Appeal's decision in ***Ilott v Mitson [2015]*** and ordered that the claimant, the deceased's estranged daughter who had been disinherited in favour of a number of charities, should receive only £50,000, the sum originally awarded by the County Court.

The Supreme Court held that all the **s3** guidelines must be considered and, in the light of them, a *"single assessment of reasonable financial provision"* should be made. The Court of Appeal had given little weight to the deceased's very clearly expressed wishes and the long period of estrangement.

The Supreme Court also rejected the Court of Appeal's approach to the issue of the effect of the award on Mrs Ilott's state benefits. The Court of Appeal's argument that the original award of £50,000 was of little or no value was rejected because a substantial part of it could be spent on replacing worn-out household equipment that the applicant could not afford. As a result Mrs Ilott would not lose state benefits because of excess capital.

Finally the Supreme Court highlighted the interests of the charities:

"but charities depend heavily on testamentary bequests for their work, which is by definition of public benefit and in many cases will be for demonstrably humanitarian purposes. More fundamentally, these charities were the chosen beneficiaries of the deceased. They did not have to justify a claim on the basis of need under the 1975 Act, as Mrs Ilott necessarily had to do."

Students are recommended to read the judgment in full.

There are two standards of provision – the surviving spouse standard and that applied in all other cases. Broadly, the spouse is treated as if the spouses were divorcing. (Civil partners are included in these sections under **CPA 2004**.) In other cases, the approach is one of maintenance.

s1(2)(a) – *such provisions as would be reasonable in all the circumstances . . . whether or not the provision is required for the maintenance of the applicant.*

In all cases other than an application by a surviving spouse, the maintenance standard applies.

s1(2)(b) – *such provisions as would be reasonable in all the circumstances of the case for the applicant to receive for his maintenance.*

The following principles have emerged from the cases.

(1) Maintenance does not mean merely subsistence (***Re Christie [1979]***).

(2) The concept denotes payments that directly or indirectly enable the applicant to discharge the recurrent cost of daily living. It does not generally include substantial capital benefit such as paying tax on a lifetime gift (***Re Dennis (Deceased) [1981]***).

(3) It was suggested in ***Re Coventry [1979]*** that maintenance means such provision as would be reasonable in the circumstances to enable the applicant to maintain themselves in a manner suitable to those circumstances.

(4) The level of support is also determined by the level of support the deceased encouraged the applicant to adopt (***Malone v Harrison [1979]***).

(5) Maintenance may denote the wellbeing, health and financial security of the applicant and immediate family, even if the only way this can be guaranteed is by the provision of capital (***Re Christie***, criticised in ***Re Coventry***). There is no doubt that the provision of a house as a home for the applicant may fall within the definition of maintenance.

11.5.1 The objective test

s3(5) states: *In considering the matters to which the court is required to have regard under this section, the court shall take into account the facts as known to the court at the date of the hearing.* This gives statutory approval to the test laid down by Megarry VC in ***Re Goodwin [1968]***. The test is not whether the deceased thought that they were acting reasonably, nor whether they did, in fact, behave reasonably according to the circumstances known to them. The question is simply whether the will or intestacy has made reasonable provision and not whether it was unreasonable on the part of the testator to have made no provision or limited provision for the dependant. The testator may have acted perfectly reasonably but, through some unforeseen circumstance, the provision proves unreasonable at death. Examples would include the birth of a child after the death of the deceased, or a steep fall in the value of property before or following the death.

Under **s3** the time to ask the question is the date of the hearing. Although the position must be considered at the death, and a prompt decision made as to whether to make an application, the objective test and time of application of the test enables the court to take account of supervening events, for example, if the applicant lost their job.

In ***Re Hancock (Deceased) [1998]***, for example, the court was able to take into account a windfall to the estate, which had the effect of making the modest provision for the applicant seem less than reasonable in relation to that made for other beneficiaries.

11.5.2 The common guidelines

s3(1) sets down guidelines that are common to all applications to assist the court in deciding whether the deceased made reasonable financial provision for the applicant, and also to help the court decide whether to exercise its discretion under **I(PFD)A 1975** and make an order.

Under **s3(1)**, the court must have regard to the following matters.

(1) The **financial resources and needs** of the applicant, any other applicant or beneficiary, now or in the foreseeable future (**s3(1)(a)–(c)**). Earning capacity, pensions and social security benefits are all relevant in ascertaining the applicant's financial resources, as are any capital assets of the applicant. In considering the applicant's financial needs, the court must take into account their financial obligations and responsibilities (**s3(6)**). If the needs of the beneficiaries are great, the application is likely to fail. In seeking to meet the applicant's needs, the court will also have regard to the type of relief that would be most appropriate, as in ***Harrington v Gill [1983]*** where, on appeal, the applicant was awarded a life interest in the house where she had cohabited with the deceased, rather than money.

NB In ***Graham v Murphy [1996]*** the court stated that the order it was making was not to provide a high standard of living for the recipient but enough for them to buy a modest property.

(2) Any **obligations and responsibilities of the deceased** towards any applicant or beneficiary entitled under the deceased's will or under the rules of intestacy (**s3(1)(d)**). Obligations include moral obligations as well as legal obligations owed by the deceased to the applicant and to other beneficiaries. The moral obligation may arise partly out of the relationship of the applicant to the deceased and partly out of the needs of the applicant. For example, normally, one spouse owes a moral obligation to the other, although the deceased was held not to owe his spouse much of a moral obligation in ***Re Gregory [1971]***. The husband left the applicant after one year of marriage and thereafter paid no maintenance to her or for their daughter.

The husband went to cohabit with another woman but, after this woman left him, he repeatedly asked the applicant to go back to him. By the time the husband died, the applicant had been living apart from him for 41 years. Even though the court accepted that the husband was solely responsible for the breakdown of the marriage, the length of separation, coupled with the lack of financial support, caused the applicant's claim to fail.

A legal or blood relationship is not necessary for a moral obligation to arise, and the obligation created by a blood relationship may not, in itself, carry much weight (***Re Callaghan [1984]***) in the case of adult children.

If the estate of the deceased is not large enough to discharge all the deceased's obligations, then the court will have to weigh up the conflicting claims. According to the decision of the Court of Appeal in ***Re Jennings [1994]***, the court should consider only the deceased's obligations and responsibilities to the applicant owed immediately before the deceased's death. It was accepted on the facts of the case that the deceased had owed legal and moral obligations to the applicant during the applicant's minority, but the applicant was now long since grown up and was married with two children, owning two companies, and living in a house worth £400,000 subject to only a small mortgage. **I(PFD) A 1975** did not intend to revive defunct obligations and responsibilities.

Stephanides v Cohen [2002] is an example of the court's attempt to resolve competing claims on an estate, as it balances the deceased's moral and legal obligations. Here, the widow of the deceased applied for an order that reasonable financial provision be made for her out of the estate. The deceased died in March 1999 (aged 84), leaving an estate that consisted of cash, shares and investments in the UK worth £92,027, cash at overseas banks totalling over £133,000 and a freehold shop valued at £275,000. The family home (worth £250,000) was held in the sole name of the deceased's son, who also held assets of around £80,000 cash and an income from an overseas trust fund of £107,000. The widow had cash and other assets worth about £167,000.

By his will, the deceased left a legacy of £25,000 to his widow and the remainder of his estate to his son. It was common ground that the will failed to make reasonable financial provision for the widow. The deceased and widow were married in 1994, when she was aged 31 and he was 79, after cohabiting for five years. This was the deceased's second marriage and his son was his only child from his previous, dissolved marriage. The son, now aged 37, was a confirmed drug addict currently engaged on an attempt at rehabilitation at a private clinic. Past attempts had failed.

The court was required to balance the two competing claims from spouse and adult child. It was satisfied that the widow's claim on the estate was considerably more compelling than that of the son's and found that the deceased had a legal obligation to provide for his widow, but only a moral obligation towards his son.

The court took into account the behaviour of both applicants. It heard that the widow had been a good and loyal wife, whereas the son, in his extensive dependency on the deceased as a result of his drug addiction, had not, in the court's opinion, been a good son. Also of importance was the fact that the widow had managed the shop since her marriage to the deceased and had transformed and revitalised the business.

The court awarded the widow the shop and £80,000 in cash from the estate and the remainder to the son under the will.

(3) The **size and nature of the net estate of the deceased (s3(1)(e))**. In ***Re Fullard [1981]*** Ormrod LJ said that the court would be reluctant to interfere in the case of small estates. In order to discourage applications with respect to very small estates where the cost of the action may exhaust a large part of the assets of the estate, judges should consider ordering the costs of an unsuccessful application to be borne by the applicant rather than, as normal, by the estate. If the estate is small, no order may be made if it would not be sufficient to make a real contribution to the maintenance of the applicant. Also, the court would be unwilling to make an order if the only effect was to relieve the Department for Work and Pensions of the need to maintain the applicant. Finally, it would limit the court's scope in making an order if the vast majority of the deceased's assets were tied up in the house, which is required for a beneficiary.

(4) Any **physical or mental disability** of any applicant or any person entitled either under the deceased's will or the rules of intestacy (**s3(1)(f)**). In ***Re Debenham [1986]*** it was said that a court will treat favourably a claim by a disabled adult child. On the facts of the case, an award was made to the 58-year-old daughter of the deceased, who suffered from epilepsy and was physically disabled.

In ***Re Watkins [1949]***, a case decided under the pre-1975 legislation, the court said that the availability of state aid, such as free hospital accommodation, was a factor to be taken into account in such cases. It was, therefore, held to be reasonable to leave nothing out of an estate of £23,000 to a mentally ill daughter who was in a mental hospital and had no hope of ever coming out. In such cases, a payment may be ordered for pocket money for the applicant (***Re E [1966]***).

(5) **Any other matter**, including the conduct of the applicant or of any other person (**s3(1)(g)**). This covers the conduct of the deceased as well as that of the applicant or any other beneficiary. The conduct can be negative or positive. In ***Re Cook [1956]*** the fact that the deceased's daughter had devoted her life to caring for him was a relevant consideration, while in ***Williams v Johns [1988]*** the applicant's conduct in causing shame and emotional distress to his adoptive mother was taken into account in dismissing his claim.

In ***Re Ducksbury [1966]*** the mother and father of the applicant daughter went through a bitter divorce, following which the daughter wrote to her father in a manner deliberately calculated to wound his feelings. Some time later, she wrote to her father apologising, saying that the letter had been written at the instigation of her mother. The court recognised that the father had a moral obligation to the applicant, now adult, and the apologetic letter had swung the burden back upon the father. The court made an income award.

In ***Sivyer v Sivyer [1967]*** a lump sum order in favour of a 13-year-old daughter, residing in the care of the local authority, was increased when the court recognised that a large proportion of the estate of the deceased father comprised a house that had been purchased largely out of the savings of the daughter's deceased mother, the second wife of the now deceased father.

Link to Practice

s1 Civil Evidence Act 1995 enables the court to admit written or oral statements as to why the deceased made little or no provision for the applicant.

It is strongly advised that a testator who wishes to exclude a potential beneficiary from benefiting under their will should make such a statement. Such statements are not conclusive since the test is an objective one but, if true, will require an applicant to make a stronger moral case in order to succeed.

When deciding whether the deceased made reasonable financial provision for the applicant, the court must consider not only the general guidelines, but also special guidelines for each class of applicant. Even the general guidelines have been interpreted differently by the courts in relation to different classes of applicant. Thus, cases on one class of applicant are of limited authority in relation to other classes, so it is important to note which category the applicant falls into and apply only those principles relevant to the particular case.

In ***Espinosa v Bourke [1999]*** the Court of Appeal reviewed earlier cases and authorities. It was held that:

- in each case, all the criteria in **s3(1)** must be applied;
- for the purposes of **s3(1)(d)**, the obligations are both moral and legal;
- an adult child capable of work would have to prove a weighty factor to show failure to make reasonable financial provision (typically, this may be an obligation owed by the deceased to the child).

The applicant daughter had given up work to care for her father. She later moved abroad, leaving others to care for him. She was expressly excluded from her father's will. Her application was based in part on a promise made by her father to his wife (who had predeceased) to leave half of the estate inherited from his wife to their daughter.

The Court of Appeal decided that the lower court had failed to give sufficient weight to this moral obligation and had had too little regard for the financial needs and limited earning capacity of the applicant. A lump sum was awarded to enable the applicant to clear her business debts so that she might then derive an income from a business which would be free of debt.

The court stressed that an application under **s1(1)(c)** by an adult child does not automatically require the applicant to show that the deceased had a moral obligation or other special circumstances.

11.6 Particular guidelines: the spouse or civil partner standard

s3 I(PFD)A 1975 also provides that, without prejudice to the common guidelines, the court will consider the following additional guidelines in relation to particular categories.

(1) **The surviving spouse or civil partner**

The court will consider:

- the age of the applicant and the duration of the marriage or civil partnership;

- the contribution by the applicant to the welfare of the family of the deceased, including any contribution in looking after the home and caring for the family; and
- the provision the applicant might reasonably have expected to receive if, on the day the deceased died, the marriage, instead of being terminated by death, had been terminated by a decree of divorce. Such provision is not to be regarded as setting an upper or lower limit on the size of the order (**s3(2)** as amended by **ITPA 2014**).

The starting point is the amount that the applicant could have expected to have received on a divorce (**s3(2)**).

Where a decree of judicial separation has been made and has continued until the death of the deceased, the application is not treated as having been made by the surviving spouse. The standard applied in such cases is one of maintenance, though, under **s14**, the court has a discretion to apply the surviving spouse standard to judicially separated spouses and to former spouses who have not remarried (**s14(1)(b)**) if:

- the deceased died within 12 months of the decree of the divorce or nullity being made absolute or the grant of the decree of judicial separation; and
- no application has been made for financial provision in the matrimonial proceedings or, if made, has not been determined at death.

Note the *dicta* in ***Re Fullard [1981]***, where the court did not envisage claims where financial arrangements on divorce had been settled by agreement in a clean break settlement (where the assets have been split between the parties and there is no continuing legal obligation to provide maintenance) unless there had been some substantial change in circumstances.

(2) **Applications by the spouse**

Applications may be successful where the deceased miscalculated what would be a fair provision for a spouse.

In ***Re Besterman [1984]*** an application was made by a widow aged 66 where the total value of the net estate was £1.5 m. The parties had been married for 18 years, during which time they had enjoyed a high standard of living. The applicant had no means of her own. By his will, the deceased left her a life interest in £100,000, personal chattels and the use of certain works of art. The deceased erroneously believed that the life interest would enable the widow to continue her life in the style to which she had become accustomed. The remainder of the estate was left to charity.

The Court of Appeal awarded the widow one-quarter of the estate (£378,000) by way of lump sum.

Oliver LJ stated: "*The correct starting point was the likely provision on divorce. The lump sum, however, should include a provision for contingencies since the order is not reviewable if the circumstances change.*"

The court stressed that each case depends upon its facts, though it did indicate guidelines:

- the length of the marriage and the relationship between the parties;
- the contribution made by the applicant to the welfare of the family;
- what the applicant would have received if the parties were divorcing at the death of the deceased;
- the age of the surviving spouse – is the spouse young enough to seek employment?

The principles enunciated in ***Re Besterman*** were considered and applied in ***Re Bunning [1984]***. The applicant wife had given up her job to help the deceased in his business. She had no resources of her own except what the deceased had given her over the years (a total of £47,000). She was young enough to resume work after consideration of the application.

The applicant had left the deceased after 15 years of marriage and some four years before his death, but the court found that there were mitigating circumstances. The deceased left all his £200,000 estate to charity. The court awarded £60,000, taking into account the factors set out in ***Re Besterman***. The court thought that on a divorce the applicant would have received half the estate, taking into account the gifts already made but excluding the house. The lump sum was made after taking into account the house, which had been sold following the death, less the costs of the application, which came out of the estate.

In ***Re Krubert [1996]*** the Court of Appeal stated that, when assessing the merits of a family provision claim by a surviving spouse, the provision that the spouse would have received had the marriage ended by divorce, rather than on death, was only one factor (though an important one) to be considered by the court. The court should decide what provision would be appropriate for the spouse, taking into account all the other factors, and then compare this with the provision that might have been ordered on divorce in order to see that no injustice is being done. The only objective is to meet the spouse's reasonable needs.

If a different approach were taken, the use of the divorce analogy and the provision of needs on a marriage breakdown, providing for housing, income and a lump sum, could deny just deserts on inheritance where the spouses have enjoyed a happy and settled marriage (*dicta* of the Court of Appeal in ***Re Besterman***). The facts of ***Re Krubert*** were that the parties had married in 1950 and bought a plot of land with the applicant's money. They built their house on this plot. The deceased had made a will leaving the spouse a life interest in the house, his personal chattels and a legacy of £10,000, leaving the remainder of the estate to his brother and sister. The court set out the above approach and applied it to award the spouse residue of the estate, but awarded her only a life interest in the house, because she was likely to move, if at all, into sheltered accommodation. The remainder interest in the house was given to the brother and sister.

NB There is no essential difference between claims by widowers and by widows (***Re Clayton [1966]***).

The House of Lords case of ***White v White [2001]*** had a major effect on family provision claims under **I(PFD)A 1975**. It was an ancillary relief case, but it is established that the provision to be made for spouses follows the principles applicable in divorce cases. ***White*** establishes that, in ancillary relief proceedings, there is no place for discriminating between husband and wife according to the roles they have played within the marriage. If, in their different spheres, they have each contributed equally to the family then, in principle, it does not matter which of them earned the money and built up the assets. This means that there should be equality of division on divorce unless there is good reason for doing something else. It was confirmed that, in assessing financial needs, the court would continue to have regard to age, health and accustomed standard of living.

Adams v Lewis [2001] applied ***White***. The deceased had been married to the claimant for 54 years and they had had 12 children. There had been one separation of 18 months. The deceased left the claimant his household goods, his personal effects and a legacy of £10,000. The claimant contended that this was not reasonable and wanted the family home. Three of her daughters opposed this. They accepted that the provision made was not reasonable, but argued that the house was too big for her.

The judge held that the will did not make reasonable financial provision for the claimant bearing in mind the duration of the marriage and the great contribution made by the claimant in caring for the 12 children and looking after the home and the needs of the deceased. He applied the principle in ***Re Besterman***, which laid down that the amount a spouse would have received on divorce is a very important factor. A divorce court would have been looking for a clean break. He applied the decision in ***White*** and said that there was no reason here to depart from the principle of equality. He ordered that the family home pass to the claimant but he reduced her pecuniary legacy to £5,000.

It is worth noting that the principle of equality is not applied rigidly in divorce cases and, of course, family provision cases should follow suit.

White was considered in ***Cunliffe v Fielden [2005]*** in the context of the death of a spouse. The appellant executors (F) appealed against an order in proceedings under **I(PFD)A 1975** that the widow (C) of the deceased (D) should be paid a lump sum of £800,000 out of D's estate. D's net estate was valued at £1.4 m. C had become D's housekeeper about 18 months before D died at the age of 66. C had no assets of her own and subsequently became D's wife 13 months before D died.

By D's will, he left his residuary estate to several beneficiaries, of which C was one, on discretionary trusts. C was offered £200,000 by the executors, but turned this down. On C's application, the High Court increased this to £800,000.

The Court of Appeal held that it was appropriate to consider ***White*** in proceedings under **I(PFD)A 1975**, but that the case did not give rise to a presumed entitlement to equal division between spouses under **I(PFD)A 1975**. This had been a short marriage and the judge had failed to take this fully into account. The court awarded £600,000.

Lilleyman v Lilleyman [2012] was another "big money – short marriage" case where the claimant widow and the deceased had been married for just over two years. He left an estate worth over £6 m. His will gave the widow limited rights to occupy both the family home and an apartment plus a fixed annuity worth £378 per month and personal chattels worth £18,000 (£17,000 of which was accounted for by his collection of Dinky toys!). The widow claimed that this provision was not reasonable and called for a substantial share in what had been their family property, in excess of her reasonable needs. In support of her claim, she relied on ***Miller v Miller [2006]***, suggesting that her life as a widow should not revert to what it was before her marriage. The defendants, who were the deceased's sons by a previous marriage and ultimate beneficiaries of the estate, submitted that reasonable provision was to be identified solely by reference to the spouse's reasonable needs, including a need for financial security for the rest of her life. They based their argument on the approach taken in ***Cunliffe v Fielden***.

The court granted the widow's claim by finding that the provision in the will was not reasonable because in this case it should not be limited to providing financial security for the rest of her life. It awarded her, in addition to the property given by the will, the entire interest in the family home and apartment, as well as the estate's future interest in another property (in all cases, the claimant could receive a lump sum representing market value if she wished). What undoubtedly influenced the court here was the fact that the relationship between the claimant and the deceased's sons had broken down completely, so if the will stood as it was, it would be very difficult for them all to maintain interests in the same property.

11.6.1 Former spouses who have not remarried

s3(2) I(PFD)A 1975 provides that the factors are:

- the age of the applicant and the duration of the marriage; and
- the contribution made by the applicant to the welfare of the deceased's family, including any contribution made by looking after the home or caring for the family. If the deceased died within 12 months after the decree absolute of divorce or nullity, and at the date of the deceased's death no order had been made or refused in relation to financial provision, the court may apply the

surviving spouse standard. If that discretion is exercised, the court must also take into account the likely level of provision on divorce.

When considering the likely success of a claim by a former spouse, the Court of Appeal decision in ***Re Fullard [1981]*** will be relevant. The applicant married the deceased in 1938. They were divorced in 1976. They had both worked throughout the marriage and had accumulated savings of about equal amounts. They settled their financial affairs after the divorce by agreement and each party acknowledged that neither would claim periodical payments from the other. Shortly afterwards, the husband died and the applicant applied. The application was rejected.

Ormrod LJ did not envisage that many post-decree cases would be the subject of family provision applications. He cited two possible situations where the court could consider a claim:

- where there have been long-standing periodical payments and the paying spouse has accumulated capital; and
- where the death of the deceased unlocks capital in a pension fund or life assurance policy.

Finally, it should be noted that, when deciding whether a claim by a former spouse should succeed, conduct of either party is generally irrelevant, unless it is extremely bad.

11.6.2 A person living in the same household as husband or wife

In relation to this additional category introduced by the **Law Reform (Succession) Act 1995**, the court must have regard to:

- the age of the applicant and the length of the period during which the applicant lived as the spouse of the deceased and in the same household as the deceased; and
- the contribution to the welfare of the family of the deceased, including any contribution made by looking after the home and caring for the family (**s3(2A)(a) I(PFD)A 1975**).

A cohabitant falling in this category will be treated less generously than a surviving spouse as reasonable financial provision is to be judged according to the maintenance standard, but some of the particular guidelines relevant to spouses are to be applied.

Under **CPA 2004**, a surviving civil partner has the same rights as a surviving spouse to claim against the estate of his deceased partner. The test of reasonable financial provision is equivalent to the surviving spouse standard.

In ***Re Watson [1999]*** the applicant had been cohabiting with the deceased at the time of his death, and for some 10 years previously. They had known each other for about 30 years but, having carers' responsibilities for their respective parents, had not been free to enter into a relationship. The deceased died intestate, leaving an estate worth between £150,000 and £200,000. It was held that the applicant's needs were for accommodation in a bungalow or ground-floor flat, in view of her age (67 years) and her arthritis. The deceased was held to have owed her some obligation and the Crown, on whom the estate would otherwise have devolved, had no real need or moral claim. Her application therefore succeeded, both in the provision of accommodation and her need for income.

In ***Lewis v Warner [2016]*** an elderly applicant who had lived in the same household as husband of the testatrix for 20 years was awarded an option to purchase the family home. The court held that the fact that the applicant was wealthier than the testatrix did not mean that the court could not order reasonable financial provision in his favour. In this unusual case, the option to purchase the family home was to be at the market value of £385,000.

11.6.3 A child of the deceased

The only particular guideline specified for this category of applicant is the manner in which the applicant was being, or was expected to be, educated or trained (**s3(3)**). This category has caused the courts some difficulty.

The court in ***Re Coventry [1979]*** cited ***Re Vrint [1940]***: "[The **Inheritance (Family Provision) Act 1938**] *was passed for the purpose of providing reasonable provision for the maintenance of the applicant. The Act was not passed for the purpose of providing legacies out of the testator's estate.*"

In ***Re Coventry*** H and W married in 1927. They purchased a house which gave W a one-third entitlement. A son (S) was born in 1931. After a period in the navy, S returned home in 1957 when W left H. From 1957 until 1961, S, in full-time employment, lived rent-free in the house but paid for food, gas and electricity. S married in 1961 and he and his wife lived in the house rent-free, the wife doing the domestic work. The marriage ended in 1975. In 1976, H died intestate and his two-thirds interest in the house was valued at £7,000, his entire estate passing on the intestacy to W. W was aged 74, living on a pension in council accommodation. S was earning a wage but had little capital and would have to find alternative accommodation.

It was held by the Court of Appeal that applications by able-bodied adult sons and daughters of the deceased should be treated with suspicion and would not succeed unless it could be shown that the deceased owed the applicant a special moral obligation. The mere fact that the parties were related or, as in this case, that the applicant was in poor financial circumstances, was not sufficient.

The cases in which the courts have considered appropriate claims by adult children include where the child is disabled (***Re Wood [1982]***), a young adult requires support to provide a start in life (***Re Collins (Deceased) [1990]***), or there is a genuine moral obligation on the part of the parent combined with necessitous circumstances, such as where the child gave up work to look after the parent.

Re Coventry was applied by the Court of Appeal in ***Re Jennings [1994]***. The applicant (H), aged 50, had succeeded at first instance in obtaining an award of £40,000 from the estate of his deceased natural father, J. H's parents had separated two years after the birth of H. J had made no financial provision for H, who had been brought up by his mother and stepfather. J died in 1990, leaving the bulk of his £300,000 estate to charities. In considering whether reasonable financial provision had been made, the Court of Appeal cited ***Re Coventry*** saying that, in the case of an adult son capable of earning his own living, there had to be some special circumstance, typically, a moral obligation of the deceased towards him, before one could say that reasonable provision had not been made.

The court rejected the trial judge's view that J's failure to discharge legal responsibilities during H's minority gave rise to a moral obligation, because the obligation was long spent. The court said that obligations and responsibilities referred to were those of the deceased immediately before the death. It was not the intention of Parliament to base an order simply upon father and son relationships. There has to be some additional factor, for example, that the adult child is in higher education or undergoing training.

If the Court of Appeal had held that reasonable provision had not been made, what provision, if any, should H receive? The court referred to ***Re Dennis (Deceased) [1981]*** and the definition of maintenance. In ***Re Jennings*** H owned two companies and enjoyed a comfortable standard of living. In the view of the court, no further financial provision was necessary to enable H to discharge the cost of daily living at the standard appropriate to him.

A case in which the court held that a moral obligation was owed to the deceased was ***Re Goodchild [1996]***. In that case, a claim that there were valid mutual wills in favour of the applicant (who was the son of the deceased) failed for lack of the necessary agreement. The court held, however, that there was a moral obligation owed to the applicant in respect of the part of the estate that would have passed to him if the mutual will had been upheld. This was because there was evidence that the deceased's mother (the first testator to die) believed that the mutual wills were valid and also that the applicant was in poor financial circumstances. Note also ***Re Abram (Deceased) [1996]*** and ***Espinosa v Bourke [1999]*** (see **11.4.3**). In both cases, the court was of the opinion that a moral obligation or special circumstances were not essential, although usually required for success.

In ***Ubbi v Ubbi [2018]*** the High Court awarded a lump sum of just over £386,000 to be paid from the testator's estate to his two minor children in their claim under **I(PFD)A 1975**. The total value of the estate was approximately £3,500,000.

The judgment includes a detailed discussion of **s3(3)** which is particularly helpful. Applications on behalf of minor children are not that common, so there is little in the way of previous guidance.

The judge said that whilst it may be desirable for children to attend private school, the test for provision under **I(PFD)A 1975** is the **expectation** that there would be a private school education. On the facts, he found no evidence of a firm intention by the testator to educate the children privately and so did not make any allowance for private school fees in the award. Provision was, however, made for housing and childcare costs, while a 65 per cent contribution by the mother towards the financial maintenance needs of the children was deducted.

11.6.4 A child of the family

In addition to the educational guideline that also applies to a child of the deceased, the court is required to consider:

- whether the deceased had assumed responsibility for the maintenance of the applicant and, if so, the extent to which, and the basis on which, the deceased assumed the responsibility, and the length of time for which the deceased had actually discharged that responsibility;
- whether in assuming and discharging the responsibility, the deceased knew that the applicant was not his own child; and
- the liability of any other person to maintain the applicant **(s3(3))**.

11.6.5 Any other person maintained by the deceased (s1(1)(e) applicants)

s3(4) (as amended by **ITPA 2014**) sets out the particular guideline for this category which requires the court to have regard:

(a) to the length of time for which and basis on which the deceased maintained the applicant, and to the extent of the contribution made by way of maintenance;

(b) to whether and, if so, to what extent the deceased assumed responsibility for the maintenance of the applicant.

(1) **The contribution made by maintenance**

The extent of the contribution made by maintenance was considered by the Court of Appeal in ***Jelley v Iliffe [1981]***. Here, the applicant, a widower, and the deceased, a widow, related by marriage, lived together in the deceased's house for eight years until the deceased died. He provided furniture, looked after the garden and did household jobs while she cooked for him, and provided him with rent-free accommodation. The Court of Appeal held that the applicant's claim should not be struck out (a litigation procedure for preventing claims with no prospect of success from proceeding to trial). Stephenson LJ stated:

"To discover whether the deceased was making such a contribution the court had to balance what she had contributed against what the applicant had contributed. If there was any doubt about the balance tipping in favour of the deceased being the greater contributor, the matter must go to trial. If however the balance was bound to come down in favour of the [applicant] *being the greater contributor, or if the contributions were equal, there was no dependency of him on her, either because she depended upon him or there was mutual dependency between them and his application should be struck out."*

NB The amended version of **s1(3) I(PFD)A 1975** (see **11.4.5**) is intended to exclude this sort of informal domestic arrangement as it was clearly not *for full valuable consideration pursuant to an arrangement of a commercial nature.*

(2) **The assumption of responsibility**

Bouette v Rose [2000] is an unusual case where Mrs Bouette had cared for her brain-damaged daughter until her death aged 14 years. The brain damage was the result of medical negligence at birth and the child was awarded £250,000 in damages. Her affairs were under the jurisdiction of the Court of Protection. A property had been purchased for the joint occupation of Mrs Bouette and her daughter. When the child died intestate, her parents were equally entitled to the funds in her estate. Mrs Bouette wished to apply under **s1(1)(e) I(PFD) A 1975** as a person maintained by the deceased. Her claim was rejected, but on appeal the court accepted the notion that the Court of Protection could act as the conscience of the patient and make provision for those to whom the patient would have felt a moral obligation had she been of full mental capacity. It was decided that Mrs Bouette had not provided valuable consideration for the benefits which she had received and her appeal was allowed on the basis that she had been maintained by the deceased.

11.7 Legally unenforceable assurances

Under **s3(5)**, the court takes into account the facts at the date of the hearing and is not entitled to take account of legally unenforceable assurances given by the other beneficiaries under the will.

In ***Rajabally v Rajabally [1987]*** the claimant was the deceased's second wife, aged 45, with two adult sons. The defendant, aged 35, was the deceased's son from his first marriage. The will left the whole estate to the widow and the three sons in equal shares. The main asset was the family home. The claimant, supported by her two sons, claimed the whole estate.

At first instance, the judge considered that the will had made reasonable provision for the claimant, but the Court of Appeal found that the judge had reached this conclusion on the basis of assurances by the claimant's sons that they were willing to transfer their share to the claimant and that the defendant was willing to be bought out. Mere assurances were not enough, however. If the parties felt that the widow was not properly provided for, they could come before the court for an order to be made.

11.8 Time limit (s4)

s4, as amended by **ITPA 2014**, provides that an application under **I(PFD)A 1975** can be made before a grant of probate or letters of administration has been issued. The application must be issued within six months of the grant of representation. The definition of a grant of representation for these purposes includes a grant of probate or letters of administration but does not include other more unusual grants which do not authorise the estate to be distributed. Such grants will include grants pending suit under **s117 Senior Courts Act 1981** (used where a grant is needed to enable the PRs to act in litigation). Similarly, grants issued outside the United Kingdom are not taken into account in relation to this time limit. Time extensions can be granted by the court, but successful applications to extend the limit are rare. PRs should not distribute the property within the six-month period, or they face the risk of personal liability. **s20(1)** protects a PR who distributes after the time limit, even if they ought to have realised that the court might grant leave to apply. Where a successful application is made outside the time limit, the applicant cannot proceed against the PRs but can pursue the beneficiaries through tracing or an application for a refund (***Re Diplock [1948]***).

The factors that the court should consider in granting an extension were considered by Megarry VC in ***Re Salmon [1980]***. The applicant, a widow, had parted from her husband in 1944 after 12 unhappy years. Although she did not see her husband again, they were never divorced. The husband died in 1978 leaving a net estate of £75,000. A grant was taken out in December 1978, the time limit expiring in June 1979. In February 1979, at the instigation of a friend, she wrote to the administrators, a bank, asking for an *ex gratia* payment. The request was rejected. In April 1979, she consulted solicitors but owing to their slowness, they did not notify the administrators of their interest in the matter until the end of October and did not issue proceedings until November 1979, by which time, most of the estate had been distributed.

In rejecting an application for a time extension, Megarry VC set out the following factors.

(1) The delay was substantial and fault was wholly on the side of the widow.

(2) There were no negotiations before the time limit expired and no warning to the bank of her interest until nearly five months after the expiry of the time limit.

(3) Almost all the estate had been distributed, therefore the beneficiaries had not merely looked at an expectation but had actually received money and had changed their positions as a result, making purchases that they would not otherwise have made.

(4) The widow probably had a right of action in negligence against the solicitors.

(5) The court should have regard to the merits of the applicant's claim for reasonable provision.

It was said in ***Re Salmon*** that the onus is on the applicant to justify an extension of the time limit. The applicant must act promptly to apply for an extension. It will be relevant to consider to what extent negotiations have taken place to settle the claim and to what extent the estate has been distributed. The final factor is whether the applicant would have a claim against anyone else if the application to extend the time limit were refused.

On the rare occasions when the court does grant leave, it is influenced by factors such as:

- the merits of the intended claim;
- whether the estate has been distributed;
- whether it is large; and
- whether there would be prejudice to other beneficiaries.

In ***Berger v Berger [2013]*** the Court of Appeal refused permission for a surviving spouse to make a claim nearly six-and-a-half years after a grant of probate was issued, because there was no identifiable trigger for the late claim. It was not a claim which had been provoked by a particular event – for example, something for which the defendants had been responsible, such as concealing assets, or something extraneous such as a dramatic fall in interest rates. While the Court of Appeal felt that the spouse had an arguable case for financial provision, this and other factors in her favour were outweighed by the undue delay.

The judgment provides a useful overview of a potential claim being made out of time, and compares the facts in previous High Court cases.

The approach taken in ***Berger v Berger [2013]*** was confirmed in ***Sargeant v Sargeant and Another [2018]*** where a widow applied more than 10 years out of time. The deceased, a farmer, had set up discretionary trusts which had the effect of providing her with very limited income only. She had been told to take independent legal advice but had not done so and was unable to provide the court with a good explanation as to why she had not applied earlier. The court rejected her application to apply out of time.

In ***Cowan v Foreman [2019]*** Mrs Cowan, the deceased's widow, sought to bring a claim against her husband's estate after the six-month period following the grant. The majority of the extremely large estate was placed in a trust which would provide the trustees with discretion to benefit Mrs Cowan and other beneficiaries. 17 months after the six-month limit from the date of the grant of probate set by **s4 I(PFD)A 1975**, Mary Cowan sought to bring a claim under **I(PFD)A 1975** on the basis that her position was not sufficiently certain, that she had no assets in her own name and that she had no control over what she would receive.

In order to allow an opportunity for mediation and thus avoiding court proceedings, the parties had agreed to enter into an a "standstill agreement". The purpose of the agreement was that both parties agreed to extend the six- month deadline to bring the claim, and that nobody would defend the claim on the basis of it being out of time.

The Court of Appeal granted Mrs Cowan permission to bring a claim under **I(PFD) A 1975**. It held that, when determining whether a claim should be brought outside the six-month period, the court had to consider all of the relevant circumstances of the case. It was necessary to decide whether the applicant's claim had a real prospect of success rather than a fanciful one. If a claim had no real prospect of success, the court would not accept a claim with no merit which was commenced outside the six-month time limit merely because the delays could not be explained and no one was prejudiced.

In relation to the negotiations between the parties and the "standstill agreement", the fact that Mrs Cowan had been encouraged to enter into "without prejudice" negotiations and the standstill agreement should be treated as a positive factor in her favour.

In ***Kaur v Bolina [2021]*** the testator, Mr Bolina, left a will which left his entire estate (valued at approximately £300,000 – £350,000) to his two adult children. The will made no provision for Mr Bolina's estranged wife, Mrs Kaur.

In December 2019, a grant of probate was obtained by the adult children, who were executors of the will. This meant that the six-month time period to bring an **I(PFD)A 1975** claim expired in June 2020.

In November 2020, Mrs Kaur's solicitors discovered that the time period had elapsed five months ago, and promptly sought permission to bring a claim out of time.

The court allowed Mrs Kaur to bring her claim out of time, taking into account the following factors.

- Mrs Kaur acted promptly to seek permission.
- Although the estate had been distributed in August 2020, the distribution was "not complex" (presumably because it had been made by and to the adult children, who were defending the claim). Moreover, Mrs Kaur notified the adult children of the claim in May 2020, before the distribution and also before the six-month time window expired.
- Mrs Kaur had an "arguable" case because she received no provision following a marriage of seven years and had limited assets and a limited income.

11.9 The property available – the meaning of "net estate" (s25(1))

The term "net estate" might be defined as all the property that the deceased owned at the date of their death and could have disposed of by their will (the testator is treated as able to dispose of the property even if they did not have the required mental capacity), less:

- funeral, testamentary and administration expenses;
- debts and liabilities; and
- inheritance tax. The amount of inheritance tax to be deducted is calculated after the court has made an order. If inheritance tax has been paid prior to the grant, the appropriate adjustments are made.

Property owned at the date of death was considered in an unusual case involving an insurance policy. In ***Lim v Walia [2014]*** the deceased and the claimant (her husband) were a married couple who held a life insurance policy which included a provision for early payment if one of the insured couple could show that they were suffering from a terminal illness. The deceased died leaving a young son from a new relationship. The husband was entitled to a grant and, because of the size of it, to the estate on intestacy. At first instance it was held that, immediately before her death, the deceased had been beneficially entitled to a joint tenancy of the terminal illness benefit, but the Court of Appeal held that she had had a severable interest in the terminal illness benefit that ceased to have a value because it was not claimed before she died. As a result, the half share of the proceeds of the life policy which was paid out on her death did **not** form part of the net estate under **s25(1) I(PFD) A 1975** and the husband therefore retained the proceeds.

The net estate available for an order is extended to include:

(1) a nomination in force at the date of death (see **1.3.4**) (**s8(1)**). In ***Goenka v Goenka, Welsh and Others [2014]*** the court held that a nomination by the deceased of a large sum payable under the NHS pension scheme created under a statutory instrument was included in the net estate;

(2) *donatio mortis causa* (see **1.3.1**);

(3) property held on a joint tenancy (see **1.3.2**).

In relation to (3), the court may order that the deceased's severable share *to such extent as appears to the court to be just in the circumstances of the case* shall be treated as part of the net estate (**s9(1)**). The date on which the deceased's severable share is to be calculated is now subject to **s9(1A) I(PFD)A 1975** (inserted by **ITPA 2014**). **s9(1A)** provides that the value is to be calculated as at the date of the hearing of the application unless the court orders it to be assessed at another date (e.g. the date of death). This amended sub-section confirmed ***Dingmar v Dingmar [2006]*** which held that the deceased's share of a jointly owned house should be calculated at the date of trial, rather than on the (much lower) value at the date of death.

The time limit for applications in respect of the deceased's share of joint property under **s9** ends six months after the date of the grant. The court has the discretion to extend the time limit.

11.10 Anti-avoidance provisions (ss10 and 11)

Prior to **I(PFD)A 1975**, a testator intent on avoiding a possible claim could, for example, give away assets prior to death or enter into a contract to leave property in any event and then not leave the property, thereby inviting an action for damages against the estate; the action would have to be resolved prior to determination of the net estate. The provisions in **ss10** and **11** seek to counter these and other steps.

11.10.1 Order for the donee to make financial provision (s10)

A court can order a donee to make financial provision for the applicant if it is satisfied that:

- the deceased made a disposition within six years of the death with the intention of defeating a claim under **I(PFD)A 1975**; and
- the deceased was not given full valuable consideration for the disposition; and
- by exercising its powers, the court would facilitate the making of financial provision for the applicant.

"Disposition" means parting with any type of property right – for example, a payment of money, conveyance, transfer, appointment and gift.

The creation of liabilities is not, in itself, a disposition – for example, where the deceased had the chance to obtain for themselves a profitable trading contract with a third party but arranged for a friend to benefit, thereby diverting the proceeds.

The enjoyment of property after the disposition does not affect the disposition. For example, where X transfers their house to Y more than six years before X's death but continues to live in the house after the transfer, this would not bring the disposition within **s10**. Compare, however, where X takes a life interest in a settlement created more than six years before their death but X retains a power of appointment over the property.

Intention is determined upon the balance of probabilities. **s12(1)** expressly provides that the intention to defeat **I(PFD)A 1975** need not be the sole intention in making the disposition.

If the deceased received consideration, this is valued at the time it was paid. It would be possible, therefore, to purchase a future right and still regard the consideration given as being for full value, thereby avoiding **I(PFD)A 1975**.

Example

X sells to Y, for £250,000, the right to his house on his death. Five years later, at death, the house is worth £280,000. Provided that the £250,000 is regarded as full consideration at the time it was furnished, this will be the value of the disposition.

The value of property caught by **s10** is the value at death. The court can make an order even if the donee has parted with the property, in which case, it is the value at the date of disposal by the donee. If the donee has died, their PRs are not liable (**s12(4)**).

11.10.2 Power to modify deceased's contract for disposition (s11)

Whereas **s10** is directed at the situation where the deceased sought to reduce their net estate by reducing their assets, **s11** deals with the situation where the deceased sought to increase their liabilities.

By **s11**, the court has the power to modify the effect of a contract entered into by the deceased to leave property by will. The conditions are:

- the deceased made a contract by which they agreed either:
  - to leave a sum of money or property to a person in a will; or
  - that a sum of money or property would be paid or transferred to a person out of their estate; and
- the contract was made with the intention of defeating a claim under **I(PFD)A 1975**; and
- at the time of the contract, full and valuable consideration was not given or promised by the donee; and
- by exercising the powers, the court would make financial provision for the applicant.

If no valuable consideration was given by anyone, intention to defeat the claim is presumed. This is to be contrasted with the position under **s10** where the intention must be proved.

I(PFD)A 1975 applies only to contracts to pass property on death. A contract to transfer property during life is outside **I(PFD)A 1975**; for example, a person could enter into an *inter vivos* covenant to pay a sum of money, but any payment to the covenantee would have to be satisfied before the net estate could be ascertained. Note, however, the *dictum* of Lord Cross in ***Schaefer v Schuman [1972]***: "[W]*hether contracts made by a testator not with a view to excluding the jurisdiction of the court under the Act but in the normal course of arranging his affairs in his lifetime should be liable to be wholly or partially set aside by the court . . . is a question of social policy on which different people may reasonably take different views.*"

There is no time limit in the case of contracts falling within **s11**, save a cut-off in respect of contracts made prior to the commencement of **I(PFD)A 1975** (1 April 1976).

The court will have regard to the circumstances in the making of the contract, the relationship (if any) of donor to donee and their respective financial circumstances.

11.11 Court's power to make orders (s2)

The court has wide powers in the making of a variety of orders under **I(PFD)A 1975**.

(1) **Periodical payments**

These can be for life or for a limited period – for example, until remarriage or a specified number of years.

(2) **Lump-sum payments**

The order can specify payment of a lump sum in instalments.
Since the applicant cannot return to the court at a later date to vary a lump-sum order, the court should take account of contingencies in arriving at an amount under the order (*obiter* in ***Re Besterman [1984]***).

(3) **Transfer of property**

The court can order the transfer of title to property – for example, a dwelling- house.

(4) **Settlement of property**

The court has wide powers to order settlements of property – for example, in making provision for infant children.

(5) **Order for acquisition of property**

The court can order a house to be purchased for the applicant.

(6) **Variation of marriage settlements**

The court has a limited power under **s6** to vary orders in respect of periodical payments. This power is limited to relevant property, that is, property supporting the periodic payments. Application to vary is not confined to the original applicant but could be made by a beneficiary of the estate, the PRs of the deceased or the trustees of any relevant property.

(7) **Variation of the trusts under the will or intestacy**

ITPA 2014 added an express power to vary, for the applicant's benefit, the trusts on which the deceased's estate is held (whether these are trusts arising on intestacy or under a will, or both).

(8) **Interim financial relief**

Under **s5**, the court can allow interim financial relief pending trial of the main **s2** claim, but only if the applicant can demonstrate *immediate need of financial assistance*.

In ***Smith v Smith and Others [2011]*** the court refused such relief, even though the applicant was the deceased's spouse, because her claim was insufficiently strong. The court said that a strong case of need must be established as the court was being asked to pre-empt the final decision.

Note that while proof of need is necessary if asking for interim relief, it is not so in determining the outcome of the main claim by a spouse or civil partner because the applicable standard of provision is that which is reasonable, whether or not required for maintenance. However, if the applicant is someone else, for whom the ordinary maintenance standard of provision applies, then need will be an important factor for the court in deciding the final outcome.

11.12 Law reform

The Law Commission's report *Inheritance and Family Provision: Claims on Death*, published in 2011 (see **10.8**) proposed changes to **I(PFD)A 1975**, many of which were implemented in **ITPA 2014**. The areas of change which were **not** included in **ITPA 2014** are set out below.

Family and dependants of a person domiciled abroad

Family provision claims have never been possible unless the deceased died domiciled in England and Wales. This precondition can prevent family members and dependants from accessing the family provision jurisdiction even if the administration of some or all of the deceased's estate is otherwise governed by the law of this country. The Law Commission recommends reform: the domicile precondition should be retained but an alternative precondition introduced so that a family provision claim can be made where the deceased left assets governed by English succession law.

Cohabitants

Currently, a cohabitee can make a claim if they have lived in the same household as the deceased as a spouse or civil partner for a period of two years immediately before the death. The Law Commission recommends reform to permit a claim by the survivor of a shorter relationship if they have had a child with the deceased. This would replace, for these couples, the current requirement that the relationship must have lasted for two years before the death, whether or not the couple had a child together.

Link to Practice

Law Commission Consultation Paper 231 – *Making a will*

The Law Commission's consultation on wills has proposed that **s8 I(PFD)A 1975** be extended to include property subject to a mutual wills arrangement (see **Chapter 7**).

11.13 Summary

(1) The law relating to family provision is contained in **I(PFD)A 1975**, as amended.

(2) *Locus standi* – under **s1(1)**, there are six categories of applicant who can apply on the ground that the deceased's will or intestacy or a combination of both fail to make reasonable financial provision for the applicant. The categories are:

- spouse or civil partner of the deceased;
- former spouse or former civil partner of the deceased who has not remarried or formed another civil partnership;
- a person living in the same household as spouse or civil partner of the deceased;
- a child of the deceased;
- a person treated as a child of the family;
- a person maintained by the deceased.

(3) To establish whether reasonable financial provision has been made, the law sets out a two-stage process.

- Has the will or intestacy or a combination of both had the effect of failing to make reasonable financial provision for the applicant?
- If so, what would amount to reasonable financial provision for that applicant?

(4) Common guidelines are set out in **s3(1)**. Particular guidelines for spouses or civil partners, former spouses or former civil partners, cohabitants, children and dependants are set out in **ss3(2)**, **(3)** and **(4)**.

(5) The time limit for an application under **s4** is six months from the date of the grant.

(6) The meaning of "net estate" is found in **s25**.

(7) Anti-avoidance provisions are found in **ss10** and **11**.

(8) The courts have the power to make various orders under **s2**:

- lump-sum payments;
- transfer of property;
- settlement of property;
- an order for acquisition of property;
- variation of marriage settlements;
- variation of the trusts under the will or intestacy.

(9) Applications for interim relief may be made under **s5**.

CHAPTER 12

Legacies and Devises

Aims of the Chapter:

By the end of this chapter, you should be able to:

- distinguish between the different types of legacies; and
- give examples of each type of legacy.

12.1 Introduction

Gifts in a will may be a **devise** of a piece of land or a **legacy** of money or physical objects. When the testator has died, such gifts can pose significant problems for executors, and it is important that lawyers are clear on the rules governing them.

The following types of legacy are considered in this chapter:

- **specific legacies** – gifts of particular things owned by the testator;
- **general legacies** – gifts of things or money not expressed as owned by the testator;

- **demonstrative legacies** – gifts expressed as being payable from a particular fund, such as a particular bank account;
- **pecuniary legacies** – gifts of money;
- **residuary legacies** – gifts of everything left over after payment of debts and other legacies.

12.2 Specific legacies

A specific legacy is defined as a gift of a particular existing item from the assets belonging to the deceased. The necessary elements were set out by Sir George Jessel MR in ***Bothamley v Sherson [1875]***: *"The gift refers to some part of the testator's assets in such a way as to distinguish it from the other assets and indicate that it is to pass to the legatee* in specie [that is, a thing not its cash value]."

Examples

"My books to A", "My Tesla motor car to B".

The specific legacy is identified by the possessive prefix "my", but this is not conclusive. Because of the doctrine of ademption (which provides that a gift of a specific item will fail if the gift is no longer owned by the testator at the date of death), the courts prefer to avoid construing gifts as specific. So, for example, if in a gift of shares the testator owned exactly the number of shares given at the date of the will and at the date of death, this will not necessarily mean that the gift will be construed as a specific gift of those particular shares (***Re Willcocks [1921]***).

In this case, the testatrix left her father £948 3s 11d Queensland 3½ per cent inscribed stock in her will. At the date of the will, she owned stock of that precise description, but she disposed of it before her death. It was held that, since the will did not refer to the stock as belonging to her at that date, it was a general legacy only and the executors were directed to purchase stock to that value for the beneficiary. Had the legacy been specific, it would have failed by ademption when the stock was sold.

There are two further cases worth considering on this point. In ***Re Gage [1934]*** the testator bequeathed to his niece "the sum of £1,150 War Loan 1929–47 and to MG the sum of £500 New South Wales stock now standing in my name". At the date of the will, the testator held exactly £1,150 War Loan but subsequently accepted a cash payment in lieu of the stock so, at death, held no War Loan at all. Was the gift specific and therefore adeemed by the cash payment?

The court held that the fact that at the date of the will the testator held the exact amount did not, by itself, make the gift specific, but the words "now standing in my name" suggested a specific nature. The gift to MG including those words was separated by the word "and"; therefore, the gift to the niece was unaffected and held to be general. The PRs were directed to buy stock for the niece.

Although the courts lean against specific legacies, the overriding factor is that one must look at the will as a whole in the light of the surrounding circumstances. In ***Re Rose [1949]***, despite the absence of the possessive word "my", the gift was held to be specific.

Generally, but not conclusively, a gift of shares will be specific if it refers to "My 500 shares in X plc to . . ." or "All my shares in X plc to . . .".

Re Eve [1956] presented interesting problems as to the nature of the gift. The will of the testator read "I bequeath to X an option to acquire from my executors at par value my shares in Z Limited". Roxburgh J referred to the definition by Sir George Jessel MR and held that the gift was not specific. The gift merely gave X the right to buy the shares; the beneficial aspect was in the price ("par value" was below market value). This was not a specific gift of the difference in values because this aspect had not been distinguished by the testator.

(1) **Income and interest**

A specific gift which takes effect immediately on the death of the testator carries with it all the income and profits accruing from the date of death and is subject to all liabilities incurred after death. So, for example, in a specific gift of shares, the legatee is entitled to the dividend income on the shares from the date of death and is subject to any calls on the shares. In a specific devise, the devisee is entitled to the rents and profits from the date of death but must bear any burdens, such as landlord repairing covenants where the land is leased. Income and profits accrue from day to day depending upon the asset.

Where a trust was created **before** 1 October 2013, including trusts created by a will or under the intestacy rules where the date of death was before 1 October 2013, the income may need to be apportioned under **s2 Apportionment Act 1870**, unless it was excluded in the will (as was normal practice in professionally drafted wills). **s2** provides that all rents, dividends and other periodical payments (payments of income rather than capital payments) are considered to accrue from day to day and shall be apportioned in respect of time accordingly. So, if the estate includes tenanted property, the rent for the period that includes the date of death, which is not collected until after death, is apportioned so that the proportion that relates to the period before the date of death is capital of the estate and that which relates to the period after death is income of the estate. Apportionment is important in various situations:

- between a specific beneficiary of the land and the residuary beneficiaries of the estate;

- between a life tenant entitled to income and a remainderman (the person receiving a residue of an estate in land).

  s1 Trusts (Capital and Income) Act 2013 disapplies **s2 Apportionment Act 1870** for all new trusts created on or after 1 October 2013 (unless the trust or will states otherwise), including trusts created under the intestacy rules or arising under a will where the date of death is **on or after** 1 October 2013.

  NB If the date of death is on or after 1 October 2013, **s1** will still apply, even if the date of the will was **before** 1 October 2013.

  In the case of contingent or deferred specific gifts, entitlement to income is governed by **s175 Law of Property Act 1925**. A contingent gift would be, for example, "to X if he reaches 25", a deferred gift would be "to X after the death of Y". Unless the testator directs otherwise, **s175** provides that a specific or deferred gift will carry the intermediate income. If X is entitled to the income under the gift but is under 18, then the income is accumulated and added to the capital.

  When a minor beneficiary is contingently entitled, it is also important to note that **s31 Trustee Act 1925** (**TA 1925**) gives the trustees the power to apply the income for the child's *maintenance, education or benefit*.

(2) **Abatement**

When the residuary estate is insufficient to meet all the liabilities of the estate, **s34** and **Part II Sch 1 AEA 1925** have the effect that the legacies are reduced *pro rata* (proportionately). The process whereby the legacies are reduced is called abatement. **Sch 1** has the effect that the general legacies abate, as a group, before the specific legacies are touched. If the general legacies are exhausted in meeting the debts, the specific legacies then abate *pro rata*. For a fuller discussion of these rules, see **Chapter 17**.

(3) **Ademption**

A specific gift will fail by ademption if the property identified in the will does not form part of the testator's estate at the date of his death (see **13.2**).

12.3 General legacies

A general legacy is one which does not specifically identify the item or object bequeathed as belonging to the testator. The distinction between a general legacy and a specific legacy does not lie in how precise the description of the asset may be. A gift of "my car" is specific, because it refers to an asset belonging to the testator, while a gift of "a silver 1995 Mercedes 200S with beige leather seats" is general, because it does not indicate a particular item in the testator's possession.

A gift of shares or stock is *prima facie* general unless a contrary intention is expressed in the will – for example, where the testator intends the legatee to take the particular identical stock.

So, if the testator leaves "my 1,000 ordinary shares in Magic plc to Fred" this is a specific legacy, whereas if the will had read "I leave 1,000 ordinary shares in Magic plc to Fred", that does not specify any particular shares, and so is a general legacy.

If the subject matter does not form part of the assets at death, the general gift operates as a direction to the PRs to purchase the equivalent asset or offer the beneficiary the equivalent in money. This means that the rule on ademption does not apply to general legacies. If residue is insufficient to meet all the debts in full, general legacies abate before specific legacies.

12.3.1 Interest on general legacies

Interest on general legacies runs from the time the legacy is payable. Unless the testator directs otherwise, the appropriate rate is linked to the basic account rate of the Courts Funds Office. The object is to compensate the legatee for any delay in paying the legacy and prevent the residuary beneficiary from benefiting unduly from this delay. The interest payable is treated as a payment in the course of the administration of the estate and not as an additional legacy. A partial payment on account of interest and legacy is treated (unless the will directs otherwise) as made first in respect of arrears of interest and then the principal sum (***Re Morley's Estate [1937]***, where the will left 922 legacies).

The normal rule is that an immediate legacy is payable one year after the death of the testator, that is, the end of the executor's year. Interest is payable from the end of that year until the actual date of payment. If the will directs that the executors set aside and invest a sum for payment of a legacy, even though the legacy may be contingent or deferred, the legacy carries interest from the end of the executor's year. This varies the rule that a contingent or deferred general legacy is payable from the date on which the contingency is satisfied or the deferment ends.

The testator may fix the time for the payment of the legacy, for example, by directing that the legacy is payable immediately from the date of death.

There are four cases where interest on a general legacy will run from the death of the testator.

(1) Where the testator gives a legacy to a creditor in satisfaction of the debt, unless the testator directs a later time for the payment of the legacy.

(2) A legacy, charged only on real property if the legacy is vested. This is a narrow rule and will not apply where the legacy is payable out of the proceeds of sale of real property where a trust for sale has been imposed.

(3) Where the legacy is given to a child of the testator or a child to whom the testator stands *in loco parentis*. The purpose of this exception is to provide maintenance for the child. This rule will not apply where the testator has, by their will, made specific provision for maintenance of the child or where the legacy is not given directly to the child but is given to trustees to hold for the child. The rule does not apply if the specified contingency has no reference to the child's infancy. If the will reads "to X at 25", the rule would not apply. The rule will apply if the legacy is not payable until the child attains majority or is contingent on the child attaining majority.

(4) Where the legacy shows an intention to provide for the maintenance of an infant beneficiary. This rule is not confined to a child of the testator or a child to whom they stood *in loco parentis*, and applies even if the contingent event does not relate to infancy.

It may be preferable for specific provisions to be made in the will as to the payment of interest on the legacy, rather than to rely on the above technical rules.

In the case of general legacies that are expressed to be contingent or deferred, the legacies do not carry income until they become payable. For example, in a gift of "£5,000 to X at 21", interest would run only from the time X attained 21. If, however, the testator directs that the legacy in the above example is to be set aside from the remainder of the estate, interest will run from the end of the executor's year.

12.4 Demonstrative legacies

This type of legacy was described by Lord Thurlow in ***Ashburner v Macguire [1786]*** as *"something of a hybrid"*. The gift is in the nature of a general legacy but points to a specific fund as the primary source.

Examples: "100 out of my 1,000 shares in ICI plc" or "£500 out of my account at Barclays".

This gift is rather like getting two bites of the cherry. As long as the specific fund exists, the legacy is paid from the specified fund. To the extent that the specified fund does not exist at the time, the legacy will be paid as a general legacy out of the general assets of the estate. This means that if the testator had left £500 out of "my Barclays Bank current account" to Fred, but the account had only contained £100 at the date of his death, the £100 is payable as a specific legacy and the remaining £400 is paid as a general legacy, assuming that residue is large enough to meet all debts and legacies. To the extent that the specified fund is sufficient, the legacy is treated as specific for the purposes of entitlement to income of the property gifted and for protection from abatement. To the extent that the fund is insufficient, the legacy is treated as general for both of these purposes.

Demonstrative legacies are rarely created intentionally but are often found in home-made wills where testators often believe that if they want to give a legacy to someone, they must then designate the bank account or some other property from which it is to be paid. Of course, it is not necessary to do this because a general legacy is payable from any available assets in the residuary estate that are not the subject of a specific gift.

12.5 Pecuniary legacies

These are gifts of money; they are usually general but can be specific or demonstrative.

Examples: "£500 to X" is general, "£1,000 out of my National Savings Certificates" is demonstrative, and "The £700 X owes me I give to Y" is specific.

AEA 1925 defines "pecuniary legacy" in **s55(1)(ix)** as including *an annuity, a general legacy, a demonstrative legacy so far as it is not discharged out of the designated property, and any other general direction by a testator for the payment of money, including all death duties free from which any devise, bequest or payment is made to take effect*. This definition sheds light on the rules on abatement discussed earlier.

12.6 Residuary legacies

The residuary legacy is what remains after the payment of all debts, liabilities, expenses and other legacies.

Immediate residuary gifts carry all income and profits from the date of death. This is also the case for contingent and deferred residuary gifts unless the testator has directed otherwise. In the case of an infant, the income may be applied for maintenance under **s31 TA 1925**, and the surplus accumulated. In other cases, the income is accumulated.

Where a trust was created **before** 1 October 2013, including trusts created by a will or under the intestacy rules where the date of death was before 1 October 2013, the rule in ***Allhusen v Whittell [1867]*** may need to be applied, unless it was excluded in the will (as was normal practice in professionally drafted wills).

The rule in ***Allhusen v Whittell*** is that where the testator settles property on persons in succession – for example, "A for life remainder to B" – it is presumed that the testator intends each of the people to enjoy the same property. In such a limitation, A is the tenant for life and *prima facie* entitled to all the income on the fund for their life and B is the remainderman, entitled to the capital of the fund after the death of A. The fund will consist of the net residuary estate, that is, after the payment of funeral and testamentary expenses, debts, liabilities and legacies.

Suppose the gross value of the fund is £300,000 with debts of £60,000. It would be inequitable to allow the life tenant to receive the income on the gross estate of £300,000. In ***Allhusen*** the court held that the tenant for life ought not to have the income arising from what is wanted for the payment of debts, because that never becomes residue. Under the rule, the true residue will be ascertained only by treating the legacies and debts as having been paid partly out of income and partly out of capital. This is to achieve equality between the life tenant and the remainderman.

s1 Trusts (Capital and Income) Act 2013 disapplies the rule in ***Allhusen v Whittell*** for all new trusts created on or after 1 October 2013 (unless the trust or will states otherwise), including trusts created under the intestacy rules or arising under a will where the date of death is **on or after** 1 October 2013.

NB If the date of death is on or after 1 October 2013, **s1** will still apply, even if the date of the will was **before** 1 October 2013.

12.7 Summary

(1) Specific legacy – the gift of a particular item from assets belonging to the deceased, for example, "my ginger cat".

(2) General legacy – one which does not specifically identify the item or object bequeathed, for example, "a ginger cat".

(3) Demonstrative legacy – the gift is in the nature of a general legacy but points to a specific fund as the primary source, for example, "£250 out of my account with the Halibut Building Society".

(4) Pecuniary legacy – gifts of money are usually general but can be specific or demonstrative, for example:

- general – "£100 to my brother";
- specific – "all the money in my safe to my cousin";
- demonstrative – "£500 out of my account with the Halibut Building Society to my granddaughter".

(5) Residuary legacy – what remains after payment of all debts and liabilities and expenses and other legacies.

Gifts of things belonging to testator, for example, "my horse, Hortense"

Legacy of specific "pot" of cash, for example, "all the cash in my safety deposit box"

Specific legacies

Gift of money payable out of specific fund, for example, "£5,000 from my Newcastle Building Society Account"

Demonstrative legacy

Gift of item not expressed, for example, "a new Cadillac car"

Gift of money, for example, "£3,300"

General legacy

CHAPTER 13

The Failure of Gifts

Aims of the Chapter:

By the end of this chapter, you should be able to:

- explain how specific gifts may be adeemed;
- describe how a beneficiary can disclaim a will;
- explain how a gift may lapse if a beneficiary has predeceased;
- describe the circumstances where a beneficiary does not inherit due to forfeiture ; and
- list other reasons for failure of gifts.

13.1 Introduction

The distinctions between specific and general legacies are important when considering how such legacies fail. This chapter considers reasons for failure. These include **ademption**, where a specific item has been disposed of before death; **abatement**, where there are insufficient funds in the estate to pay all the legacies; and **lapse**, where a beneficiary has predeceased the testator.

Other reasons for failure include **disclaimers**, where a beneficiary refuses to accept a legacy, and **forfeiture**, where special rules apply when the beneficiary has killed the testator.

13.2 Ademption

Where a **specific gift** is made, the gift will fail for ademption if the subject matter of the gift does not form part of the testator's estate at the date of death. Ademption may occur because the testator sells or gives away the subject matter of the gift or because the property is destroyed during the testator's lifetime.

The disappointed beneficiary receives nothing in compensation. So, if there is a specific gift of a ring which is stolen before the testator's death, the beneficiary is not entitled to any proceeds resulting from an insurance claim – the proceeds will go to the residuary estate. A will might contain an express provision to cover the case where a specific asset might be disposed of and replaced with something similar, for example "I give my house The Willows or any house I may own at the date of my death to X". Even here, the gift will fail if the deceased owned no house at that date, perhaps because they had gone into residential care.

Where it is unclear whether the death of the testator or the destruction of the property occurred first, the property is deemed to have perished before the testator so that the gift is adeemed (***Durrant v Friend [1852]***). Suppose the testator dies in a fire at home leaving a specific gift of a piano by will. The gift will adeem as it will be assumed that the piano was destroyed before the testator died.

Property may change in nature. In ***Re Slater [1907]*** the gift in question was one of stock (a form of share) in Lambeth Waterworks. Subsequent to the date of the will, the stock was taken over by the Metropolitan Water Board and Metropolitan stock was given in lieu. If the gift was specific, the will took effect from the death and the Metropolitan stock was so different in character that there was ademption. Sir Herbert Cozens-Hardy MR said that ademption would not occur if the subject matter of the gift had changed in form only but remained substantially the same thing.

Change in the nature of the asset has proved a particular problem in relation to shares. These difficulties arise because companies frequently change the types of shares owned by their shareholders. There are various technical reasons for such changes, including the need to raise more money to finance the capital of the company, but the effects are that a shareholder who owns a certain number of shares in a particular share category may have them replaced by a different number of shares in a different share category. This change might have been imposed on the shareholder without any opportunity to object.

In ***Re Clifford [1912]*** the will included a legacy of "twenty-three of the shares belonging to me" in X Co Ltd. At that time, the testator held 104 £80 shares in the company. Before the testator died, the company changed its name and sub-divided each share into four £20 shares. It was held that this was a change in form and not a change in substance and so the beneficiary took the shares which represented those originally given – that is, 92 £20 shares.

In ***Re Leeming [1912]*** the testator left a legacy of "My 10 shares" in Y Ltd. Before his death, the company went into liquidation and formed itself into a new company with the same name. The testator was issued with 20 £5 ordinary shares and 20 £5 preference shares to replace those originally issued. Once again, it was held that ademption did not occur because the change was in form and not in substance. The securities were of the same kind and were in essentially the same company. A change from shares into debenture (loan) stock would be a change in substance, because a debenture holder is a creditor rather than an owner of the company.

Another case of a change in form is ***Re Dorman [1994]***. The will included a legacy of the balance on the testatrix's bank deposit account. The testatrix appointed an attorney who, without her knowledge and without knowing the terms of the will, closed the account and opened a new account (a capital advantage account) with the same bank in order to obtain a higher rate of interest. Normally, the closure of the account would have caused the legacy to adeem but it was held that, under the circumstances, the change could be regarded as one of form only. This was a rare occasion where the court allowed the intention of the testatrix to override the strict rule.

In ***Soukun v Hardoyal and Others [1999]***, however, a specific gift of money from a life assurance policy was held to have adeemed, where the original policy taken out by the testator had expired prior to his death and the new one could not be said to be the old policy in a different form.

A contract to sell the subject matter of a specific gift will cause a gift to fail for ademption even though the contract is not completed until after the testator's death. The contract is legally binding on the PRs. This means that the beneficiary may enjoy the property until the contract is completed, but has no right to the proceeds of sale. This will not be the case where the testator made a contract to sell the subject matter of the gift before the will was executed. In this case, the beneficiary will be entitled to the proceeds of the sale (***Re Calow [1928]***).

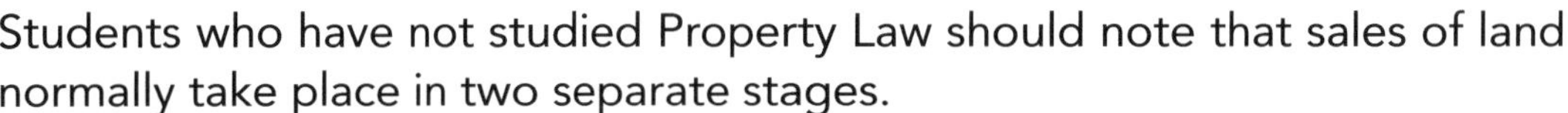

Link to Practice

Exchanging contracts and completing – sales of land

Students who have not studied Property Law should note that sales of land normally take place in two separate stages.

(1) Exchange of contracts – this is when the seller's and buyer's conveyancers exchange signed copies of the contract (each party signs their own copy). The contract is legally binding from this point.

(2) Completion – this is when the seller hands over the keys to the buyer who gains possession of the land. Completion will often take place a week to 10 days after exchange.

Ademption will therefore apply if the seller/testator, overcome by the stress of moving house, dies after exchange of contracts but **before** completion.

The principle of ademption by subsequent contract also applies where the contract is conditional, the sale being uncompleted at the death, but completed later when the condition is met, such as when a satisfactory mortgage is obtained by the buyer.

In ***Re Sweeting (Deceased) [1988]*** the testator made two specific devises of a plot of land and of a yard, both of which adjoined his house. Shortly before his death, he exchanged two contracts of sale, one for the house and the other for the yard, but he died before either contract could be completed. The contract for the sale of the yard was conditional on the simultaneous completion of the contract for the sale of the house, which, in turn, was conditional on certain releases being obtained from the testator's wife and the cancellation of a land charge. The wife had given the necessary consents before the death and both contracts were completed after the death. The court concluded that the rule in ***Lawes v Bennett [1785]*** (see **13.2.1**) did apply, with the result that the specific devises were adeemed and the proceeds of sale fell into residue.

Nicholls J said: *"For my part I can see no rational basis for applying the rule in the case of an option but not applying it in the case of a contract of sale containing conditions such as those present in the yard contract and the house contract. If the rule applies where an option is not exercised until after the testator's death, with the consequence that conversion and ademption occurs at that time, why should the rule not apply equally (or, indeed,* a fortiori [Latin meaning: all the more]*) where a contract exists at the death but subject to such conditions which are subsequently fulfilled or waived?"*

The Court of Protection has briefly considered the increasingly common issue of ademption, arising when a testator's property is managed before death by a person acting on his behalf because of his failing health and the item has been disposed of by the attorney rather than the testator. In ***Public Guardian v JM [2014]*** Senior Judge Lush said: "*The law regarding ademption caused by an attorney is a minefield and over the last twenty years there have been a number of conflicting judgments in several Common Law jurisdictions.*" He observed, however, that problems can be resolved by making a statutory will during the testator's lifetime. (**NB** The Court of Protection has the power under the **Mental Capacity Act 2005** to make a statutory will on behalf of a person who has lost mental capacity.)

13.2.1 Ademption and the option to purchase

Suppose the testator, T, gave Y an option to purchase Blackacre exercisable within three months of the grant of the option. In T's will, Blackacre is the subject of a specific gift to X. In such a case:

- the exercise of the option, even after T's death, converts the real property (i.e. land) into personalty (i.e. money) from the date of the grant of the option (***Lawes v Bennett [1785]***);
- the specific devise of Blackacre to X is therefore adeemed, although rents and profits due from the date of death until the exercise of the option will go to X (***Re Marlay [1915]***). The proceeds of sale go to residue (subject to contrary provision in the will).

It is seen that, for the purpose of determining the entitlement to the sale proceeds, the asset is deemed to have been converted from the date of the grant of the option, whereas in determining entitlement to income, the asset is treated as converted at the date of the exercise of the option. The specific devisee, X, would take the proceeds of sale if:

- the will is made after the grant of the option (***Drant v Vause [1842]***);
- the will is confirmed by codicil after the grant of the option (***Emuss v Smith [1848]***); or
- the making of the will and the grant were contemporaneous (***Re Pyle [1895]***).

13.2.2 Interpreting gifts (s24 Wills Act 1837)

s24 Wills Act 1837 (**WA 1837**) sets out the rules for construing how gifts in a will should be applied. Essentially, a will "speaks from death", that is, it must be interpreted as if the testator had made it just before dying in the light of the property they owned at that date. This principle does, of course, rarely match the reality that the will may have been made many years earlier when the testator's assets were quite different. **s24** does, however, also provide that this principle will not apply if the will shows a contrary intention. **s24** states:

Every will shall be construed with reference to the real and personal estate comprised in it to speak and take effect as if it had been executed immediately before the death of the testator, unless a contrary intention shall appear in the will.

It follows that, in the absence of a contrary intention, property acquired after the date of the will may pass under a devise or bequest in the will. So, in ***Re Kempthorne [1930]*** "all my freehold land" passed the freehold land that the testator owned at death and not just that at the time the will was made.

In ***Re Bancroft [1928]*** the testator bequeathed "all my rights in connection with the play *Diplomacy*" to X. Subsequent to the will, the testator entered into a contract selling the film rights to the play, but he died before the contract was completed. It was held that the words were spoken from the death, therefore X received the benefit of the contract.

By contrast, in ***Bergliter v Cohen and Others [2006]*** a clause in the testator's will allowing B to occupy one of his "homes" for life was invalid as the testator did not occupy that property as his home at the time of his death.

Contrary intention

(1) **s24** states that the contrary intention must appear from the will itself. In practice, the court is willing to take account of evidence of the surrounding circumstances to construe the gift.

(2) Words indicating the present time, such as the use of the word "now", can amount to contrary intention – does the word suggest the date of the will, therefore contrary intention, or is the word used as additional description?

In ***Re Edwards [1890]*** the testator bequeathed to A "my leasehold house and premises . . . where I now reside". After the date of the will, part of the premises was separated and let to a tenant by the testator.

The court held that contrary intention under **s24** applied, and A could take the whole property. The words "where I now reside" were construed as referring to the date of the will, because the property could be identified only if the words "where I now reside" were included.

By contrast, in ***Re Willis [1911]*** the testator left a legacy of "all my freehold land at X and known as Y and in which I now reside". The testator later purchased two further plots of land which fell within the general description, so the question was whether they fell within the legacy. On these facts, the property was clearly described without the reference to the present time, and so they did not amount to a contrary intention under **s24** and therefore the beneficiary took the additional pieces of land.

(3) If the gift comprises property that is capable of being increased and decreased ("all my stocks and shares", "all my land in Kent", "all my personal chattels", etc.), the use of the word "my" will not show a contrary intention to exclude **s24**, so all the property within the description at the date of death passes in the absence of other evidence to the contrary.

(4) Where the will refers to a single specific asset and the circumstances show that the testator meant that particular asset, then there will be a contrary intention. This was demonstrated in ***Re Gibson [1866]*** where there was a specific legacy of "my one thousand North British Railway preference shares". After the will was executed, the testator sold these shares and subsequently bought a greater number of North British Railway preference shares. The court held that the wording of the gift had shown contrary intention and it was therefore adeemed. Similarly, in ***Re Sikes [1927]*** a gift of "my piano" was, in the light of evidence of the surrounding circumstances, taken to mean the piano owned at the date of the will.

Of course, on that construction, if it was the case that the testator had in fact sold the original piano and replaced it with a new one by the time of his death, then the gift of the original piano would fail for ademption (**13.2**). The beneficiary could claim the new piano only if there were words in the will which made it clear he was entitled to any replacement.

The effects of republication under **s34 WA 1837** (see **9.2**) must be considered in determining whether the specific property passes. A good illustration is ***Re Reeves [1928]***. The will contained a bequest of "my present lease". At the date of the will, the lease in question had three-and-a-half years to run. On expiry, the testator effected a renewal and later executed a codicil confirming his will. The words of description were construed as speaking from the date of the codicil which had republished the will, so the legatee took the new lease.

s24 does not apply to the description of persons (e.g. "to my brother's wife"). The description of a beneficiary (or executor) is taken as the person answering the description at the date of the will (***Re Whorwood [1887]***). However, note the position regarding class gifts (**13.4.2**).

The will may contain a contrary intention, however. In ***Re Daniels [1918]*** a gift to "the Lord Mayor of London for the time being" was construed as referring to whoever held the office of Lord Mayor at the date of the testator's death.

13.3 Disclaimer

A beneficiary is not obliged to take the gift but can disclaim. For example, "I leave my pet elephant, Oscar, to my brother Henry" is a specific gift and Henry would be liable to house and feed Oscar from the date of death. The beneficiary cannot disclaim if, by his conduct or by deed, he has accepted (***Re Hodge [1940]***). A beneficiary cannot accept part of a gift and disclaim the rest where the gift is single and undivided (***Guthrie v Walrand [1882]***) but can disclaim one if they are separate legacies.

A disclaimer can be retracted (withdrawn) provided that no one has altered their position as a result of the disclaimer. It is not possible for a beneficiary to disclaim before the death of the testator. No question of retraction arises; the disclaimer is simply ineffective (***Smith v Smith [2001]***).

The effect of a disclaimer has always been that if a beneficiary under a will or intestacy disclaims, then the property passes as if the gift or entitlement had failed. The application of this seemingly straightforward rule has given rise to some uncertainties in the past and so, for deaths on or after 1 February 2012, it has been given statutory effect by the **Estates of Deceased Persons (Forfeiture Rule and Law of Succession) Act 2011** (**EDP(FRLS)A 2011**).

s1 EDP(FRLS)A 2011 provides for what happens if a person entitled on intestacy disclaims (see **10.4.6**).

s2 deals with the situation where the disclaiming person is a beneficiary in a will. It says that if a person disclaims a benefit under a will, that person is treated as if they had died immediately before the testator. Subject to what is said below, the terms of the will should then be considered to determine who is entitled to the property by applying the usual rules of construction. So, for example, a non-residuary gift to the testator's brother will be treated as having lapsed and fall into residue unless the will contains a substitution provision that can apply in the assumed circumstances, because it is worded to take effect if the brother "dies before me" (or there is similar wording).

However, this effect of **s2** is not entirely certain because it states that the fictional predeceasing of the disclaiming beneficiary is for the purpose of *this Act*, which is a reference to **WA 1837**. So, it is quite clear that if the person disclaiming is a child or issue of the testator, **s2** will have implications for the application of **s33 WA 1837** (see **13.4.3**). However, it is not so certain that the fiction will apply if the person disclaiming is someone else, because apart from **s33**, there are no other provisions in **WA 1837** that can affect the devolution of the gift. That being the case, the outcome of the disclaimer must be determined by applying the existing law.

Suppose T's will contains a gift to his brother, B, and there is a substitution provision saying "if my brother dies before me, then this gift is to pass to his wife". After T dies, the brother disclaims the gift.

(1) If **s2 EDP(FRLS)A 2011** does apply to the disclaimer, then the wife can claim the gift because the fictional predeceasing of B will activate the substitution in her favour.

(2) However, if **s2** is held not to apply, then the gift falls into residue. The wife cannot claim because her substitution was expressed as taking effect if B died before T, which he had not done. She could claim only if the substitution was drafted in wider terms, for example, by saying "if this gift fails for any reason" rather than being limited to the brother predeceasing.

Since **s2** refers to a person who disclaims (as opposed to limiting it to a child or issue of the testator), it would appear that it was intended to apply regardless of the identity of the beneficiary (this view is consistent with the explanatory notes provided by the Law Commission when the Bill was published). However, to have that effect, **s2** should have been worded to say the fictional predeceasing of the disclaiming beneficiary was for the purpose of "the will" rather than *this Act* (or, alternatively, not prescribe any purpose at all). If so, **s2** would clearly apply, whether or not the person was a child or remoter issue of the testator.

The limitations on disclaimers and possible uncertainty in some cases can be largely avoided by entering into a written post-death variation (traditionally called a deed of family arrangement, although a deed is not strictly necessary and the parties do not necessarily have to be family). A variation allows a beneficiary of full age and capacity, who is entitled, to redistribute their entitlement in the estate to whomsoever they want, whether to bring in a beneficiary who was omitted from the will or to provide additional benefit for a needy beneficiary. (In fact, the motive is often to save inheritance tax on the estate.) This method can be used to give up part of a benefit or be used after a legacy has been accepted. If infant beneficiaries are to make a variation, the court must approve the variation and will do so only if satisfied that it is for the infant's benefit. It should be noted that these points on disclaimer and deeds of variation apply equally on intestacy.

13.4 Lapse

If a beneficiary predeceases the testator, the gift to that beneficiary will lapse. Lapse cannot be prevented by a general declaration against lapse, but where there is a substitutional gift (a gift over), the property will pass to the beneficiary of the gift over. Republication of a will by subsequent codicil after the death of the beneficiary will not save the gift from lapse.

Although the use of the word "lapse" is best confined to situations where the beneficiary predeceases the testator, lawyers may also talk about a gift lapsing if the beneficiary is living at the deceased's death but has only a contingent entitlement to the property and dies before satisfying the contingency. So, if T leaves £10,000 to X "contingent on X reaching 18" and X survives T but then dies aged 15, the legacy fails. The £10,000 would then fall into the residuary estate for distribution unless there was an effective substitutional gift in the will that said what was to happen to the legacy if X failed to reach 18.

Note that if there was no contingency attached to X's gift (or any other requirement that they had to survive for a certain period), then it would be a **vested** gift. As such, the death of X after T would not cause the gift to lapse. Instead, the £10,000 would be treated as an asset belonging to X and so would devolve, in his case if aged 15, as part of X's estate on intestacy.

13.4.1 Joint tenancy and tenancy in common gifts

If a gift is made to beneficiaries as joint tenants and one of them predeceases the testator or witnesses the will, their share will pass to the surviving joint tenants. The gift will lapse where the sole surviving joint tenant predeceases the testator and there is no substitutional gift. In contrast, if a gift is made to beneficiaries as tenants in common, the share of a beneficiary who predeceases the testator will lapse (***Page v Page [1728]***). Most gifts by will to more than one person are to them as tenants in common ("To A and B equally" or "To A and B in equal shares").

13.4.2 Class gifts

These are defined by Lord Selbourne in ***Pearks v Moseley [1880]*** as:

"A gift to several persons uncertain in number at the time of the limitation who answer to a general description and who are to take one divisible subject in proportionate shares the size of which will vary according to the number who ultimately answer the description."

A gift of "£90,000 to my children" would be a class gift, because the size of each child's share is determined by the total number of children who benefit. On the other hand, a legacy of "£10,000 to each of my children" is not a class gift because the benefit that each takes is fixed by the will and will be the same however many children survive.

The doctrine of lapse does not apply to class gifts, and those members of the class who survive the testator, or who otherwise make up the class will inherit, whether the gift is expressed as a joint tenancy or a tenancy in common (e.g. "To all my children in equal shares"). However, see **13.4.3** concerning **s33(2) WA 1837**.

In order to determine membership of the class, certain class-closing rules, rules of construction used in interpreting the will, are set out in ***Pearks v Moseley***. These have evolved because of the need to avoid lengthy delay in distributing the estate, which would be caused if one had to wait to see whether new members entered the class, thereby reducing the share of the other members of the class. The rules apply subject to anything to the contrary that might be expressed in the will.

The rules deal with a number of situations.

(1) If the gift is an **immediate vested** gift to each member of the class (e.g. "to all my nephews and nieces"), the class closes at the testator's death, if any member of the class is alive at that time, so no one born later (apart from a child *en ventre sa mère* at the testator's death) can take (***Viner v Francis [1789]***). If no member of the class was alive at that time, the class remains open indefinitely (***Weld v Bradbury [1715]***).

(2) If the class gift is a **vested remainder** after a life interest (e.g. "to A for life then to all my nephews and nieces"), the class closes when the life tenant dies, if any member of the class is alive at that time (***Ellison v Airey [1748]***). If no member of the class has obtained a vested interest at that time, the class remains open indefinitely. If the life interest fails through normal rules (e.g. lapse), the gift will be interpreted as if it were an immediate legacy. The answer may be different if the life interest ended by disclaimer, because then the life tenant could influence (perhaps unfairly) who would take the gift over. The better answer seems to be that the class should continue to close on the death of the life tenant in that situation (***Re Harker's Will Trust [1969]***, ***Re Kebty- Fletcher's Will Trust [1969]***).

(3) If the gift is an **immediate contingent** legacy (e.g. "to all my nephews and nieces who reach the age of 18"), the class closes at the testator's death if any beneficiary has then satisfied the contingency (the rule in ***Andrews v Partington [1791]***). The other beneficiaries alive or *en ventre sa mère* at that date will also inherit if they eventually satisfy the contingency. If no beneficiary had satisfied the contingency when the testator died, the class closes when the first beneficiary satisfies the contingency.

    In ***Blech v Blech [2004]***, one of the rare modern cases on this aspect of the law, B died in 1977 having made a will in 1975 in which she left property on trust for her three children. She also executed a codicil establishing a trust for such children of her son, R, "as shall survive me and reach the age of 21".

    At the date of B's will, R had only two children. After B died, R divorced and went on to have two more children with his second wife. R sought summary judgment as to the meaning of the phrase "as shall survive me" and whether it precluded the children born to R after B died.

    Patten J held that the two additional children were entitled to inherit. The circumstances showed that B intended to make a gift to all of R's children. At the date of B's will, R's children were very young and B must have anticipated that he might go on to have more.

(4) If the legacy is a **contingent remainder** (e.g. "To A for life, with remainder to such of my nephews and nieces who reach the age of 18"), the class closes on the death of the life tenant if any beneficiary has then satisfied the contingency and no beneficiary born afterwards can inherit. Otherwise, the class remains open until the first beneficiary does satisfy the contingency.

These are rules of construction that are applied to ascertain the testator's intention when no intention was made clear on the face of the will. The well- drawn will makes it plain when the class is to close: for example, "To such of my nephews and nieces as survive me and reach the age of 18" or "To my wife for life, with remainder to such of my nephews and nieces as survive her and reach the age of 18".

13.4.3 s33 Wills Act 1837

s33 WA 1837, as amended, provides an exception to the doctrine of lapse if property is left in a will by a testator to their children or remoter issue (i.e. grandchildren, or great-grandchildren). **s33(1)** states:

Where:

(a) *a will contains a devise or bequest to a child or remoter descendant of the testator; and*

(b) *the intended beneficiary dies before the testator, leaving issue; and*

(c) *issue of the intended beneficiary are living at the testator's death, then, unless a contrary intention appears in the will, the devise or bequest shall take effect as a devise or bequest to the issue living at the testator's death.*

s33(4)(b) provides that the illegitimacy of any person is to be ignored, and so a legacy to an illegitimate child of the testator may be saved by **s33** and illegitimate issue of the beneficiary may save the gift from failure.

Living at the death will include unborn children *en ventre sa mère* at the death of the testator (**s33(4)(b)**).

An example of how **s33(1)** is applied is where the will states "I give £10,000 to my son, Jacob". If Jacob predeceases the testator, leaving two children, Rebecca and Miriam, they will each receive £5,000. They will therefore inherit Jacob's legacy *per stirpes* (**s33(3)**).

s33(2) provides that, where a member of a class of children or remoter issue of the testator predeceases the testator, leaving issue living at the death of the testator, the gift takes effect as if the issue were included in the class.

An example of how **s33(2)** applies is where the will has left the residue "to such of my sons as shall survive me". The testator, Noah, had three sons, Jacob, Reuben and Joseph, but Jacob has predeceased leaving his children, Rebecca and Miriam. Here, Rebecca and Miriam are treated as being included in the class gift with Reuben and Joseph and will receive one-sixth of the residue each while Reuben and Joseph receive a third each.

Contrary intention

In all cases, **s33** can be excluded by a contrary intention shown by the will. If the testator does not want issue to take the entitlement of one of their children, they can make those wishes clear in the will, ideally by express words. Professional will-writers should always seek the testator's instructions on whether issue should benefit or not and then word the will accordingly. It would be wrong for a lawyer to assume that the testator invariably wants issue to benefit. Even if the testator does want issue to take, it is better to say that expressly on the face of the will rather than rely on **s33**.

Sometimes the words used in the will might give rise to doubt as to whether **s33** has been excluded, as in ***Rainbird v Smith [2012]***. The will had left the residue "upon trust for such of them, my daughters, R, J and S, as shall survive me, and if more than one, in equal shares absolutely".

One of the daughters predeceased and the question was whether **s33** caused the bequest to the predeceased daughter to pass to her children, or whether instead the property was taken by the two surviving daughters. The trustees sought clarification and the court had no hesitation in finding that the language "such of them, my daughters, R, J and S, as shall survive me" combined with "and if more than one, in equal shares" made it plain that the testator's intention was to leave the residue only to those daughters who actually survived, rather than that share devolving on the predeceased daughter's own children. In particular, the words "and if more than one, in equal shares" showed that the amount each daughter would get was intended to increase if any of the other daughters predeceased the testator. Consequently, there could be no application of **s33** to allow the dead daughter's share to pass by substitution to her children because there was clear evidence in the will that the testator wanted to leave residue only to those daughters living at his death.

Refer back to Noah's estate earlier in this section illustrating a class gift where a child (Jacob) predeceases leaving two children, Rebecca and Miriam. That example says that **s33(2)** applies to allow Rebecca and Miriam to be included in the class gift. Why is that different from ***Rainbird v Smith*** where it did not apply? The earlier example is subtly different because it is a gift expressed in simpler terms by just saying "to such of my sons as shall survive me". Crucially, it does not include any additional words along the lines of "and if more than one, in equal shares", which were important to the finding of a contrary intention in ***Rainbird v Smith***.

Cases involving **s33 WA 1837** are rare. However, in ***Hives v Machin [2017]*** the testatrix made a will leaving the residue of her estate to such of her three sons, Peter, Eric and Christopher, "who shall be living at the date of my death" in equal shares.

Christopher and Eric died before their mother. Eric left a child, Joanna. Peter argued that the plain interpretation of the will is that, since only he was living at the date of his mother's death, he should take the entire estate, and that **s33** should not apply. Joanna argued that there was nothing in the will specifically excluding **s33**, and that it should therefore apply, with the result that she would take half of the estate.

The case turned on whether the wording in the will was sufficient to exclude **s33**. The court decided that it was not, but evidence was sought as to the testatrix's intentions, in the hope that this would clarify the matter. Unfortunately, the lawyer who drafted the will acknowledged that, when taking instructions, he had not explained the implications of **s33** to the testatrix. The court said that it was therefore impossible to infer that she had wanted **s33** to be excluded. The section applied, and Joanna took half of the estate.

Applying s33

Note the following important points.

(1) The statutory substitution in favour of the beneficiary's surviving issue applies only if the gift was to the testator's child (or remoter issue such as a grandchild) in the first place. Do not fall into the trap of applying **s33** if the gift is to another relative, for example, a brother.

(2) **s33** is expressed to apply only if the child (or remoter issue) predeceases the testator. It will not apply if they survive and die afterwards. There is an exception to this rule where a person is treated as having predeceased even though they do not – see (5).

(3) Where **s33** does apply and the issue of the initial beneficiary take that beneficiary's entitlement (as in the example above regarding Jacob's legacy of £10,000) there is nothing in **s33** to say that the issue must subsequently attain 18 or marry or enter into a civil partnership. Students often suggest that there is this requirement but it arises from confusion with the statutory trusts arising in favour of issue in intestacy cases.

    The only situation where the issue might have to satisfy a contingency is where it was a class gift, in which case, any issue joining the class by virtue of **s33(2)** would need to satisfy the contingency imposed by the testator, like the other class members.

(4) Even if the circumstances for the application of **s33** appear to be present, do not apply it automatically – it takes effect subject to any contrary intention in the will. Sometimes, a testator, having been told about the effect of the section, will expressly provide that it is not to apply. In the same way, an express provision in the will, even if giving rise to the same outcome, will take precedence over **s33**.

(5) There is one situation now where **s33** can apply even if the child (or remoter issue) dies after the testator. That situation arises under **s2 EDP(FRLS)A 2011**

if the testator dies on or after 1 February 2012. The Act is intended to preserve the inheritance rights of a person's descendants if that person disclaims an inheritance (see **13.3**) or is disqualified from receiving an inheritance as a result of the forfeiture rule (see **13.5**). In either case, **s2** provides that for the purpose of **WA 1837**, the property will devolve as if the person disclaiming, or being disqualified, had died immediately before the deceased so that if the person in question was a child (or remoter issue) of the testator, then the property will pass to that person's living issue under **s33** (subject to a contrary intention in the will).

13.4.4 The statutory presumption as to survivorship: *commorientes*

This statutory presumption deals with the situation where two or more persons leave property to one another but the circumstances of their deaths are such as to indicate no evidence as to who died first. This rule is important in deciding whether lapse has occurred. At common law, the courts refused to speculate as to the order of deaths; therefore, as one could not prove that one survived over the other, the gifts failed. In ***Underwood v Wing [1855]*** the testator left property "to X if my wife shall die in my lifetime". The testator and his wife died when they were both swept off the deck of a ship in a storm. As there was no evidence as to who died first, X could not benefit.

s184 Law of Property Act 1925 (**LPA 1925**) provides that where *two or more persons have died in circumstances rendering it uncertain which of them survived the other or others, such deaths shall (subject to any order of the court), for all purposes affecting title to property, be presumed to have occurred in order of seniority, and accordingly the younger shall be deemed to have survived the elder.*

The leading case on the meaning of "uncertain" is ***Hickman v Peacey [1945]*** in the House of Lords. Two brothers left property to each other. They died when a bomb hit the house where they were sheltering during the Second World War. Could one say that there was uncertainty when the deaths were, in lay terms, instantaneous? Yes, declared the House of Lords – the slightest degree of uncertainty is all that is required to invoke the presumption.

Per Lord Macmillan: *"Can you say for certain which of these two dead persons died first? If you cannot say for certain, then you must presume the older to have died first. It is immaterial that the reason for your inability to say for certain which died first is either because you think they died simultaneously or because you think they died consecutively but you do not know that sequence."*

Any satisfactory evidence as to the actual order of deaths will exclude the operation of **s184**. The burden of proof is the balance of probabilities (***Lamb v Lord Advocate [1976]***).

In ***Lamb***, the Court of Session in Scotland, considering the Scottish equivalent of **s184**, said that the court must first be satisfied that, on the evidence before it, the order of deaths is, in fact, uncertain.

If, on the balance of probabilities, the actual order of deaths emerges, the court will give effect to that without resorting to **s184**. In ***Lamb*** a husband and wife were both killed when the house in which they were staying caught fire. The husband, who was the elder, had been gassed in the First World War, and was in poorer health than the wife. The circumstances in which they died could not be established with certainty, but the court found that the most likely explanation was that the wife, who was the more active of the two, managed to get out of the house to summon assistance and, having done so, went back into the house to help her husband. By that time, the husband had been asphyxiated and the wife then died. Although it could not be said for certain that the wife had briefly survived the husband, the balance of probabilities pointed to that conclusion and therefore there was no scope to invoke the statutory presumption.

Re Scarle [2019] is a rare recent example of a *commorientes* case. Mr and Mrs Scarle were an elderly and frail couple who both died from hypothermia in their home at some point between 4 October 2016 and 9 October 2016. Mr Scarle was aged 79 years and Mrs Scarle was aged 69 years. The dispute was between Mr Scarle's daughter, representing his estate, and Mrs Scarle's daughter, representing her estate. The medical evidence relating to the times and dates of their deaths, based on rates of decomposition of the bodies and the temperatures of the rooms in which they were found, was unable to prove which of the couple died first. Mr and Mrs Scarle's house and bank account were both in their joint names and the key issue was whether **s184 LPA 1925** would apply.

The judge held that the burden of proof, where the order of death is uncertain, was on the party seeking to establish otherwise. The civil standard of proof applied – on the balance of probabilities. Mr Scarle's daughter was unable to establish that Mrs Scarle had died first on the balance of probabilities. The judge therefore held that **s184 LPA 1925** applied and the jointly owned assets passed to Mrs Scarle's daughter.

The doctrine of *commorientes* applies also where a person dies intestate. So, if a father and son died in the same accident and the father died intestate without leaving a surviving spouse, **s184** would apply to allow the son to inherit along with any surviving brothers and sisters. If the son left a will that left all his estate to a named charity, both his own assets and the assets that he inherited from his father would pass under his will.

s184 does not apply where spouses or civil partners die intestate in respect of their property passing under the intestacy rules (see **10.4.3**). **s46(2A) AEA 1925** states that the surviving spouse or civil partner must survive for at least 28 days before being able to inherit under the intestacy rules. If the spouse or civil partner does not survive for at least this period, whether or not there is any uncertainty over which spouse/civil partner died first, the second spouse or civil partner to die is treated as having predeceased the intestate spouse or civil partner. **NB** Where spouses or civil partners die intestate owning property as joint tenants, **s46(2A)** does not apply to the joint property. Instead, **s184** will apply and the joint property will pass to the estate of the younger spouse/civil partner by survivorship outside the intestacy rules.

Rather than relying on the application of the statutory presumption, it is good practice to consider the inclusion of a survivorship clause when drafting a will. Such a period is appropriate because it prevents **s184** having to be applied, and deals with the situation when the beneficiary survives the testator for a short period only when the assets given would pass under the beneficiary's will or intestacy. The period is not so long that it would delay the distribution of the estate. A survivorship clause is used mainly in relation to major non-residuary gifts (perhaps the house), or a gift of the entire estate to a particular beneficiary, with a gift over in the event that the beneficiary does not survive the testator.

Care should be taken in the wording of a survivorship provision, and professional advice should be sought. The dangers of the well-meaning, intelligent individual using a form to make their own will are illustrated in ***Re Rowland [1962]***. A husband and wife provided in their respective wills that each was to take the property of the other save "in the event of the decease of my wife (husband) preceding or coinciding with my own".

The Court of Appeal, by a majority, held that the statutory presumption applied on a construction of the word "coinciding". This applies where the deaths were simultaneous. Here, the spouses died in a shipwreck where it was impossible to prove who died first.

13.5 Forfeiture

Link to Practice

Criminal law – murder/manslaughter distinction

The criminal law categorises homicide (killing a human being) into a number of different crimes. The most important of these are murder and manslaughter.

Murder is the most serious form of homicide and the prosecution must prove that the defendant intended to kill or cause serious harm. The judge will be **required** to impose a life sentence.

Manslaughter covers killing in a range of circumstances where the defendant is considered to be less blameworthy. These circumstances include a loss of control (previously provocation), diminished responsibility and gross negligence. The judge has a **discretion** in sentencing and, within certain guidelines, can impose a sentence which reflects the particular circumstances of the crime.

The common law has developed a series of principles based on public policy, denying benefit to a person who seeks to benefit from crime. These principles extend to the perpetrator of the crime and to those claiming property through them. ***Gray v Barr [1971]*** set out the broad principle *"that no man should be allowed to profit at another person's expense from his own conscious and deliberate crime"*.

This principl e was applied to murder in ***Re Crippen [1910]*** and extended to manslaughter in ***In the Estate of Hall [1911–1913]***.

Key Cases

The notorious Dr Crippen

Dr Crippen was an unhappily married American doctor who killed his wife and buried her under the floorboards of his house in London. When the police became suspicious, he fled and was eventually arrested with his girlfriend Ethel (who was disguised as a boy) on an ocean liner heading for Canada. After his conviction for murder, he made a will leaving all of his estate to Ethel. After his execution, Ethel claimed the estate of Mrs Crippen (***Re Crippen [1910]***) but was unsuccessful.

Prior to the **Forfeiture Act 1870**, the criminal's interest was forfeited to the Crown. Since 1870, the law will not assist a criminal to recover property from the estate of the person they killed, whether the deceased left a will or died intestate. The rule applies in all cases of murder (unless the beneficiary was insane) and in manslaughter cases where it was a case of deliberate, unlawful, intentional violence (***Re H (Deceased) [1990]***).

The **Forfeiture Act 1982** (**FA 1982**) gives the court a discretionary power to grant relief to those convicted of crime except in the case of persons found guilty of murder (**s2(1)**). In ***Dunbar v Plant [1997]*** it was held that the survivor of a two-person suicide pact would not be subject to forfeiture as **FA 1982** allowed the court to exercise discretion.

In ***Amos v Mancini [2020]*** the High Court considered whether the law of forfeiture applied where an elderly woman was convicted of causing the death of her husband by careless driving. It held that the forfeiture rule did apply in cases of causing death by dangerous driving, but **s2(1) Forfeiture Act 1982** (**FA 1982**) should be used to waive its effect here. As a result, the widow received a legacy under her husband's will and his share of their jointly owned house passed to her by survivorship.

s2(5) FA 1982 provides that the court may make an order to modify the effect of the forfeiture rule. The interpretation placed on **s2(5)** by Vinelott J in ***Re K (Deceased) [1985]*** enabled the court in the case to grant total relief from the rule.

In ***Re K*** the deceased was shot by his wife on 30 September 1982, two weeks before **FA 1982** came into force (13 October). She was convicted of manslaughter on 4 May 1983.

The court was prepared to grant relief from the forfeiture rule on the basis that there was evidence that the defendant had been provoked into the killing. The court had power to dispense with the forfeiture rule altogether or to modify it in any way it thought fit under the circumstances.

In ***Re Land [2007]*** it was held that there is no discretion to extend the time limit for an application for relief from forfeiture and that the rule of public policy applied to all cases of unlawful killing except where there is a finding of criminal insanity. These two rulings are unexceptional, but the court also held that **s3** gave the court a discretion to mitigate the effect of the rule even where the will had made provision but the forfeiture rule had taken this away. ***Re Royse [1985]*** held otherwise but the court observed that, at the relevant date, **s3** was not in force.

Application for relief under **FA 1982** must be brought within three months of conviction (**s2(3)**).

The time limit for applications for relief from forfeiture was considered in ***Challen v Challen [2020]***. Here, the applicant, an abused wife who had killed her husband, pleaded not guilty to murder but guilty to manslaughter by reason of diminished responsibility on 5 April 2019. On 29 May the prosecution indicated they were willing to accept that plea and on 7 June the plea was formally accepted and she was sentenced accordingly. She brought her claim under **FA 1982** on 6 September 2019. The judge held that, for the purposes of **s2(3)**, the "conviction" was the date on which the guilty plea to manslaughter was formally accepted and the defendant was sentenced. As a result, the application was within the three-month time limit and the judge was able to modify the effect of the forfeiture rule in this case.

The statutory rules on forfeiture do not preclude a killer from applying for provision under the **Inheritance (Provision for Family and Dependants) Act 1975** (**I(PFD)A 1975**) unless they have been convicted of murder (**ss3** and **5 FA 1982**).

13.5.1 Reform of the consequences of the law of forfeiture

In ***Re Jones [1998]*** the deceased left her estate by will to her son with substitutional gifts to nephews in the event of the son predeceasing his mother. The son was convicted of the manslaughter of his mother and so forfeited his right to inherit. It was decided that to construe the will as though the son had predeceased his mother, when in reality he had not, was incorrect. Therefore the gifts in the will to the nephews could not take effect because the condition on which they were given had not happened. So, the estate was dealt with on intestacy.

Forfeiture has also been considered in the context of the intestacy rules. In ***Re DWS (Deceased) [2001]*** the son murdered both his parents, both of whom died intestate. The public policy rule meant that he could not inherit, as there is no relief from forfeiture where the conviction is for murder (as opposed to manslaughter). The son's son claimed to be entitled to the estates of his grandparents under **s47 AEA 1925**. It was held that, on a true construction of this section, the issue of the child of an intestate could inherit only if the child had actually predeceased the intestate. The wording could not be made to extend to a situation where the child failed to inherit for other reasons and had, as a matter of fact, survived the intestate. The grandfather's estate, therefore, passed as if he had had no issue and the grandson could not inherit.

In response to the perception of unfairness resulting from ***Re Jones*** and ***Re DWS (Deceased)***, **EDP(FRLS)A 2011** applies if the deceased dies on or after 1 February 2012. The Act is intended to preserve the inheritance rights of a person's descendants if that person disclaims an inheritance (see **13.3**) or is disqualified from receiving an inheritance as a result of the forfeiture rule.

s1 EDP(FRLS)A 2011 provides that if a person entitled on intestacy is so disqualified, then the property will devolve under the intestacy rules as if that person had died immediately before the intestate. So, if that person leaves issue capable of taking under the statutory trusts, they will do so. Otherwise, the entitlement will devolve as though the beneficiary had never existed. This means that if the intestates in ***Re DWS (Deceased)*** died today, **s1** would allow the child of the disqualified son to take under the statutory trusts.

s2 deals with the situation where the disqualified person is a beneficiary in a will. The outcome is exactly the same as the case where a beneficiary disclaims a gift (see **13.3**). It therefore clearly has implications for the application of **s33 WA 1837** (see **13.4.3** (5)) and possibly also where the disqualified beneficiary is someone other than the testator's child or remoter issue.

EDP(FRLS)A 2011 preserves the power of the court to modify the effect of the forfeiture rule (except in the case of murder) if the justice of the case so requires it.

13.6 Other reasons for the failure of gifts

13.6.1 Abatement

As discussed in **Chapter 12**, if the residuary estate is insufficient to meet all the liabilities, the general legacies are used to meet them. The general legacies abate *pro rata*, but they may be completely exhausted. In these cases, the legacy fails by abatement, either wholly or partly.

13.6.2 Beneficiary witnesses will

A gift in a will is void, though the will itself is still valid, if a beneficiary or the beneficiary's spouse or civil partner is one of the attesting witnesses (**s15 WA 1837**) (see **3.6**).

13.6.3 Uncertainty

A gift in a will cannot take effect if either the subject matter or the beneficiary cannot be ascertained with certainty after applying the usual rules of construction (see **Chapter 14**).

A good example of a gift failing for uncertainty of subject matter is ***Boyce v Boyce [1849]***. The testator left his houses to trustees in trust for his wife for life, and after her death the trustees were to allow his daughter, Maria, to choose one of the houses. The remaining houses were to pass to his other daughter, Charlotte. Maria died in the testator's lifetime and Charlotte survived him. Since Maria was obviously unable to choose which house to have, it was impossible to know which houses Charlotte was entitled to receive and so the gift failed for uncertainty.

Gifts of "some of my best table linen" (***Peck v Halsey [1726]***) and "of a handsome gratuity" (***Jubber v Jubber [1839]***) have been declared void for uncertainty. However, now that it is possible to admit extrinsic evidence of a testator's intention under **s21 Administration of Justice Act** (**AJA 1982**) (see **14.5.2**), it may be possible to establish what the testator intended. Even so, this is not always possible – see, for example, ***Anthony v Donges [1998]*** discussed in **14.4**.

A gift that allows a beneficiary to choose items – for example, "Each of my nieces may select one book from my library" – is not void for uncertainty as long as the subject matter from which the choice is to be made is sufficiently identified. It is sensible if giving such a right to provide that, in the event of any dispute, the decision of the PRs is final.

An early example of a gift failing for uncertainty as to the beneficiary was a gift to "the son of A". This failed because A had several sons (***Dowset v Sweet [1753]***). Once again, it may now be possible to ascertain the testator's intention by admitting evidence under **s21 AJA 1982**, and the court will often do what it can to prevent intestacy. For example, in ***Harris v Estate of Cooper (Deceased) [2010]*** extrinsic evidence was admitted to establish exactly who the testatrix had meant by "my surviving relatives". See also ***Pinnel v Anison [2005]***, discussed in **14.5.2**, where the court said that it would be reluctant to find a gift void for uncertainty.

There is an exception to the rule that a gift fails if the beneficiary is not sufficiently identified. In the case of gifts to charities, provided it is clear from the will that the gift was intended to be used for exclusively charitable purposes, it does not necessarily matter that the exact charity or charitable purpose cannot be ascertained from the terms of the will. In such cases, the court can direct a scheme to give effect to the testator's wishes, rather than allowing the gift to fail.

13.7 Summary

(1) A gift may fail by ademption where a specific gift is made. The gift will fail for ademption if its subject matter does not form part of the estate of the deceased at the date of their death.

(2) **s24 WA 1837** provides that a will speaks from death as regards property unless a contrary intention appears in the will – for example, where the testator refers to "my ginger cat" in a will, it is taken to mean their ginger cat at the time of writing the will.

(3) A beneficiary can disclaim a gift before accepting it, but only after the death.

(4) Where a beneficiary predeceases the testator, the gift to that beneficiary will lapse and form part of the residue.

(5) Where a gift is made to beneficiaries as joint tenants and one of them predeceases the testator, their share will pass to the surviving joint tenant. Contrast the position with tenants in common. Note the position where there is a class gift.

(6) **s33 WA 1837**, as amended, provides that where a gift is left to a child or remoter issue of the testator and the beneficiary predeceases the testator, if the intended beneficiary leaves issue, they can inherit the beneficiary's gift unless there is a contrary intention in the will.

(7) The statutory presumption as to survival is called *commorientes*:

- **s184 LPA 1925** – where two or more people die in circumstances rendering it uncertain who died first, there is a presumption that the deaths occurred in order of seniority;
- **s46(2A) AEA 1925** – where a spouse or civil partner dies intestate, the other spouse or civil partner must survive them by 28 days in order to inherit.

(8) A principle based on public policy is that where a beneficiary under a deceased's will or intestacy is found guilty of murdering the deceased, they cannot inherit. ***In the Estate of Hall [1911–1913]*** extends this principle of forfeiture to manslaughter. **FA 1982** gives the court discretion to grant relief except in cases of murder. Note the effect of **EDP(FRLS)A 2011**.

(9) Other reasons for failure include:

- abatement;
- beneficiary witnessing the will; and
- uncertainty.

CHAPTER 14

Construction of Wills

Aims of the Chapter:

By the end of this chapter, you should be able to:

- outline the main principles for the construction of wills;
- consider how to interpret particular words and phrases used in wills;
- explain circumstances where extrinsic evidence has been allowed; and
- describe how gifts by description to children are interpreted.

14.1 Introduction

It is not always possible to say what the particular words used in a will actually mean. The testator may, for example, have used imprecise words ("my relations"), there may be uncertainty ("my car to Henry" when, at death, the testator owns two cars or there are two potential beneficiaries both called Henry), or there may be ambiguity of meaning ("I give Henry my money").

There is also, inevitably, a degree of subjectivity, which can make it very hard to predict the outcome of any judicial decision on the meaning of an unclear provision.

The courts are guarded over their approach to the construction (interpretation) of wills because they do not want to be, in effect, writing the will for the testator. However, the cautious, narrow, linguistic approach that is sometimes adopted does not always reflect the testator's wishes. Inevitably, the problems tend to appear more often in home-made wills, where it can be seen what the testator meant to say but their objective is not necessarily achieved when the court applies the strict legal meaning of a particular word or phrase.

In this chapter, the general approach of the judiciary is explained and the main principles of the rules of construction are considered.

We will also consider the approach the courts have taken to interpreting particular words and phrases. The rules relating to extrinsic evidence (evidence from outside the will) and **s21 Administration of Justice Act 1982** (**AJA 1982**) are also reviewed. Problems in deciding whether a gift is absolute or limited are considered in the light of **s22 AJA 1982** and the obscure rule in ***Lassence v Tierney [1849]***, together with various subsidiary rules of construction. Finally, we will discuss certain rules affecting gifts by description to children and other relatives.

14.2 Two broad approaches to the construction of wills

The traditional approach of the courts was best put by Viscount Simon LC in **Perrin v Morgan [1943]:**

"The question is not, of course, what the testator meant to do when he made his will, but what the written words he used mean in the particular case . . . what are the 'expressed intentions' of the testator."

Following this approach, if the testator has failed to express themselves in clear and unambiguous terms, the court must undertake the task of interpretation in the light of the actual words used by the testator. It is not for the court to attribute to a testator an intention that cannot be fairly deduced from such wording. The court is not allowed to use guesswork as a substitute for construction.

By contrast, in ***Marley v Rawlings [2014]*** (see **2.7.1** and **2.7.5**) Lord Neuberger took a more liberal approach. His summary of the role of the court when interpreting a will argued that it was essentially the same as interpreting a commercial document.

"When interpreting a contract, the court is concerned to find the intention of the party or parties, and it does this by identifying the meaning of the relevant words,

(a) *in the light of*

  (i) *the natural and ordinary meaning of those words,*

  (ii) *the overall purpose of the document,*

  (iii) *any other provisions of the document,*

  (iv) *the facts known or assumed by the parties at the time that the document was executed, and*

  (v) *common sense, but*

(b) *ignoring subjective evidence of any party's intentions."*

He added:

"When it comes to interpreting wills, it seems to me that the approach should be the same. Whether the document in question is a commercial contract or a will, the aim is to identify the intention of the party or parties to the document by interpreting the words used in their documentary, factual and commercial context."

Lord Neuberger's comments were *obiter* but are, nonetheless, very persuasive. In ***Brooke v Purton [2014]*** the High Court considered a will which had created a discretionary trust which was designed, in part, to save inheritance tax. The solicitor drafted a clear explanation of what the trust was intended to achieve in a letter to the testator but, unfortunately, used the wrong precedent clause in the will. David Donaldson QC held that the clause in question could be interpreted in order to achieve the result which the testator had clearly intended. He referred to Lord Neuberger's comments in ***Marley v Rawlings [2014]*** in which he stated that wills should be interpreted in the same way as other commercial documents.

In ***Wales v Dixon and Others [2020]*** the testator had left his residuary estate to *"such all of my nephew's and niece's children"*. The question for the court was whether this definition was confined to the testator's seven blood relatives (the grandchildren of his brother and sister) or whether it also included the children of the testator's deceased wife's nieces and nephews, so expanding the number of beneficiaries to 15.

Master Teverson, applying ***Marley v Rawlings [2014]***, held that the court should take into account the context and circumstances of the case and the background facts known to the testator at the time of making the will, noting in particular:

- the fact that the testator and his wife had been married for 46 years;
- both the testator and his wife had previously made wills including the other's family;

- the whole of his wife's estate had passed to the testator;
- the absence of any extrinsic evidence as to why the testator would have wanted to exclude his wife's family after her death; and
- the continuing contact between the testator and his late wife's family.

It was held that the testator had indeed intended to benefit the wider class of beneficiaries.

14.3 The rules of construction

The rules of construction are numerous. The judge can usually find some form of construction to support their reasoning to arrive at what they consider a just result. When the judgment is delivered, it appears as a logical sequence starting with the principles when, in many cases, the judge has made up their mind at the outset and select the principles to support their reasoning.

The function of the court is to interpret the words used by the testator and not to make the will itself. The court looks at the will as a whole and not simply at the part in issue. In this way, other provisions may make it easier to determine the intention of the testator. The testator may, for example, have given a definition of a word in a later clause.

The general principle is that the intention of the testator is deduced only from the will itself. To assist it, the court adopts rules of construction – rules of convenience to arrive at a solution to the meaning of the gift.

If the words in the will have a clear meaning, effect will be given to them even if this was not the intention of the testator.

In ***Scale v Rawlins [1892]*** the testator left three houses to his niece for life and, provided that she should die leaving no children, the houses were to pass to certain nephews. The niece died leaving children. Did they take the property? No, for, although this was probably the intention of the testator, the will did not say so and the houses passed on intestacy.

NB If it could be shown that there was a misunderstanding by the draftsman when presented with instructions, it could now be possible to invoke the limited powers of the court to rectify the will under **s20 AJA 1982** (see **2.7.5**).

14.4 The meaning of words and phrases

(1) **Usual meaning**

A word is first given its ordinary grammatical meaning. This is to safeguard against words becoming too general in expression. The meaning of the word is the meaning attributable at the date of the will, that is, the dictionary definition (***Perrin v Morgan [1943]***).

(2) **Secondary meanings**

A secondary meaning may be indicated:

(a) by a definition clause in the will itself; or

(b) by the application of a statutory rule (see **14.8**); or

(c) if, when the will is applied to the surrounding circumstances, it becomes clear that the testator has used a particular word in a secondary sense, as in ***Re Davidson [1949]*** where a residuary gift to "my grandchildren" was held to include the children of the stepson of the testatrix, for the will had described him as "my son" and one of his children as "my granddaughter".

In ***Re Smalley [1929]*** the testator left his property to "my wife Eliza Ann Smalley". His lawful wife was called Mary Smalley but he lived with a woman called Eliza Ann. The court held that the testator had used the word "wife" in a secondary (non-legal) sense, meaning "common law wife".

Another example concerns the shortest known litigated will in ***Thorn v Dickens [1906]***. The will read "all to mother" but his mother had died when the will took effect. Who did the testator mean? If his mother had died after the date of the will but before the testator, the gift would have lapsed, but evidence of the surrounding circumstances showed that the testator was aware that his mother had died before the will was executed. The evidence indicated that the testator was referring to his wife.

Again, in ***Re Fish [1894]*** a gift to "my niece Eliza Waterhouse" was construed, in the light of extrinsic evidence, as meaning the testator's wife's great-niece of that name.

The secondary meaning will often emerge from looking at the circumstances applying when the testator made the will. James LJ in ***Boyes v Cook [1880]*** described **the armchair rule** thus: *"You place yourself so to speak in the testator's armchair and consider the circumstances by which he was surrounded when he made his will."*

One of the best examples of the application of the armchair rule is ***Charter v Charter [1874]***. By his will, the testator left property to "my son Forster Charter". The will in context at death showed that his son, Forster, had died some years before the will was executed. The testator was survived by two sons, William Forster Charter and Charles Charter. William claimed the property on the basis that his middle name was Forster, but application of the armchair rule revealed that William saw his father infrequently, whereas Charles lived with his father and the testator frequently referred to Charles as "Forster".

It should be borne in mind that, if in each of the above cases effect could have been given to the words used, that would have been done, irrespective of the testator's intention. Also, all these situations are now covered by **s21 AJA**

1982, in that the wills were either meaningless as they stood or there was a latent ambiguity (i.e. the words used appeared to be clear in themselves, but they could be given more than one interpretation on the facts).

(3) **Words with more than one meaning**

In cases of ambiguity, the court will adopt the most probable meaning (Lord Atkin in ***Perrin v Morgan [1943]***). This gives a wide discretion to the judge.

In ***Re Everett [1944]*** the expression "stocks and shares" was held to pass all the shares in limited companies but not redeemable debentures (debentures are an alternative form of investment by way of a loan to a company). Compare ***Re Purnchard's Will Trusts [1948]*** where the same expression was held to include all the testator's investments.

In construing the meaning of the word "money", one considers the meaning at the date of the will and the effect of the rest of the will (***Perrin v Morgan***, where the word was held to pass all the residuary personalty), coupled with the meaning to that particular testator, given his level of education and standing in life.

Per Goulding J in ***Re Barnes [1972]***: "[T]*he use of a word like 'money' varies between persons of different classes, possibly between different parts of the country. Certainly in the mouth of one and the same individual under differing circumstances, and a judge would need to be more of a philologist than I am to feel confident in relying in all cases on his own knowledge of the contemporary use of the English language. Nonetheless it seems to me the House of Lords* [in **Perrin v Morgan**] *has directed that a judge should apply his own knowledge of the language in the light of such context and circumstances as may assist him."*

(4) **Technical words and phrases**

This is a dangerous area, particularly for the testator who makes a home-made will and, thinking that legal pomposity is important, adds technical words or phrases when they know little or nothing of their meaning.

Where a testator uses a word or phrase that has acquired a technical (legal or scientific) meaning, there is a strong presumption that the words will carry the technical meaning; in ***Re Cook [1948]***, for example, "all my personal estate whatsoever" was held not to include the testator's realty (land).

Distinguish, however, technical words and phrases which merely convey description. "Male issue" is a technical phrase meaning the male descendants in the male line, whereas "male descendants" is not a term of art but a descriptive phrase meaning males descended through both the male and female line (***Re Drake's Will Trust [1970]***). "Next of kin" is not a technical phrase; it is construed as the nearest blood relations.

If the will referred to the next of kin who would benefit on an intestacy, this would be construed as meaning the statutory next of kin.

"Relations" and "family" are both wide terms and could fail for uncertainty. Alternatively, the court could construe the terms as meaning those who would benefit on intestacy but sharing *per capita* rather than *per stirpes*.

Perhaps the most misused expression is "personal property". Particular problems were caused where land was held on trust for sale and, as a result, was regarded as being personal property. This situation, which was especially inappropriate in respect of the family home, has been altered by **s3 Trusts of Land and Appointment of Trustees Act 1996**, which provides that land held on a trust of land is now to be regarded as real property, while personal property held on trust to acquire land is to be regarded as personal property, which reverses the old rule. Leasehold land still remains personal property.

(5) **Custom**

Where the testator belonged to a special group of people and the word or phrase has a special meaning among that group, then the special meaning will be adopted. In ***Shore v Wilson [1842]*** the testator was a member of a religious sect, and the term "godly preachers" was given the meaning current among members of the sect.

(6) **Punctuation**

The use of punctuation in a will is dangerous, for a comma or colon could place a meaning on a gift which the testator did not intend. The court will take account of punctuation, words in capitals and blanks, in seeking to identify subject matter and objects.

In ***Gauntlett v Carter [1853]*** the testator devised his estate "Bullen Court, Strand and Maiden Lane". The property "Bullen Court" was off the Strand – was "Strand" part of the description of "Bullen Court" or did it indicate another property owned by the testator in the Strand? The court concluded that the testator meant another property, for there was a comma before "Strand", thereby indicating a separate description.

(7) **Considering the document as a whole**

The court exercises great caution over reading words into a will and does so only if it is clear from the will itself (*"from the four corners of the document"*) (***Re Whitrick [1957]***).

In ***Re Whitrick*** the testatrix left her entire estate to her husband and provided that "in the event of my husband . . . and myself both dying at the same time" her estate should be held on trust for X, Y and Z equally. The testatrix's husband predeceased her. On a literal reading of the words in the will, the gift over to X, Y and Z failed and the property passed on her intestacy (compare ***Scale v Rawlins [1892]*** at **14.3**). The Court of Appeal, however, said that it was clear from the will as a whole that the testatrix intended the gift over to take effect if her husband predeceased as well as their dying at the same time and therefore the court held that the property should pass under the gift over to X, Y and Z.

Compare this with ***Anthony v Donges [1998]***. In this case, the testator put a clause in his will stating that his widow should have "such minimal part of the estate as she might be entitled to under English law". The court held that the clause was void for uncertainty and the widow should make an application under the **Inheritance**

(Provision for Family and Dependants) Act 1975 (**I(PFD)A 1975**). Interestingly, the testator was a solicitor.

The power of the court to supply, omit or change words, as part of the process of construction, is very limited. It may be obvious from the will that an error has been made in its wording, but a court of construction cannot supply, omit or change words if the will leaves the substance of the intended wording in doubt unless **s20 AJA 1982** applies, allowing the court to add wording to a will under its power of rectification (see **2.7.5**).

14.5 The admission of extrinsic evidence

14.5.1 The general rule

Generally, the court construes only the words written in the will itself by using the established rules of construction. It will not readily admit extrinsic evidence, that is, evidence from outside the will such as the testator's personal circumstances, letters to relatives, or things said (or alleged to have been said) by the testator, as a means of discovering the testator's intention. The main reason is that to do so would effectively make **s9 WA 1837** redundant. As was seen in **Chapter 3**, **s9** lays down strict formalities for the way in which testamentary wishes must be executed in a written will. If the full extent and meaning of the will could be construed by looking at external matters, then why bother to have the formalities in **s9**?

However, the courts have established circumstances which justify taking account of extrinsic evidence, particularly where failure to do so might mean that the will is ineffective. Notable cases where extrinsic evidence has been allowed are:

- if the words used in the will are not apt to fit the surrounding circumstances – the armchair rule, as in ***Boyes v Cook [1880]*** (see **14.4**(2));
- if there is a latent ambiguity – this occurs if the words on the face of the will seem clear but when effect is given to them, it is found from the surrounding circumstances that the words can apply to two or more people or items of property, as in ***Re Jackson [1933]*** (see **14.5.2**);
- to rebut certain equitable presumptions that would otherwise apply (outside the scope of this course).

The position now is that **s21 AJA 1982** specifically allows extrinsic evidence, not only in the case of the armchair rule and a latent ambiguity but also if the will is meaningless or there is a patent ambiguity.

14.5.2 s21 Administration of Justice Act 1982

s21 AJA 1982 has codified the rules concerning the admission of extrinsic evidence and renders many of the earlier cases on construction obsolete.

The section operates by setting out three alternative conditions prior to the admission of extrinsic evidence, including evidence of declaration as to the testator's intention.

(1) **s21(1)(a)**: *insofar as any part of the will is meaningless.*

This is a narrow linguistic concept. The lack of meaning must be apparent from the face of the will, such as where the testator has used a code.

(2) **s21(1)(b)**: *insofar as the language used in any part of it is ambiguous on the face of it.*

This represents a change in the law where the court is now permitted to admit extrinsic evidence to resolve a patent ambiguity (i.e. words which are clearly ambiguous just by reading them). This rule would permit evidence of the testator's intention to be admitted in cases such as ***Perrin v Morgan [1943]***, where such expressions as "my money" or "my effects" are used.

Re Williams [1985] was the first reported case to consider **s21(1)(b)**, although the admission of extrinsic evidence did not help in this instance.

By her home-made will, the testatrix set out a list of 25 names in three groups. There was no common pattern among the groups; they were uneven and each contained next of kin, close relatives and organisations. There was nothing in the will to indicate the purpose of the list or proportions of benefit. The day before her death, the testatrix wrote to her solicitors asking them to give various legacies to the members of the groups. Since the will was ambiguous on the face, the letter could be admitted under **s21(1)(b)**, even though it was of no assistance and the court held that each group took in equal shares.

Nicholls J said that extrinsic evidence could be admitted under **s21(1)(b)** to show which of two or more possible meanings the testator attached to a particular word or phrase, as long as that meaning was one that the word or phrase as read in its context was capable of bearing. If the meaning was one that the word or phrase cannot bear, then the court cannot apply the provisions.

There have been other cases on the interpretation of **s21(1)(b)**.

In ***Tyrrell v Tyrrell [2002]*** the testator was elderly but there was no concern about his capacity to execute a will. He had a large number of relatives and friends whom he wanted to benefit under his will. Instructions for the will were taken by a legal clerk with a firm of solicitors.

The family were aware that the testator intended to leave his residuary estate to his four grandsons. After the testator's death, it was found that the residue had been left to two of the grandsons, the wife of one of the grandsons and a non-existent person whose name was similar to another family member. There was evidence that the testator frequently became confused as to the names of family members. For this reason, the court held that the clause dealing with residue did not reflect the testator's intentions and would be amended so that the four grandsons inherited.

In ***Spurling v Broadhurst [2012]*** the court determined the true construction of the residuary gift which was to be divided between some, or all, of the 13 beneficiaries. The testator (T) was unrelated to the beneficiaries of the residuary gift but had been close to and loved and supported both families involved, whom he treated as his adopted families. His will read:

"I give the rest of my estate to . . . D1, D2, the living grandchildren of D1, and C1 in equal shares."

That clause was ambiguous in two ways:

- it was unclear if it was C1 or his grandchildren who were to benefit;
- it was unclear if the grandchildren referred to were entitled to individual shares equal to those of D1 and D2 (and possibly C1), or to share one of four equal shares.

Relevant to both issues was whether the comma after "the living grandchildren of D1" gave a special meaning to the wording of the gift.

The executors suggested four possible interpretations of the words in the will, either:

(a) the residue was to be divided into 13 shares, with each one passing to each of the 13 beneficiaries, being D1, D2, the seven grandchildren of D1 and the four grandchildren of C1;

(b) the residue was to be divided into four shares, with one passing to each of D1, D2 and C1, and with one further share being divided between the seven grandchildren of D1;

(c) the residue was to be divided into four shares, with one passing to each of D1, D2 and C1, and with one further share being divided between D1's seven grandchildren and C1's four grandchildren;

(d) the residue was to be divided into 10 shares, with D1, D2, C1 and D1's seven grandchildren each receiving one of those shares.

In making the declaration, the court said as follows.

(i) It was able to rely on **s21(1)(b)**, which provides that if the language used in any part of a will is ambiguous on the face of it, extrinsic evidence, including evidence of the testator's intention, may be admitted to assist in its interpretation.

(ii) On the evidence, T was close to both families and had spent significant time with each over the years. He had contact with the grandchildren of D1 and C1, he had nobody else to leave his money to, and he had a special fondness for D1 and D2. He also had a wish to help the younger members of his adopted families, with whom he had a special affinity and with whom he found it easier to relax than with adults. There was no evidence demonstrating any special affinity to one family over another, and such a measurement was impossible and unattractive.

Taking the strands together, T had wished to make special provision for D1 and D2, and subject to that to provide for the grandchildren whom he knew, namely the living grandchildren, to benefit substantially equally. That finding pointed to the suggested solution ((a) above), that the residue was to be divided into 13 shares, since that was the only way of ensuring substantial equality between each of the grandchildren living at his death, since there were seven grandchildren on one side, and only four on the other.

(iii) The comma after "the living grandchildren of D1" had no special significance because the will was handwritten and may well have been written in a hurry. As the Judge said, "*the Testator was by then very ill with cancer, and may not have been at his most grammatically punctilious. In short, I do not think I should place great weight on the comma.*"

Accordingly, the court declared that T's residuary estate was to be divided into 13 equal shares, with each of the beneficiaries receiving one share.

(1) **s21(1)(c)**: *insofar as evidence other than evidence of the testator's intention shows that the language used in any part of it is ambiguous in the light of the surrounding circumstances.*

This is in effect the old rule on latent ambiguity (it also accounts for the armchair rule), but it goes further, by providing that extrinsic evidence (apart from evidence of the testator's intention) can now be admitted to raise the possibility that such an ambiguity exists.

Note that evidence of the deceased's intention cannot be introduced to raise the ambiguity in the first place because only evidence of the surrounding circumstances is admissible at this stage. However, once the ambiguity has been identified, extrinsic evidence of the testator's intention is admissible to attempt to resolve it.

A good example of the admission of evidence in the case of a latent ambiguity is ***Re Jackson [1933]***. The testatrix left property to "my nephew Arthur Murphy". At the date of the will, there were three nephews, all called Arthur Murphy and known to the testatrix. Two were legitimate, the third illegitimate. Evidence of the surrounding circumstances had revealed the ambiguity and extrinsic evidence showed that the testatrix intended that the illegitimate nephew should take the property.

As the law stood at that time, evidence could not be adduced from outside the will in order to create the ambiguity. So, in ***Re Jackson***, if there had been only one legitimate Arthur Murphy, he would have taken, for the law as it then stood would not (in the absence of clear evidence from the will) have recognised the illegitimate nephew. However, if the facts were repeated today, evidence that there was more than one Arthur Murphy would now be allowed, under **s21(1)(c) AJA 1982**, to show the ambiguity existed.

In ***Pinnel v Anison [2005]*** the applicant, P, the executor of the estate of the deceased (D) sought determination of a latent ambiguity in D's last will. D left his residuary estate to his brother, P, and sister, H, in equal shares. D had not had a lot of contact with his family in the last years of his life.

D put the address of H in the will correctly; however, H was not a relative of D but a friend. D had one surviving sister (X) who lived at a separate address. Looking at extrinsic evidence of D's relationship with X and H, the most logical explanation was that D had mistakenly put H into the will as residuary beneficiary instead of X. Briggs J held that, on the basis of the extrinsic evidence available, this was the case. The will would be amended accordingly.

Lord Neuberger in ***Marley v Rawlings [2014]*** referred to **s21(1) AJA 1982** as not only confirming his view that a will should be interpreted in the same way as a commercial contract, but that it goes further by allowing the admission of extrinsic evidence, including evidence of the testator's intention in certain circumstances.

"In my view, section 21(1) confirms that a will should be interpreted in the same way as a contract, a notice or a patent, . . . In particular, section 21(1)(c) shows that 'evidence' is admissible when construing a will, and that that includes the 'surrounding circumstances'. However, section 21(2) goes rather further. It indicates that, if one or more of the three requirements set out in section 21(1) is satisfied, then direct evidence of the testator's intention is admissible, in order to interpret the will in question."

The ***Royal Society v Robinson [2015]*** is a creative example of how **s21(1)(c) AJA 1982** can be used. Here the testator had made a Swiss will dealing with his Swiss assets. He then made an English will which stated:

"(b) this Will and any Codicil to it shall be construed and take effect according to English law; this Will and any Codicil to it shall extend only to property of mine which is situated at my death in the United Kingdom."

The difficulty arose on death because most of the testator's assets were in off- shore accounts in Jersey and the Isle of Man. Jersey and the Isle of Man do not form part of the United Kingdom under **Sch 1 Interpretation Act 1978**. As a result, the off-shore accounts would pass under a partial intestacy rather than to The Royal Society, the residuary beneficiary.

The court held that "United Kingdom" could be interpreted more widely in this case, applying **s21(1)(c)**. First, the testator's assets at the date he made the will were almost exclusively in offshore accounts and, second, he had corresponded with his solicitors about the age at which his minor beneficiaries should take their specific legacies, fixing this at 25 after saying he did not want them to inherit too early. This made it unlikely that the testator intended his major assets to pass to them on intestacy, which would be the consequence if 'United Kingdom' had its technical meaning.

Once the possibility of a secondary meaning (i.e. an ambiguity) was established, extrinsic evidence of the testator's intention was admitted. There was then no difficulty in finding that he had intended his offshore accounts to be included – for example, when giving instructions about his assets, he had listed them under the heading "my assets in England". Also, he had over many years demonstrated his intention that the Society should inherit his whole estate and when he made the 2006 will (with wording identical to the 2009 will) he had no true UK assets.

Consequently, the reference to "United Kingdom" in the will was given the wider meaning to include Jersey and the Isle of Man, as intended by the testator.

Nodes (deceased), Re [2021] was a case about interpretation of wills and the admissibility of extrinsic evidence. Here, the High Court found that a clause in a deceased's will which gave his widow and co-director shares in his company should be construed as giving "each" of them a 26 per cent share, rather than that the shares of "both" of them should amount to 26 per cent in total. The court applied the approach set out by Lord Neuberger in ***Marley v Rawlings and another [2014]*** and found that the clause in question was ambiguous both:

- on its face (noting the difficulties with the word "both");
- in light of surrounding circumstances (a previous will had given each of them a 26 per cent share in the company).

Extrinsic evidence of the deceased's intention could therefore be admitted under **s21(c) Administration of Justice Act 1982** and the court was able to consider the evidence of the testator's widow and of the co-director, the will file and the evidence of the solicitor who prepared the will. The court found that this clearly showed that the testator's intention was for each of the widow and co-director to have a 26 per cent share. The solicitor who had prepared the will was criticised, amongst other things, for not considering and acting on the conflict of interest issues as both the testator and his wife were his clients, and not complying with various provisions of the STEP Code for Will Preparation or the Law Society's File Practice Note (e.g., not making a note of the meeting at which instructions were given, nor sending a note of it to the clients).

Re Bracey (deceased) Bracey v Curley and another [2022] is an example of how hard courts will try to give effect to what is believed to be the intention of the testator. In this case, it was very clear from a variety of evidence that the testator intended to leave a particular residential property to his son, subject to his wife's right to occupy until her death. Unfortunately, the solicitor drafting the will adapted a precedent and did not quite get the wording right, and so did not allow for the possibility of the wife pre-deceasing the testator. The court held that the proper interpretation of the will was to construe a gift of the house to the son; alternatively, **s21 Administration of Justice Act 1982** could be used to admit extrinsic evidence of the testator's intentions; or if not the will could be rectified under **s20** of that Act.

14.6 Deciding if a gift is absolute or limited

14.6.1 s22 Administration of Justice Act 1982

s22 AJA 1982 provides that: *Except where a contrary intention is shown it shall be presumed that if a testator devises or bequeaths property to his spouse in terms which in themselves would give an absolute interest to the spouse, but by the same instrument purports to give his issue an interest in the same property, the gift to the spouse is absolute notwithstanding the purported gift to the issue.*

In ***Harrison and Another v Gibson and Others [2006]*** the testator (T) made a home-made will. He was married at the time of his death and had four adult children. In his will, the testator had written: "The bungalow I leave in trust to my wife. If she falls on hard times it could be sold to raise cash." He subsequently crossed out the second sentence and added the word "deleted" over it. He then added: "On her death the bungalow is to be sold and the cash raised is to be equally divided between my children. No doubt if mum runs into money problems you can sort everything out. Like selling the bungalow."

T died in 2002. His wife made a will and left the bungalow on trust in favour of three out of the four children as one of the children had predeceased both his parents. In addition, the shares to these three children were not equal. The two children receiving larger shares argued that T's will passed the bungalow to the wife absolutely so the uneven shares in her will stood.

The third child contended that the wife took only a life interest under T's will and therefore, on her death, the children took in equal shares.

Hart J stated that **s22** allowed the court to look beyond the words of the will themselves to the context of the will as a whole. The key words in T's will here were: "The bungalow I leave in trust to my wife." In his opinion, looking at the background to the case, the statutory presumption had been displaced here and T intended that his wife should have a life interest in the property rather than an absolute interest. On her death, therefore, the three surviving children inherited **equal** shares in the bungalow.

14.6.2 The rule in *Lassence v Tierney [1849]*

This rule deals with the position where a badly drafted will has made a gift to a legatee absolutely and has also imposed a trust on the same property in favour of other beneficiaries. Consider the following example.

Case Study

Greenacre

A house called Greenacre is given to John absolutely. Later in the will, Greenacre is given to trustees to hold on trust for John for life and then for John's children. The residue of the will is given to Sheena. John outlives the testator and, when he dies, he has no children.

The rule states that in this situation, where the trust of the property fails (when John dies childless), the property will pass to the beneficiary who was given the initial absolute gift. Greenacre would pass to John (and his estate on his death) and not pass to the residuary beneficiary, Sheena.

The rule was applied in ***Hancock v Watson [1902]*** where the testator gave the residue of his estate to be held on trust for his wife for life and then to be divided into five shares. Two of those shares were given to D. The will then went on to state that "the two fifth portions allotted to [D] shall remain in trust, and that she be entitled to take only the interest of the shares so bequeathed to her during her natural life". On the death of D, the will provided for other beneficiaries to inherit the two portions. After the deaths of the testator, then his wife and then D, a dispute arose as to whether the two-fifths portions passed to the other beneficiaries or under D's own estate. The House of Lords held that, because the will stated "I give" and referred to the shares being "allotted" to D, the will had made an absolute gift to D. On D's death, the two shares therefore passed under her own estate and not to the other beneficiaries.

14.7 Subsidiary principles of construction

(1) **Inconsistent clauses**

If two parts of a will are mutually inconsistent then, in general, the later clause is to prevail (***Re Hammond [1938]***). This principle gives a wide discretion to the court, and one might describe it as a mere rule of thumb (***Re Potter's Will Trust [1944]***).

This arbitrary rule will not apply:

(a) where, on construction of the will as a whole, the testator shows that the first clause was to be effective;

(b) where there are two persons and each could take a half, as in ***Re Alexander's Will Trust [1948]*** where clause (i) gave a bracelet to A and clause (ii) gave the same bracelet to B; A and B share the property.

NB Extrinsic evidence would be admissible here because there was an ambiguity. In ***Re Bywater [1881]***, where there were conflicting clauses, there was some evidence that one clause had been admitted in mistake. Where this is the case, **s20 AJA 1982** (see **2.7.5**) would now allow rectification of the will.

(2) **The court "leans against" intestacy**

The court will attempt a construction that leads to a sensible meaning and, as far as possible, avoids an intestacy.

See, for example, ***Harris v Estate of Cooper (Deceased) [2010]*** and ***Pinnel v Anison [2005]***, discussed in **13.6.3**, where the court was able to give effect to seemingly uncertain words.

(3) **Ejusdem generis**

Where wide words of description are used in conjunction with narrow words, the scope of the wide words will be cut down by the narrow words.

In ***Re Miller [1889]*** the testator made specific bequests of his books, wine and plate. He then made a residuary gift of "all the rest of my furniture and effects at my residence". The word "effects" construed on its own could mean all the personal property, but the court held that it was to be construed *"as the same kind"* (*ejusdem generis*) as books, wine and plate, so the residuary gift did not include certain share certificates and bank notes found at the testator's residence.

(4) **Falsa demonstratio**

Falsa demonstratio non nocet cum corpore constat – a false description does not vitiate an instrument if the true part describes the subject with sufficient certainty.

If, in the description of a gift, the object is described with sufficient certainty, any additional words that are shown to be inaccurate will be ignored. The important issue is that even though the description is wrong, it is possible to see the intention of the testator.

In ***Blague v Gold [1880]*** the will contained a devise of a house described as "the corner house in the tenure of A and B". In fact, the house was in the tenure of A alone.

The court held that there was sufficient true description to pass the gift; the reference to B was disregarded.

In ***Blake v Blake [1923]*** the testatrix bequeathed to her niece "all the shares in any company I have that are absolutely my own". She then went on to enumerate certain shares but not others. Subsequent to the will, she became entitled to other shares.

The court held that the enumeration of certain shares did not cut down the previous bequest "all the shares" but the niece was entitled only to those shares held at the date of the will, the court treating "absolutely my own" as part of the description of the shares and contrary intention to exclude **s24 WA 1837** (see **13.2.2**).

An extreme example of the application of the doctrine is seen in ***Re Price [1932]***. By her will, the testatrix bequeathed to X a holding of government stock, "my £400 five per cent War Loan 1929–47". The surrounding circumstances showed that she had never held any War Loan but had held £400 National War Loans (a different stock) but she had converted this stock to other government loans shortly before making the will.

The court took account of the poor education of the testatrix and her inadequate instructions to her solicitor regarding the nature of her investments. Eve J held that she meant "war loan" in a general way, meaning any securities which helped the war effort. Most of the references in the gift were excluded as *falsa demonstratio*, so the gift read "my £400 . . . war loan" and the term "War Loan" was then read in a secondary sense.

Note the approach by Goulding J in ***Re Barnes [1972]*** (see **14.4**(3)) where he took account of the limited education of the testatrix in interpreting the word "money".

The principle has been extended to a situation where the description in the will is wholly false but the context of the will and the evidence of the surrounding circumstances show unambiguously what the testator intended. The description in the will is then rejected and effect is given to the gleaned intention.

An example is the decision in ***Re Fleming's Will Trust [1974]***, where the testator held a house on a long lease and made a will leaving "my leasehold house 54 Narcissus Road" to named beneficiaries. Two years later, the testator purchased the freehold reversion but the freehold and leasehold interests were not merged. Did the beneficiaries receive the freehold?

Templeman J said that where the testator makes a gift of property, it is likely that he intends to give whatever estate and interest he has in the property at the date of his death. Merely referring to the estate or interest he holds at the date the will is made does not disclose a contrary intention and, therefore, the beneficiaries took the freehold.

14.8 Gifts by description to children and other relatives

A will need not identify beneficiaries by name. Often the testator resorts to describing beneficiaries when making a will, particularly if they want to benefit a class determined at a future date, such as at their death. In some cases, it may not be possible to name individual beneficiaries anyway, typically if the testator wishes to benefit people who have yet to be born. So, the use of a class gift (see **13.4.2**) – for example to "my children" or to "my nephews and nieces" – is very common.

However, care is needed to avoid any misunderstanding, not only on the part of the testator but also by his PRs when administering the estate. For example, in ***Harris v Estate of Cooper (Deceased) [2010]*** the will left residue equally to "my surviving relatives". Given its ordinary meaning, the word "relatives" extends to all persons related to the testatrix, however remotely. The judge recognised that to give the word that meaning would invariably lead to the gift failing for uncertainty because it would be impossible to identify everyone entitled to benefit. The problem was resolved by resorting to extrinsic evidence, admissible under **s21 AJA 1982**, to find the true intention if part of the will was meaningless or ambiguous (see **14.5.2**). By doing so, the judge was able to say that the testatrix intended the expression to mean her three closest first cousins, whom she knew well, and not all her worldwide relatives.

It is important to note that a gift to "my nephews" etc., without more, is construed as including only the testator's nephews (taking account of the statutory rules below) and not those on their spouse's, civil partner's, or cohabitee's side of the family, even though extrinsic evidence might show they have been treated as the testator's own. In particular, a reference to "my children" does not include stepchildren, in the absence of adoption (see **14.8.3**) or other express words in the will. It follows that a testator wishing to benefit relations who are not otherwise within the terms of a gift must include express words in the will to show an intention that excludes the normal rules.

Prima facie, a gift to "children" (or, indeed, other relations as above) is construed at common law as including only legitimate children (or persons tracing relationship through legitimate links) and not those who were born illegitimate or have been adopted. However, there are now statutory rules that extend the common law meaning to determine the full extent of relationships described in a will.

These statutory rules are subject to a contrary intention expressed in the will. Although the rules were introduced relatively recently in keeping with changing social attitudes to illegitimacy, there is nothing contrary to public policy if the testator wants the old common law rules to apply to their will.

14.8.1 Children whose parents were never married

For a will or codicil executed before 1970, the common law rule is that a gift to "children" (or other relations) is construed *prima facie* as embracing only legitimate children. For wills made after 31 December 1969, the position is now determined by statute.

s19 Family Law Reform Act 1987 (**FLRA 1987**) applies to any will, codicil or *inter vivos* dispositions of property made on or after 4 April 1988, so that references in any such document are construed without regard to *whether or not the father and mother of either* [person] *or the father and mother of any person through whom the relationship is deduced have or had been married to each other at any time.* This means a reference to "my children", "my brother's children", "my nieces", etc. includes both legitimate and illegitimate persons within the description, whether or not they need to trace their pedigree through any illegitimate relationship. So, a gift "to my grandchildren" includes all the testator's grandchildren, even the illegitimate child of an illegitimate child. (**s15 FLRA 1969** applies to wills or codicils made after 1969 but before 4 April 1988. It contains provisions broadly the same as those in **FLRA 1987**.)

The rules are applied subject to any contrary intention shown in the will and so it is always open to a testator to make it clear that they do not want any illegitimate person to benefit. This might be shown, for example, by a clause saying that **s19 FLRA 1987** is not to apply.

Note that if the rules do apply, there is no specific protection for PRs and trustees who distribute in ignorance of the existence of a rightful illegitimate claimant. Such protection is still available to PRs and trustees who follow the standard practice of advertising for claimants under **s27 Trustee Act 1925**, or use the ***Benjamin*** order procedure (see **16.3.3.1** and **17.7.1**).

14.8.2 Legitimated children

Under the **Legitimacy Act 1976** (**LA 1976**), a legitimated child (that is born outside marriage but then the parents marry), is entitled in the same way as if born legitimate, subject to a contrary indication in the will. **LA 1976** also provides rules on deemed birth corresponding to those for adopted children (see below), so that if a disposition under a will depends upon the date of birth, the child is treated as if born on the date of the parent's marriage.

14.8.3 Adopted children

The position of adopted children is now governed by the **Adoption and Children Act 2002** (**ACA 2002**).

ACA 2002 applies to adoption orders (whether made before or after the testator's death) made by a court in the UK, Isle of Man or Channel Islands and to certain foreign adoptions. **s67** confirms the status of an adopted child by providing the child is to be treated as the legitimate child of the person who adopts him or her and consequently such an adopted child is to be treated as not being the child of anyone other than of the adoptive parent. **NB s4 Inheritance and Trustees' Powers Act 2014** has amended **s67** and provides that, where a child's natural parent has already died leaving a contingent interest under their will (or under the intestacy rules) to the child, the subsequent adoption of the child will **not** result in the child losing their rights under the contingent interest (see **10.5**(3)).

ACA 2002 also contain rules of interpretation that apply when a disposition depends on a date of birth. Subject to any contrary intention being shown, the disposition is construed as if:

- the adopted child had been born at the date of adoption;
- two or more children adopted on the same date had been born on that date in the order of their actual births.

So, if there is a gift to "such of X's children living at my death" and X adopts a three-year-old child one year after the testator's death, that child would not be included in the gift because the child was not X's child at the time of the testator's death. The child is excluded in the same way as any natural child would be under the class closing rules (see **13.4.2**). However, it is provided these rules do not affect any reference in the gift to the age of a child. So, if a gift is contingent on attaining the age of 21 years, an adopted child who is within the class of entitlement achieves a vested interest on reaching the age of 21 and not 21 years after the adoption.

As with the statutory rules on illegitimacy, it is open to the testator to show a contrary intention that a person who might benefit as a result of adoption should not take. So a clause saying "to my sister's natural children" would include her legitimate and illegitimate children but would exclude an adopted child who had not been born to her naturally.

In ***Hardy v Hardy and Another [2013]*** by clause 4 of his will the testator, T, directed his residuary estate to be held in trust "for such of my children as shall survive me and attain the age of 21 years". T had three natural children, A, B and C who all survived and attained age 21. However, A had been adopted by his natural mother and T's brother, so by reason of **s67 ACA 2002**, A would no longer qualify as one of T's children within the meaning of clause 4 unless there was a contrary indication. Fortunately, in clause 1 of the will, T appointed A and B as his executors and trustees, describing them as "my sons". The court ruled that on the true construction of the will, the description of A in the will as one of T's sons was a very clear indication of T intending to regard A as his child and, therefore, as one of his children within the meaning of clause 4 of the will, contrary to the usual effect of **s67**.

14.8.4 Same-sex marriages

Although **s11 Marriage (Same Sex Couples) Act 2013** (see **6.7.1**) states that marriage has the same effect in relation to same-sex couples as it has in relation to opposite-sex couples, **Sch 4** makes it clear that **s11** does not alter the effect of any "private legal instrument" made before 13 March 2014. A "private legal instrument" includes a will, codicil or trust document.

So, for example, a legacy in an existing will (i.e. made before 13 March 2014) which is expressed to be contingent on "marriage" or "marrying" will be construed as an opposite-sex marriage only. Similarly, a reference in a trust deed made before 13 March 2014 to a "widow" will be taken to mean a woman whose marriage to a man has ended on that man's death; it will not include a woman whose marriage to another woman ended with the other woman's death.

For any will or trust document made on or after 13 March 2014, "marriage", or any marriage-related term, will have a wider meaning than before, unless it states otherwise.

Suppose the testator instructs you to draft a new will that includes a legacy to their son, contingent on the son attaining 25 years of age, or marrying earlier, and a discretionary trust of their residuary estate. The testator wishes to include as potential beneficiaries of the discretionary trust not only their own "children and grandchildren" but also their "husbands, wives, widows and widowers". When advising the testator, the draftsman must remember that these terms will include same-sex spouses, unless the will expressly states otherwise. As always, clear instructions must be taken from the testator and the will drafted accordingly, to ensure that it reflects the testator's actual wishes.

14.8.5 Other related rules

(1) **Children born following fertilisation techniques and surrogacy arrangements**

At common law a child's legal parents are their genetic parents. However, the **Human Fertilisation and Embryology Act 2008** contains complex provisions to determine parentage in cases of assisted reproduction or where there has been a surrogacy arrangement.

HFEA 2008 is outside the scope of this textbook.

(2) **Gender recognition**

The **Gender Recognition Act 2004** (**GRA 2004**) provides that transsexuals, who have obtained a full gender recognition certificate from a gender recognition panel, will have full legal recognition under English law in their acquired gender. It applies only to a will made after the Act came into force in 2005 (**s15**). Hence, if a will made after this date makes provision for "my nieces", then someone born a nephew will be eligible to benefit after acquiring female gender recognition under **GRA 2004**.

GRA 2004 is outside the scope of this textbook.

14.9 Summary

(1) Will construction – a summary of recommended approaches:

- Is the will clearly expressed?
- put the will in context;
- if there is doubt as to the meaning, look at the circumstances surrounding the testator when they made the will;
- in cases of doubt, is there any extrinsic evidence admissible under **s21 AJA 1982**?

(2) The meaning of words and phrases:

- first, give words their usual meaning;
- there may be a secondary meaning when applying surrounding circumstances;
- words may have more than one meaning – if so, the court will adopt the most probable one;
- technical words and phrases – there is a strong presumption that the words will carry this meaning even if this is not what the testator intended;
- the court must consider the document as a whole.

(3) Subsidiary principles of construction:

- inconsistent clauses – generally, the later one prevails;
- the court will attempt a construction which leans against intestacy and leads to a sensible meaning;
- *ejusdem generis* – where wide words of description are used in conjunction with narrow ones, the scope of the wide ones will be cut down by the narrow ones;
- *falsa demonstratio* – if, in the description of a gift, the object is described with sufficient certainty, any additional words that are shown to be inaccurate will be ignored.

(4) Gifts to children and others by description (subject to any contrary intention:

- for the purposes of succession, an adopted child will be treated as the child of the adoptive parents. Under **s4 Inheritance and Trustees' Powers Act 2014**, children who are subsequently adopted will retain any contingent rights to their deceased natural parent(s)' estates under the intestacy rules or their wills;
- an illegitimate child is treated as a full family member for the purposes of construing gifts in a will.

CHAPTER 15

Personal Representatives: Obtaining the Grant

Aims of the Chapter:

By the end of this chapter, you should be able to:

- outline the roles of executors and administrators;
- define who an executor *de son tort* is;
- describe when a grant may be revoked; and
- outline the effects of foreign grants.

15.1 Introduction

Until a grant of representation – either a grant of probate or a grant of administration – has been issued to the PRs of the deceased, there is relatively little they can do to progress the actual administration of the estate. The grant is confirmation of the validity of any will and the appointment of the executors named in it, or that the deceased died intestate. If there are no executors, the grant also constitutes the court's authorisation of one or more administrators to deal with the estate.

There are three main grants of representation:

- probate – issued to the executors who prove the will;
- administration with will annexed (administration *cum testamento annexo*) – issued to administrators where there is a will but no proving executors;
- administration on intestacy – issued to administrators.

In this chapter, we will consider the roles of executors and administrators.

The key difference between an executor and an administrator is that an executor is the person chosen by the deceased to deal with the estate. The executor takes their authority from the will, whereas, at death, the powers of the administrator are limited to those necessary to obtain the grant. The administrator takes their authority from the order of the court, which is the grant. We will also review the unusual role of an executor *de son tort* who acquires some legal responsibility for administering the estate, despite not being appointed in the will, because he or she has intermeddled with the assets of the estate.

We will briefly consider the special treatment of very small estates and then discuss grants of probate and administration in more detail. In addition, we will review grants *de bonis non administratis* where the original PRs have died before the estate has been completed.

Revocation of the grant will also be considered – this may be needed, for example, where the PR has been dishonest or has lost capacity.

Finally, we will review the circumstances in which grants issued in England and Wales may be used in other jurisdictions and when foreign grants will be needed.

15.2 Executors

Executorship is essentially a personal office. It cannot be assigned (***Re Skinner [1958]***). The executor is appointed by the will of the deceased. The appointment can be either express or implied. The will may nominate someone to appoint an executor, who may be the nominee themselves.

In ***In the Goods of Cringan [1828]*** the testator authorised his legatees to appoint two executors.

Difficulties can arise if the appointment is ambiguous: either patent ("I appoint one of my brothers") or latent ("I appoint my brother" where evidence of the surrounding circumstances reveals two brothers). To resolve ambiguities, the court will admit extrinsic evidence under **s21 AJA 1982** (see **Chapter 14**).

An executor may be appointed to deal with the whole estate (a general executor) or appointed to a specific part of the estate, for example, in connection with the continuation of a business owned by the deceased or as literary executor, as in ***Re Orwell [1982]***. The appointment may be limited in time – for example, during the minority of an infant, substitutional ("I appoint X but, if he should go and live in France, then I appoint Y") or conditional ("I appoint X on condition that he acts with Y").

15.2.1 Appointment of a firm

It is common for a testator to appoint a firm of solicitors to act because, although they may wish to appoint "their" solicitor, it is generally a good idea to appoint two executors (because they are often also to be trustees and two trustees are needed to give a good receipt for the proceeds of sale of land). In addition, although two individual solicitors may be named, they may leave the firm or predecease the testator. In this situation, it is a good idea to appoint the firm to act as executors. There are various pitfalls which should be avoided when drafting such an appointment. First, the firm is a partnership with no legal identity, so the appointment should be of "the partners in the firm". The second problem is that membership of the firm is ascertained at the date of the will under the principle in ***Re Whorwood [1887]***, so the will should refer to the "partners in the firm at the date of my death". The final problem is that the firm may be taken over or amalgamated before the testator dies and so the will should refer to the firm or the firm that represents it at the date of the testator's death. Also, since the firm may be large, the clause usually includes a statement of the testator's wish that no more than two members of the firm shall obtain probate. Such a clause was approved by the court in ***Re Horgan [1969]***.

The appointment of the partners in a firm of solicitors does not become invalid if the partnership subsequently converts into a limited liability partnership. It is nonetheless sensible to use a precedent clause allowing for this possibility.

Solicitors are now permitted to practise as incorporated bodies. Any reference to a firm in, for example, the clause adopted in ***Re Horgan*** should include reference to an incorporated practice as recognised by the Solicitors' Regulation Authority. Care should be taken where a practice is incorporated and the testator wishes to appoint the practice to act as executor under the will. By **r36(4) Non-Contentious Probate Rules 1987** (**NCPR 1987**), a corporate body cannot take out a grant in its own right unless it is a trust corporation. The incorporated practice would have to nominate someone to act on behalf of the practice or appoint an attorney.

It used to be the case that where a professional person or firm was appointed executor, the will had to include a professional charging clause. The provisions of the **Trustee Act 2000** now provide for remuneration to professionals, although the inclusion of a charging clause is still the usual practice.

15.2.2 Implied appointment of the executor

The testator may not use express words but may name someone requesting the person to carry out acts that only an executor would do. This is termed an appointment "according to the tenor (of the will)".

In ***In the Goods of Baylis [1865]*** a will directed that named persons were to pay the debts of the estate and hold it on trust for the deceased's children. They were held to be executors.

By contrast, in ***In the Estate of McKenzie [1909]*** appointment as a trustee without an instruction to pay debts was held **not** to be an appointment as an executor.

15.2.3 Passing over and substitution of executors

s116 Senior Courts Act 1981 (**SCA 1981**) gives the court the power to pass over an executor (refuse to issue a grant in their favour) in special circumstances where it is expedient to do so. The court will appoint a replacement administrator.

Examples include circumstances where:

- the executor is insolvent;
- the executor is incapable of acting – for example, serving a prison sentence (***Re S [1968]***);
- all those with an interest in the estate, as well as those entitled to a grant, request that their nominee be appointed (***Re Potter [1899]***);
- the executor refuses to take out a grant of probate although they have accepted office by intermeddling (commencing the process of administering the estate) (***Re Biggs [1966]***);
- the executor cannot be found; in ***In the Goods of Wright [1898]*** the executor disappeared after a warrant of arrest had been issued for him for embezzlement;
- the executor is of bad character (***Re Crippen [1911]***), where the executor was serving a sentence for murder).

In ***Khan v Crossland [2012]*** the testator had appointed a firm of will-writers as executors with whom he had very little contact. The beneficiaries were all adults and were united in requesting that the executors be replaced following a breakdown in trust. The court exercised its discretion under **s116** to appoint them as replacements.

In ***AB v Dobbs [2010]*** the court emphasised that the power to pass over executors should be exercised only in extreme cases.

Under **s50(1) Administration of Justice Act 1985** (**AJA 1985**) an executor or a beneficiary may apply to the court for an order to replace an existing executor with a substitute. This order is often used after a grant has been issued where there has been a breakdown in trust between the beneficiaries and the executor which is likely to affect the administration of the estate. In ***Re Steele [2010]*** the executor was replaced because of such a breakdown in trust, even though the executor had not committed any wrongdoing. However, an order can also be applied for if there is a falling out among the executors themselves. In ***Goodman and Another v Goodman and Another [2013]*** the court said an order could be applied for under **s50(1)** even though no grant of probate had issued to the executors appointed by the will. This was because an executor's authority stems from the will itself (see **16.2**). In this respect, so far as executors are concerned, an application under **s50(1)** is an alternative to an application under **s116 SCA 1981**.

s50 AJA 1985 was also considered in ***National Westminster Bank v Lucas and Others [2014]***. The bank had been appointed as the executor of the paedophile Jimmy Savile. Under his will, the Jimmy Savile Charitable Trust was the residuary beneficiary. Although his estate was substantial, there were a large number of claims from the testator's victims which, it was anticipated, were likely to exceed the value of the estate. There were also a number of third party defendants, including the BBC and NHS hospitals, who were claiming an indemnity from the estate in respect of claims by the victims against them.

The bank and the third party defendants developed a scheme for managing the litigation under which, it was hoped, the individual claims by the victims could be dealt with fairly and with the minimum of legal costs. Unfortunately the trust objected to the scheme and applied under **s50 AJA 1985** for the bank to be replaced as executor. Sales J refused the application using the analogy of a company *"which faces a real risk of being unable to pay its creditors, where the directors are bound to consider the interests of the creditors and not simply those of the shareholders"*.

15.2.4 The number of executors

Although a testator can name any number of executors in the will, **s114(1) SCA 1981** provides that a maximum of four may obtain a grant *in respect of the same part of the estate*. A person could, for example, appoint four people to be general executors and two more in respect of their literary estate. The four would obtain a grant of probate to the estate (apart from the literary assets for which a separate grant would be issued to the two literary executors).

15.2.5 The persons who may be appointed as executors

In general, anyone can act as an executor. The exceptions are as follows.

(1) A minor cannot act until attaining majority. If the minor is appointed sole executor, then a limited grant would issue *cum testamento annexo durante minore aetate* (with will annexed limited during the minority) to the minor's parent with parental responsibility or guardian. If the minor is aged 16 or over, they can nominate anyone from their next of kin. On attaining majority, the minor applies for a cessate grant. The original grant ceases.

If there are others appointed with the minor, then probate is granted to the others with power reserved for the minor to prove when they attain majority. On attaining majority, the former minor is granted double probate (see **Glossary**) which runs concurrently with the original grant.

(2) A person of unsound mind cannot act. If the person is named sole executor, there would be a grant of letters of administration with will annexed limited during the disability (*durante dementia*). If there are others named who can act, power is reserved to the person so that they can obtain probate if the disability ends. If the period of disability ends, there would be a grant of double probate.

(3) A person being in known financial difficulties is not, in itself, a bar, but if that person becomes insolvent, a receiver will be appointed unless there is another executor.

(4) The court has an inherent power to pass over unsuitable executors without citation (**s116 SCA 1981**) (as **15.2.3**).

Where a trust corporation, such as a bank, is appointed, the corporation can act either alone or in conjunction with others. All the major clearing banks have trustee divisions and their booklets give examples of specimen appointments. The court must be satisfied that it has the power in the Memorandum of Association to act as executor and a copy of the resolution appointing the nominees must be filed with the court.

A corporation aggregate (made up of groups of persons associated for some purpose and having rights, duties and the capacity of succession) which is not a trust corporation, such as an ordinary limited company, cannot take out probate in its own name but must act through nominees. The grant is of letters of administration for the use and benefit of the corporation.

15.2.6 Chain of representation

Generally, the office of executor is for life. If property falls into the estate many years after the completion of the administration, the executor is duty bound to deal with it. Where a sole or last surviving executor dies in office having taken out the grant of probate, **s7 AEA 1925** provides that the duties pass to their executor without the need for a further grant of probate with respect to the original estate, provided that the executor of the original executor also takes out probate to the estate for which they were appointed.

Example

A is named executor to the will of T. A proves T's will by obtaining probate then dies, having appointed B to be his executor. Provided that B proves the will of A, B becomes executor by representation to the estate of T. B must agree to act with respect to both estates (***In the Goods of Perry [1840]***).

Example

T appoints two executors, X and Y, and Y proves the will with power reserved for X to prove at a later date. If Y dies before completing the administration, having appointed Z to be his executor, Z should cite X to determine whether X wishes to prove the will of T; otherwise, Z would become executor by representation to the estate of T (by proving Y's will) only to be removed from that task should X subsequently wish to prove in the estate of T.

The chain of representation will be broken where the sole or last surviving executor dies:

- before obtaining a grant of probate of the original will; or
- intestate; or
- leaving a will but not appointing executors; or
- leaving a will appointing executors who are unable or unwilling to act.

15.2.7 Acceptance of office

A person who takes out probate and so proves the will or does anything in connection with the estate which, if they had not been named executor, would have constituted them an executor *de son tort* will be deemed to have accepted (see **15.4**). If a person fails to take out the grant after having accepted the office, they may be cited to compel them to accept or refuse. Collecting assets or paying debts would be sufficient to amount to acceptance, rendering the person liable as executor (***Re Stevens [1897]***), although the court will not consider trivial acts in relation to the estate as amounting to acceptance (***Holder v Holder [1968]***), such as arranging the funeral.

15.2.8 Renunciation

A person appointed may renounce probate, for example, if they do not feel able to carry out their duties, either because of lack of time or they just do not want to act. The renunciation is not final until it is filed in the Principal or District Probate Registry.

Renunciation as an executor does not preclude the person applying for a grant of administration to the estate in another capacity, for example, as a creditor, unless the court expressly says to the contrary.

Once a formal renunciation has been made, it may be retracted only with the consent of the court (**r37 NCPR 1987**). Consent will be given only if it can be shown that it will be for the benefit of the estate. In ***Re Gill [1873]*** the executor renounced on the basis of incorrect advice. The court would not permit a retraction because the applicant could not show that it would be for the benefit of the estate. In ***Re Stiles [1898]*** a retraction was allowed where the co-executor who had taken out probate absconded.

One cannot accept one appointment and renounce others under the chain of representation. In these circumstances, it might be better to renounce probate of both estates and, if entitled, apply as an administrator of the second estate (***Re Toscani [1912]***).

15.3 Administrators

Administration with will annexed

Where a testator dies leaving a valid will and there is no executor able to prove the will of the deceased, application must be made for administration of the estate with will annexed (*cum testamento annexo*). The order of entitlement to this grant is set out in **r20 NCPR 1987** (which also authorises an executor to take out a grant of probate).

(1) The executor is entitled above all others and would be granted probate. All later classes are entitled to the grant of administration with will annexed.

(2) The trustees of the residuary estate (if any).

(3) The residuary beneficiaries and those entitled on intestacy where there is any property undisposed of by the will.

(4) The PRs of residuary beneficiaries or of anyone entitled to property undisposed of by the will where such persons have died after the deceased.

(5) Any other beneficiary under the will or any creditor of the deceased.

(6) The PR of any beneficiary who dies after the deceased or of a creditor.

Where more than one person is entitled to a grant in any category, a grant may be issued to any of them without notice to the others. This is unlike the position with executors where, if not all of those appointed wish to apply for the original grant, notice must be given to those who do not apply and this stated in the oath or statement of truth. Power is then reserved to the other executors to take probate at a later stage (a grant of **double probate**). An executor who does not wish to act may always renounce, but this is not essential, and the power reserved procedure allows the executor to come in and prove the will should the others become unable, for whatever reason, to continue the administration.

Where more than one person is entitled to a grant in the same category, the court has power to select the most suitable person on behalf of an infant in the same category.

Administration – full intestacy

Where the deceased has died without a valid will, that is, totally intestate, the order of entitlement to a grant follows the order of beneficial entitlement on a total intestacy (**r22 NCPR 1987**). Clearing off will be used, as under **r20**, for higher categories of relative. If no one has a beneficial interest in the estate, a grant may be issued to the Treasury Solicitor, claiming *bona vacantia* on behalf of the Crown (**r22(2)**) or, if the Treasury Solicitor is cleared off, a creditor of the intestate may take out a grant.

The order under **r22** is as follows.

(1) The surviving husband or wife or civil partner of the deceased.

(2) The children of the deceased (and the issue of a child who has predeceased).

(3) The parents of the deceased.

(4) The brothers and sisters of the whole blood of the deceased (and the issue of any brothers or sisters who have predeceased).

(5) The brothers and sisters of the half blood of the deceased (and the issue of any who have predeceased).

(6) Grandparents.

(7) Uncles and aunts of the whole blood (and the issue of any who have predeceased).

(8) Uncles and aunts of the half blood (and the issue of any who have predeceased).

It is important to note that, under **r22**, a person who falls within the various classes of relative specified in the intestacy rules is entitled to a grant only if they are entitled to share in the estate, so the applicant is selected from the beneficiaries. If no one is entitled under these rules or such persons renounce, a grant may be issued to a person who would be a beneficiary in the event of an accretion to (increase in) the estate. If the spouse or civil partner were solely entitled to a small estate, but did not wish to act, the issue could take a grant under this rule. If a beneficiary dies after the deceased without taking out a grant, their PRs may take a grant on their behalf.

As under **r20**, an application by a living person is preferred to one by the PRs of a deceased one, and an application by an adult is preferred to one on behalf of an infant. An application by the PRs of a deceased spouse or civil partner would have a lower priority than one by other living beneficiaries, unless the spouse or civil partner was solely entitled to the estate.

A few points are relevant to applications under **r20** and **r22**. **s116 SCA 1981**, discussed at **15.2.3**, gives the court an equivalent power to pass over applicants for a grant of letters of administration with will annexed and applicants for a grant of letters of administration. Similarly, an administrator or a beneficiary can seek an order for the appointment of a substitute administrator under **s50(1) AJA 1985** (see **15.2.3**). However, since administrators derive authority from the court through the issue of a grant (see **16.2**), this right is effectively limited to situations where a grant has already issued at the time when the order is sought. Before the issue of a grant, an application would need to be made using **s116 SCA 1981**. There are equivalent provisions for infant applicants and applicants of unsound mind to those discussed at **15.2.5**.

Number of administrators

A minimum of two individuals or a trust corporation (e.g. a bank) must be appointed as administrators or administrators with the will annexed where there is a child beneficiary under 18 years or a life interest, unless the court considers it expedient to appoint only one (**s114(2) SCA 1981**). If an appointee dies, the court has power to appoint another administrator while a minority or life interest exists if application is made (**s114(4)**).

15.4 The executor *de son tort*

An executor *de son tort* [French: of his own wrong] is a person who is not a true executor but who, without authority, acts as if they are the PR of the estate of the deceased – the **intermeddler** in the estate. Someone who obtains estate property or releases (forgives) a debt without lawful authority will be liable to the creditors to the extent of the assets they have received (**s28 Administration of Estates Act 1925** (**AEA 1925**)). Their lawful acts bind the estate.

Examples of acts making someone an executor *de son tort* include carrying on the business of the deceased (***Hooper v Summersett [1810]***) and collecting the deceased's debts (***Sharland v Mildon [1845]***). Acts of necessity or charity, such as arranging a funeral or feeding the deceased's livestock, would not make someone an executor *de son tort*. In ***Pollard v Jackson [1994]*** a tenant of the deceased who kept the parts of the property occupied by the deceased tidy and burnt his rubbish was held not to be an executor *de son tort*.

A person can be liable, however innocently they have acted. In ***New York Breweries Co Ltd v Attorney-General [1898]*** an English company was held to be liable for allowing a transfer of shares to foreign PRs without requiring production of an English grant of probate.

The executor *de son tort* is liable to the extent of the assets they have received but they can plead as a defence that they dealt with those assets in the way a lawful PR would have done.

Authorities on this topic are rare, but an application of the principle occurred in ***IRC v Stype Investments (Jersey) Ltd [1982]***. The Inland Revenue successfully contended that, by remitting sale proceeds of English real property out of the jurisdiction, the trustees had diverted funds thereby placing them out of the reach of the PRs of the deceased constituted in England.

15.5 Small estates

Certain types of estate may be administered without the need for a grant, for example, where the assets consist of National Savings or building society accounts to a maximum of £5,000 (**Administration of Estates (Small Payments) Act 1965**).

15.6 Grants of probate and administration

Applications for non-contentious probate or common form are made to the Family Division. Contentious probate matters, that is, where there is some dispute over the will or the estate, are referred to the Chancery Division.

Common form

The primary duty of the PRs is to collect in and value the assets of the deceased and assess all *bona fide* debts and any inheritance tax due on the estate.

The documents to be filed with the court at one of its Probate Registries are listed below.

(1) The **application** on form PA1P (where there is a will) or on form PA1A (where there is no will) signed by the PR giving details of, *inter alia*, the dates of birth and death of the deceased, domicile, testate or intestate distribution and confirming that the PR will duly administer the estate according to law and will render a true account of the administration and indicate the gross and net values of the estate.

(2) Any **original will** (and any codicils) or a **copy** or **reconstruction** where the original cannot be found and the presumption of *animus revocandi* has been rebutted. Two A4 copies of the will, which must not be stapled, must also be enclosed.

An engrossed copy of the will in the form in which it is to be proved must also be sent where parts of the will are not admissible to probate (e.g. there are inadmissible alterations or the will has been mutilated but not revoked).

A photocopy of the will bearing the court seal will be attached to the grant. The court may blank out certain parts of the copy, for example, for reasons of national security or where the words used by the testator are distressing to members of the family and have no disposing effect.

(3) If required, **form IHT 421** to show prior payment of inheritance; the HMRC account on **form IHT 400** giving details by inventory of the estate is sent to HMRC first. Payment of the inheritance tax due on the value of the estate situated in the UK (unless the instalment option is applicable) must be made before the documents are lodged with the court.

Regulations came into force on 2 November 2020 that required all solicitors and probate practitioners to submit non-contentious probate matters online.

Applications by private individuals may still be made by post.

Guidance issued by Her Majesty's Courts and Tribunals Service (HMCTS) on how to use the online system can be found at **https://www.gov.uk/government/publications/myhmcts-how-to-apply-for-probate-online**.

The Registrar or District Judge has the power under **NCPR 1987** to call for further proof by way of affidavit evidence. The main affidavits are listed below.

(1) **Knowledge and approval** (**r13 NCPR 1987**) – any situation where there is doubt that the testator had knowledge of the contents of the will, for example, in the case of a blind or illiterate testator.

(2) **Due execution** (**r12 NCPR 1987**) – **s9 Wills Act 1837** says that no form of attestation is necessary. Where the will does not contain the standard form attestation clause, or if the will is signed in an unusual place, the Registrar or District Judge may call for further proof, usually from the witnesses, if available,

by way of affidavit of due execution. The standard form clause, if included in the will, recites the requirements of **s9** and allows due execution to be presumed (see **3.5**).

(3) **Terms, condition and date of execution** (**r14 NCPR 1987**) – this applies where the will is mutilated in some way that could suggest that another document may have been attached, or there has been attempted revocation by destruction, or the will is not dated. The Registrar or District Judge can call for affidavit evidence for clarification, usually from those who had custody of the will or were instrumental in its preparation. In the same way, where there are unattested alterations, affidavit evidence will be called for.

15.7 Administration *de bonis non administratis*

This special grant translates literally as "of the goods not yet administered". The grant applies where the administration of the estate has not been completed and the original PRs die in circumstances where the chain of representation (see **15.2.6**) is broken. The persons who may apply for the grant *de bonis non* are the same as the order in **r20** and **r22 NCPR 1987**, depending upon whether the grant is with will annexed or on total intestacy.

15.8 Revocation of grants

The court has power, under **s121(1) SCA 1981**, to call in (revoke) a grant which should not have been made or one that contains an error.

Reasons for revocation

(1) A grant to the wrong person where, for example, it is believed that the deceased died intestate and a later valid will is found and proved.

(2) A grant issued on the basis of a false statement: in ***In the Estate of Napier [1809]*** a grant was issued in the belief that the person had died when he was still alive.

(3) Where the issue of the grant was irregular, for example, a grant issued without due notice to a caveator.

(4) If the PR leaves the jurisdiction in circumstances and they are unlikely to return, as in ***In the Goods of Loveday [1900]***. The deceased died intestate leaving a widow and six children by a former marriage. The widow obtained letters of administration but subsequently disappeared before completing the winding

up of the estate. The grant was revoked and a grant *de bonis non* was issued to one of the children.

Contrast ***Loveday*** with ***In the Estate of Cope [1954]***, where an application was made to revoke a grant issued to A and B on the basis that they had not made full disclosure of assets in the HMRC account and had shown as a liability against the estate a debt allegedly due to A which the applicant disputed. The court refused, as these were not special circumstances. The remedy was to order an inventory under **s25 AEA 1925**.

(5) Where the PR becomes incapable through physical or mental infirmity: if one of the PRs becomes incapable, the grant is revoked and a new grant is issued to the remaining PRs. If the only PR becomes incapable, the grant is not revoked, but a grant of letters of administration *de bonis non* is issued for the use and benefit of the incapable person.

(6) If the PR wishes to retire, for a reason which is satisfactory to the court.

(7) Where there is a serious breach of duty prejudicing the beneficiaries, such as dishonesty.

Additionally, the court has power in contentious proceedings to revoke a grant of probate on evidence that it should not have been made as a result of proof of lack of capacity, intention or non-compliance with the correct formalities for execution. In ***Re Wilson (Deceased) [2013]*** the court revoked a grant of probate on hearing subsequent evidence from her nieces that established that the deceased lacked both capacity and intention at the time she made her will. The court revoked the grant of probate, declared that the deceased had died intestate and granted letters of administration to the nieces, her closest relatives. It also ordered rectification of the entries at HM Land Registry to remove the names of those who had benefited under the will and to replace them with the names of the nieces in their capacity as administrators.

15.8.1 Effect of revocation

s27 AEA 1925 protects third parties who dealt in good faith with the PR whose grant is revoked. Further, the PRs themselves are entitled to be indemnified from the estate, provided that they have acted in good faith.

This section means that all payments by and to the PR prior to the revocation of the grant are valid, if made in good faith (i.e. the payer had no reason to believe that the grant might be revoked). **s27(1) AEA 1925** also provides that a PR who acts in good faith under a revoked grant is protected from liability. This would not prevent those correctly entitled from recovering the assets from the beneficiaries.

Contracts for sale remain binding and enforceable by the estate even if a grant is revoked (**s39 AEA 1925**). A purchaser from a PR is also protected by **s37 AEA**

1925, which provides that a conveyance of property (including land) from PRs is valid in favour of a purchaser in good faith and for value, despite any later revocation of the grant. "Conveyance" is defined in **s55** to include a mortgage, legal charge, lease or assent, but some writing is required. If no writing is present, the purchaser may rely on the rule in ***Hewson v Shelley [1914]***, which protects a purchaser in good faith and for value.

15.9 Foreign grants

If the deceased owned property outside England and Wales, there must be compliance with the requirements as to probate of the country in which the assets are situated. This will often mean that another grant or alternative process will have to be taken out in the country in question. Where a grant has already been taken out in another country this, by itself, may not be sufficient for the court in England and Wales and another grant will have to issue in this country.

s1 Administration of Estates Act 1971 (**AEA 1971**) provides that grants issued in England and Wales, Scotland and Northern Ireland will be recognised automatically in any of the other countries specified, provided that the deceased was domiciled at the date of their death in the country in which the grant was taken out. So, if a person died domiciled in England and Wales, the grant could be used to deal with assets in Scotland.

A grant issued in the majority of Commonwealth countries may be resealed in England and Wales, irrespective of the domicile of the deceased (**Colonial Probates Act 1892**).

In any other case, a fresh grant will have to be taken out in the country in which foreign assets are situated.

15.10 Summary

(1) There are three main grants of representation:

- probate issued to an executor who proves the will;
- administration with the will annexed – where there is a will but no proving executor;
- administration on intestacy.

(2) Executors:

- it is a personal office, so cannot be assigned;
- an executor can be appointed by implication;
- an executor may be passed over in certain circumstances (**s116 SCA 1981**);
- the maximum number of executors obtaining a grant is four in respect of the same part of an estate;
- minors and people of unsound mind cannot obtain a grant;
- a person appointed may renounce probate.

(3) Administrators:

- where the deceased died leaving a will but there is no executor able to prove the will, the order of entitlement to the grant is set out in **r20 NCPR 1987**;
- where the deceased died without a valid will, the order of entitlement to the grant is set out in **r22 NCPR 1987**.

(4) An executor *de son tort* is a person who, without authority, acts as if they are the PR of the estate.

(5) An application for a non-contentious grant of probate or common form must be accompanied by:

- the statement of truth or oath;
- the original will (if any);
- the HMRC account, as required.

The following affidavits may be required by the Registrar or District Judge:

- knowledge and approval;
- due execution;
- terms, condition and date of execution.

(6) Revocation of grants: the court has the power, under **s121(1) SCA 1981**, to call in a grant that should not have been made or one that contains an error.

CHAPTER 16

Personal Representatives: Powers and Duties

Aims of the Chapter:

By the end of this chapter, you should be able to:

- distinguish the legal status of executors and administrators;
- list the duties of personal representatives; and
- detail the powers personal representativesunder the relevant legislation.

16.1 Introduction

In this chapter, we will first distinguish the legal status of executors and administrators.

We will then review the legal duties of PRs, which are primarily to:

- collect in the assets of the deceased;
- pay the debts of the deceased;
- distribute the estate to the beneficiaries.

Finally, we will consider the powers which PRs have under the **Administration of Estates Act 1925** (**AEA 1925**), the **Trustee Act 1925** (**TA 1925**) and the **Trustee Act 2000** (**TA 2000**).

16.2 Distinguishing executors and administrators

It is important to distinguish the offices of executor and administrator.

(1) **Executors**

Executors takes their authority from the will, since they are appointed by the will. The effect of the grant of probate is to confirm the executor's authority. Proof of the executor's authority may be required by the court, by those holding assets of the estate or by those purchasing assets from the executors. The only situations in which it is absolutely essential to produce the grant are when it is required by the court and in order to prove title to land. This means that the executors could issue proceedings or exchange contracts for the sale of land prior to the grant, so long as the grant is produced before the action is concluded or the sale is completed. Although, in theory, the executors can carry out all acts in the administration of the estate prior to the issue of the grant, apart from obtaining judgment or completing a sale of land, in practice, most institutions holding substantial assets will insist on seeing the grant before money is released.

The property of the deceased vests in the executors when the deceased dies (**s1(3) AEA 1925**, in relation to real property, and ***Woolley v Clark [1822]*** for personal property). **s1(1)** provides that the deceased's estate shall devolve on the deceased's PRs for the time being, which means that if the PRs change (e.g. on revocation of the original grant), the assets will devolve automatically on the new PRs.

(2) **Administrators**

Administrators derive their authority from the grant, whether or not there was a will, so have no authority to act until the issue of the grant. On the death of the deceased, the estate vests in the Public Trustee (**s9(1) AEA 1925**, as amended by **s14 Law of Property (Miscellaneous Provisions) Act 1994**). It follows that, until the grant is issued, the administrators have power to do only what is necessary to obtain the grant.

Once the grant has been issued, the doctrine of relation back may apply to protect the lawful acts of the administrators. This would permit the administrators to sue for trespass to the deceased's land or to sue for recovery of any of the deceased's assets which have been misappropriated by a third party. This doctrine is limited to action taken to protect the estate. In ***Ingall v Moran [1944]*** the prospective administrator issued proceedings to recover damages under the **Fatal Accidents Acts** in respect of the deceased's death in a motor accident. It was held that the later issue of the grant did not validate the issue of the proceedings because they were not issued for the protection of the estate and so the action was struck out. The action could have been validly commenced under a limited grant taken out prior to the proceedings.

In ***Milburn-Snell and Others v Evans [2011]*** the Court of Appeal upheld this principle by striking out an action started before a grant had been obtained by the daughters of a deceased who claimed as his "administrators" acting on behalf of his estate. Furthermore, because the proceedings were a nullity from the outset, the court refused to allow the pleadings to be amended using a provision in the **Civil Procedure Rules 1998** (**CPR**), which was available only where proceedings had been validly constituted.

16.3 Duties of the personal representatives

The duties of the PRs are set out in **s25 AEA 1925**, as amended by **s9 AEA 1971** and in **TA 2000**. These duties must be performed with due diligence, and **s1 TA 2000** imposes a duty *to exercise such care and skill as is reasonable in the circumstances.*

In general, the duties of a PR are:

- to collect and safeguard the assets;
- to pay the debts of the deceased;
- to distribute the estate to the beneficiaries correctly entitled.

16.3.1 Collection of assets

s25(1) AEA 1925 imposes the duty *to collect and get in the real and personal estate of the deceased and administer it according to law.* The assets must be collected by taking legal action, if need be. This would include suing for recovery of debts owed to the deceased. They must collect the assets as soon as reasonably possible, although secured debts need not be collected immediately if the security is adequate, unless the money is required for payment of debts. This duty relates only to those assets that devolve on the PRs.

How far a beneficiary can insist on a PR litigating on their behalf was considered in ***Re Clough-Taylor, Coutts & Co v Banks [2003]***. The deceased had been an artist.

A friend removed a screen from the deceased's house after her death, claiming that she had given it to him during her lifetime. The first defendant claimed that it had belonged to the deceased at the date of her death and therefore passed to the first defendant under the deceased's will. She also claimed that the executor bank was under a duty, by virtue of **s25 AEA 1925**, to take proceedings to recover the screen. The court held that the executor was entitled not to commence a claim against the deceased's friend given that there was a real risk that it would be unsuccessful, incurring significant costs for the estate. Instead, the executor could assign the screen and the claim itself to the first defendant (the specific beneficiary of the screen). The first defendant would then be able to make the claim but would bear the financial risk of losing.

Power v Bernard Hastie & Co Ltd and others [2022] reinforces the principle that executors are entitled to pursue court actions commenced before the death of the testator. The applicant here was the nephew and executor of the estate of the claimant. He said that he should be substituted as the claimant in the proceedings for damages due to an asbestos related illness in the place of his deceased uncle, so as to be able to pursue an application under a provisional damages order (PDO) made in those proceedings. The defendants asserted that the right to pursue such an application did not survive the claimant's death. The court held, among other things, that a beneficiary's right to apply for further damages under a PDO passed on death to their estate, and could be pursued by their executor. Therefore, the applicant was substituted as the claimant and enabled to pursue an application for further damages under the PDO.

s1(1) AEA 1925 provides that land owned by the deceased will devolve on his PRs unless the deceased's interest came to an end on their death; this is also generally true of assets other than land. Applying this rule means that certain property in which the deceased had an interest or connection at their death will not devolve on the PRs. If property does not devolve on them, they do not have any duty to collect it because it will not pass under the terms of the deceased's will or intestacy.

Property that does **not** devolve on the PRs includes the following.

(1) Property held by the deceased as a beneficial joint tenant – provided that there has been no severance, the property will pass to the survivor under the right of survivorship. If the property is held as tenants in common in equity, then, on the death of the deceased, the deceased's severable share passes to the PRs.

(2) Property held or enjoyed by the deceased under a life tenancy – where the deceased was a life tenant, the property will devolve according to the terms of the trust instrument and not to the deceased's PRs.

(3) Property which is the subject matter of a *donatio mortis causa* – this is held on trust by the donee until the donor dies.

(4) Money arising under insurance policies on the life of the deceased but written in favour of others, either by means of the implied trust under **s11 Married**

Women's Property Act 1882 or by means of an express trust, which passes to the beneficiary named without the need for a grant of representation.

(5) Lump sum payments under the deceased's pension scheme (the death in service benefit) – such schemes are generally discretionary and the pension money is paid directly to those nominated by the deceased.

(6) Foreign property.

Note that, by the **Law Reform (Miscellaneous Provisions) Act 1934** (**LR(MP)A 1934**), all causes of action vested in the deceased at their death survive for the benefit of their estate. Exemplary damages (damages awarded as a punishment for particularly bad conduct) will not be awarded to the estate, however, and, if the action relates to the cause of the death, damages are calculated without reference to any gain or loss to the estate caused by death except that a reasonable sum is allowed for funeral expenses. Actions in contract and tort survive, apart from an action for defamation and a contract for personal services (such as a jockey's contract of employment which ended on the death of the racehorse owner who employed him, as in ***Graves v Cohen [1930]***). In addition, the PRs may bring an action under the **Fatal Accidents Act 1976** on behalf of the dependants of the deceased, where the death of the deceased was caused by an event in respect of which the deceased could have sued if they had lived. Any damages recovered under such a claim belong to the dependants and do not form part of the estate.

Note that the danger here is that if the PRs are seen to have delayed, they can be made personally liable for failing to collect if loss is suffered by the estate. In ***Caney v Bond [1843]*** the testator had lent £500 to a friend on a promissory note. After the death of the testator, the PR did not call in the loan immediately, believing the friend to be good for the money. £100 was paid voluntarily by the debtor and he would have paid the balance if he had been asked to do so. Two years elapsed and the debtor died insolvent. The executor was held to be personally liable for the loss. He should have acted earlier by calling in the whole of the outstanding debt.

If the security is inadequate, then the PRs will have to consider a favourable time for realisation. Provided that they act honestly and prudently, they will not be personally liable for loss.

In ***Re Chapman [1896]*** the estate consisted of several mortgages on agricultural land. Owing to a depression, the value of the land fell and, at death, the value was insufficient to cover the mortgages. The executors were held not liable for loss after their decision to wait for a more favourable time for realisation.

Under **s15 TA 1925**, PRs have wide powers to compound liabilities or compromise claims. These include powers to:

- accept any property, real or personal, before the time at which it is transferable or payable;

- pay or allow any debt or claim on any evidence that they think sufficient;
- accept any composition (agreement with a debtor) or security (item of value handed over pending payment of a debt), real or personal, for any property, real or personal, claimed;
- allow time for payment of any debt;
- compromise, compound, abandon, submit to arbitration, or otherwise settle any debt, account, claim, or thing whatever relating to the estate.

The exercise of the discretion under **s15** must be active. A PR who has failed to collect a debt owing to negligence or carelessness cannot rely upon **s15** for protection from liability.

Once the PRs have collected in the assets, they owe a duty to take reasonable care to preserve them. This means that they should consider exercising their power to insure (see **16.4.4**).

16.3.2 Payment of debts

It is the responsibility of the PRs to pay the funeral expenses, testamentary and administration expenses, and debts and liabilities incurred by the deceased in their lifetime.

The PRs must be aware of which assets are available to them for the payment of debts. These are defined in **s32(1) AEA 1925** and include:

- property in which the deceased had a beneficial interest;
- property subject to a general power of appointment exercisable by will;
- income and assets arising after death.

Property not available to PRs for the payment of debts includes:

- property in respect of which the deceased was a beneficial joint tenant;
- property not passing into the hands of the PRs, for example, where the property has perished or has been stolen and no blame can attach to the PRs;
- trust property, such as a life policy in favour of a named beneficiary;
- foreign property.

The liabilities must arise out of the obligations entered into by the deceased and not as a result of obligations incurred by the PRs (***Homer's Devisees Case [1852]***).

Inheritance tax due on the free estate must be paid to HM Revenue & Customs before applying for the grant unless the instalment option applies. This creates a short-term cashflow problem since, until the grant is obtained, balances on bank accounts or investments in the name of the deceased cannot be transferred to the estate account operated by the PRs. The PRs can be held personally liable for the inheritance tax due (***IRC v Stannard [1984]***). In practice, a bank or building society where the deceased held an account may be prepared (subject to the account balance being sufficient and against an indemnity from the PRs) to make funds available to pay the inheritance tax.

The debts must be paid promptly (***Re Tankard [1942]***). Uthwatt J said: *"It is the duty of the personal representatives to pay the debts with due diligence having regard to the assets in their hands. They should have special regard to the debts which carry interest and can be personally liable for an unnecessary order for costs made against the estate."*

This means that the PRs should give priority to the payment of debts that carry interest so as to minimise the loss to the estate and should not unnecessarily defend actions for debt brought against the estate. Actions in contract and tort survive by and against the estate (**LR(MP)A 1934** – see **16.3.1**). The PRs would be liable if they paid debts that were unenforceable (e.g. a claim under a contract for land which was unenforceable for not being in writing) or a claim that was statute-barred. The limitation period for actions in contract or tort is six years, and 12 years in relation to land and covenants.

There is no rule that the debts should be paid within the executor's year (one year from death). "Due diligence" means that they should be paid as soon as assets are available to pay them and the full extent of the liabilities has been ascertained. After the end of the executor's year, the PRs may still be justified in not making payment (perhaps because no assets are yet available), but in this case the onus is on the PRs to justify the delay.

16.3.2.1 The ascertainment of debts

The PRs must ensure that they have taken all reasonable steps to ascertain the debts payable. Failure to do so can render them personally liable. In order to gain protection from the claims of creditors or beneficiaries of whom they may not be aware, the PRs must advertise in the manner laid down by **s27 TA 1925**, which requires:

- advertisement in the *Gazette* (see https://www.thegazette.co.uk/wills-and-probate/content/299);
- advertisement in a newspaper in the area where any land that belonged to the deceased is situated; and
- such other advertisements as the court would have directed in an administration action. If, for example, the deceased carried on a business, it would be usual to advertise in a newspaper circulating in the area where the business was situated.

A time limit of not less than two months must be stated in the notice for claims to be made. Only when the time limit specified in the advertisement has expired can the PRs distribute the estate without being personally liable for claims of which they are unaware. The PRs must also make the searches that a purchaser of land would have made. Even then, a disappointed creditor or beneficiary can recover assets by tracing them into the hands of the beneficiary who wrongfully received them (**s27(2)**).

s27 also protects the PRs against claims by unknown beneficiaries, but not where a beneficiary is known about but cannot be found (see **16.3.3.1**).

s27 TA 1925 was discussed in ***Aon Pension Trustees v MCP Pension Trustees [2010]***, which concerned the extent to which trustees of a pension scheme that was being wound up were protected by **s27** advertisements. Here, the trustees had forgotten the existence of 32 members of the scheme. The Court of Appeal held that the trustees were not protected by the **s27** advertisements, even though none of the members concerned responded to them. The trustees were treated as having had notice of the members' existence, so **s27** offered no protection.

16.3.3 Distribution of the estate

s44 AEA 1925 provides that the PRs do not have a duty to distribute before the end of the executor's year (12 months from the date of death). This means that any direction to make earlier payment contained in the will (e.g. to pay a legacy "as soon as convenient after the date of my death") may be ignored by the PRs. Indeed, it may be most unwise to rush into making payment in case the estate turns out to be insolvent. The effect of such a direction is only to make interest on the legacy payable from the time that the will directed payment.

16.3.3.1 The ascertainment of beneficiaries

The PRs must correctly identify and find those entitled to benefit as well as ascertaining the extent of their entitlement. If the existence of a beneficiary was unknown to the PRs, such as in the case of unknown illegitimate relatives, the PRs will be protected if they advertise and search under **s27 TA 1925**. Distribution may be delayed because the PRs cannot be sure who is entitled. For example, it may be that they know of the existence of a beneficiary whom they cannot find. In such circumstances, since they are aware of the beneficiary, **s27** will not protect them but they may apply to the court for a ***Benjamin*** order for protection.

In ***Re Benjamin [1902]*** the testator left a residuary gift to X, who disappeared nine months before the testator died. Despite advertisements, X did not come forward to claim his share. The court permitted the distribution of the estate on the footing that the beneficiary had predeceased the testator. The principle in ***Re Benjamin*** can be extended to the ascertainment of creditors as well as beneficiaries.

The court may include other terms, such as ordering distribution where a child has predeceased the testator, on the basis that the child did not leave issue who survived the testator (thereby excluding the operation of **s33 Wills Act 1837** (**WA 1837**)).

In ***Re Gess [1942]*** the administrators of a Polish national who died domiciled in England were unable to advertise for Polish claimants because Poland was occupied by the Germans during World War II. They knew of some debts and applied to distribute the remainder of the estate. The court allowed distribution subject to a contingency fund to meet known Polish liabilities without the requirement of further advertisements.

The court will direct what, if any, enquiries are to be made by the PRs, which usually involves placing **s27** advertisements in case the beneficiary should respond. Once these have been completed to the satisfaction of the court, the court will direct the estate to be distributed on the footing set out in the order. This may be, for example, that the beneficiary predeceased the deceased without leaving issue.

The PRs are then authorised to distribute the estate to the existing beneficiaries and are protected from liability for doing so. If the missing beneficiary later appears, they may recover their share from any overpaid beneficiary.

The PRs have two alternatives to obtaining a ***Benjamin*** order.

(1) They may take out an insurance policy against the possibility of the missing beneficiary appearing, the premium being paid from the estate. This policy would indemnify them against liability if they were to be sued by the missing beneficiary. This is likely to be the cheapest option.

(2) They may take an indemnity from the beneficiaries who may be being overpaid, so that they will reimburse the PRs if the missing beneficiary appears. However, there is the risk that the indemnity may be difficult to enforce. An indemnity signed by a child beneficiary will not be valid.

In ***Evans v Westcombe [1999]*** the court recommended that PRs, particularly of small estates, should not be discouraged from obtaining missing beneficiary insurance cover. Such indemnity insurance offers a fund to meet the claim of a missing beneficiary in exoneration of the PRs or the beneficiary who has been overpaid.

An insurance policy can be more effective than a ***Benjamin*** order, and in a small estate the insurance premium can be less than the costs incurred in the ***Benjamin*** order procedure. If a ***Benjamin*** order is not sought, taking insurance cover can avoid sums of money being tied up indefinitely to await the claim of a long-lost beneficiary.

NB s27 TA 1925 affords no protection against claims under the **Inheritance (Provision for Family and Dependants) Act 1975** (**I(PFD)A 1975**).

The **Presumption of Death Act 2013** (**PDA 2013**) sets out a court-based procedure that enables those left behind when someone goes missing to obtain a declaration from the High Court that the missing person is deemed to have died. The High Court can make that decision if satisfied that the missing person has died or is not known to have been alive for a period of at least seven years. The court can also say when the person is deemed to have died, which could be extremely important in determining rights to property interests. The procedures for an application under **PDA 2013** are set out in **CPR PD 57B**.

In ***Greathead v Greathead [2017]*** the High Court identified factors supporting its determination that a missing person could be presumed to have died on the day they disappeared, including:

- they were suffering from a clinical mental illness;
- they were not able to look after themselves properly;
- they were in a very low mood having previously suffered suicidal ideation (thoughts);
- they may not have been taking any necessary medication;
- they disappeared without warm clothes, access to money, a passport, or mobile phone;
- they had nowhere else to go (so far as known);
- there were severe frosts and heavy snow shortly after they disappeared;
- they had a sore knee and limp, meaning they could not have travelled far on foot;
- their money remained untouched since their disappearance;
- they had not been seen or heard of since 2005, despite extensive searches.

When such a declaration has been made, a copy will appear in a new register of presumed deaths, which will be linked to the register of actual deaths. This certificate will be conclusive as to the presumed death, and is effective for all purposes and against all persons. Therefore, PRs trying to find a missing beneficiary could, in appropriate cases, rely on a declaration of presumed death obtained by a third party in other proceedings, rather than seeking further protection through a ***Benjamin*** order or indemnity insurance. Such a declaration would also, presumably, allow a death to be sworn by those seeking to obtain a grant of representation.

In ***Re Fisher [2023]*** the executor was a friend of the deceased and therefore did not come within the category of person that would require the court to automatically hear her application for a declaration of presumption of death under the

Presumption of Death Act 2013 (**PDA 2013**). The High Court however held that an executor had sufficient interest to apply, even though the will had not yet been proved. **PDA 2013** does not define the term "sufficient interest" and there was no previous authority on the point. The court therefore had to determine whether the claimant, as a person who intended to prove a will, had "sufficient interest" in the determination of the application for the purposes of **s1(5)(b) PDA 2013**.

The court noted that an executor owed fiduciary duties to the creditors and beneficiaries of the estate and did not act out of pure self-interest. Therefore, in considering the executor's position, the court was also considering the position of the beneficiaries of the estate. It also noted that an applicant for a presumption of death declaration could not obtain any rights in relation to the missing person's estate merely by obtaining the declaration, as there still needed to be a successful probate application, in which the will could be challenged if appropriate. There was therefore no risk to the estate in allowing the application to be made. The declaration would also be useful even if it turned out that the will was not valid, as it would still be necessary to show that the missing person was presumed to be dead.

16.4 The powers of the personal representatives

The PRs have a number of powers when administering the estate, some of which are commonly amended by the will, particularly when the estate contains continuing trusts (whether a life interest or a trust for infant children). A number of these powers will be familiar to those who have studied trusts; others relate particularly to PRs.

The powers of trustees apply also to PRs, whether or not they are also trustees, because "trustee" in **s35(1) TA 2000** is defined to include a PR.

AEA 1925 powers:

Alienation of property	**s39** – PRs have powers to sell, mortgage or charge personal property; for land, the functions of trustees are given to PRs by **Part 1 Trusts of Land and Appointment of Trustees Act 1996** (**TLATA 1996**).
Appropriation	**s41** – PRs may appropriate any part of the estate in or towards satisfaction of any gift, provided that no specific beneficiary is prejudiced; note the trust law rule against self-dealing (***Kane v Radley-Kane and Others [1998]***).
Appointment of trustees of infant's property	**s42** – PRs may appoint a trust corporation or two to four persons as trustees of the infant's property (but only if the infant is absolutely and not contingently entitled).

Postponement of distribution	**s44** – PRs are not bound to distribute the estate before the end of the executor's year, so beneficiaries cannot insist on earlier payment.

TA 1925 powers:

Maintenance	**s31** (as amended by **s8 Inheritance and Trustees' Powers Act 2014 (ITPA 2014)**) – where property is held for an infant beneficiary (vested or contingent) and the gift carries the right to the intermediate income, the PRs may apply the **income** for the **maintenance, education or benefit** of the infant and must accumulate the income not so applied.
Advancement	**s32** (as amended by **s9 ITPA 2014**) – PRs have a discretion to apply up to the **whole** of the **capital** for the **advancement or benefit** of a beneficiary (whether or not an infant) who has a vested or contingent interest in the capital.

TA 2000 powers:

Investment	**s3** – gives authority for PRs to make any kind of investment that could be made if they were absolutely entitled to the property.
Delegation	**ss11–23** – provide for the delegation of certain powers to an agent (e.g. solicitor, banker, stockbroker, etc.), at such remuneration as the PRs think fit.
Insurance	**s34** – gives the same power to insure as that of a beneficial owner.
Duty of care	**s1** – imposes a duty *to exercise such care and skill as is reasonable in the circumstances.*

16.4.1 General powers of administration

s39 AEA 1925, as amended by **TLATA 1996**, provides that the PRs will have all the powers of trustees of land when administering land or the proceeds of sale of land in the estate. **s6 TLATA 1996** gives trustees of land all the powers of an absolute owner, including the power to purchase land as an income- producing investment, as a residence for a beneficiary or for any other reason. They must, however, consider the interests of all the beneficiaries before so doing. Further, they have power under **s6** to convey land to adult beneficiaries who are absolutely entitled (as a group, if more than one) with or without their consent, and power under **s7** to partition land among beneficiaries entitled as joint tenants or tenants in common. These powers may be amended or excluded by the will or be made subject to obtaining the consent of any person.

A consent provision is most important when making a property available for residence by a beneficiary. Prior to **TLATA 1996**, it was customary to include a power to purchase a home for a beneficiary, but now it is less important because of the extended powers in **s6**. It is still wise to include such a power because, otherwise, the PRs could not purchase land using personalty in the estate which did not represent the proceeds of sale of land.

TA 2000 confirms and extends this power to allow PRs to purchase land anywhere in the UK (although not abroad).

s39 AEA 1925 gives the PRs power to sell, mortgage or lease any property in the estate.

An important point to note is that, by virtue of **s5 TLATA 1996**, if the will imposes a trust for sale of land, a power to postpone sale is always implied and it is no longer permissible to direct that assets shall be sold "as soon as possible after my death". The PRs will always have power to postpone sale.

16.4.2 Investment

Under **s3 TA 2000**, trustees are empowered to undertake a wider range of investments than was previously authorised. Trustees can invest in investments that they might choose if they were absolutely entitled to the assets. In making investments, trustees must have regard to the duty of care imposed by **s1** – trustees must exercise *such care and skill as is reasonable in all the circumstances*. They must also take account of the standard investment criteria set out in **s4**, which directs the PRs to consider the suitability and diversification of the investments. **s5** requires that trustees take appropriate advice before exercising their powers of investment unless they reasonably conclude that it is unnecessary.

In respect of land, **s8** gives PRs the power to buy freehold or leasehold land in the UK either as an investment or for occupation by a beneficiary. This duty can be restricted by a provision in the testator's will.

The duties of professional solicitor trustees in managing investments on behalf of a trust were considered in ***Daniel and Another v Tee and Others [2016]***. Here, the solicitors relied on the advice of independent financial advisers and invested heavily in technology/IT shares prior to their collapse in value in 2000/2001. Although the court held that the claimants had breached their duty of care by not adopting a realistic investment strategy and investing in a wider range of investments, it was not possible to show that the losses incurred had been caused by the breach of duty. The importance of periodic reviews of investment decisions was emphasised, as well as recording the results of those discussions.

16.4.3 Appropriation

s41 AEA 1925 gives the PRs power to appropriate any asset of the estate in full or part satisfaction of a legacy, provided this does not prejudice a specific legacy.

The asset is valued at the date of appropriation, but if its value exceeds the legacy, the power is not available (***Re Phelps [1980]***), although the asset may be transferred for full value; it is treated as a sale. The PRs must employ a qualified valuer where necessary. The power of appropriation saves the PR the trouble and expense of realising assets if they do not wish to do so and the beneficiary agrees to accept the assets in lieu of a cash legacy left to them.

Obviously, the PR does not have power to appropriate an asset that is already bequeathed specifically to another beneficiary. Apart from this restriction, the power may be exercised to satisfy a settled legacy (a legacy where the gift is not absolute, e.g. a gift to X for life, remainder to Y), including one which is contingent or deferred.

The PRs must obtain the consent of the beneficiary in whose favour the appropriation is to be made. If the beneficiary is an infant or is mentally incapable, the consent and receipt of their parent, guardian or receiver are needed. If the legacy is held on trust, the consent of the trustee or the person entitled to income is needed. When exercising the power, the PRs must take into account the interests of all the beneficiaries, including those whose consent is not required, and unborn beneficiaries (**s41(5)**). The practice when drafting a will is to exclude the need to obtain the consent of the beneficiary.

16.4.4 Insurance

Previously, the power to insure assets was given by **s19 TA 1925**. The type and level of insurance was limited to fire cover for up to two-thirds of the market value of the property. **s34 TA 2000** amended **s19 TA 1925**. Trustees now have the same authority to insure as would a beneficial owner. The limits as to the type and level of cover have been removed.

16.4.5 Appointment of trustees of an infant's legacy

s42 AEA 1925 allows the PRs to appoint two trustees or a trust corporation to receive a legacy on behalf of an infant who is absolutely entitled. Otherwise, the PRs must continue to hold the legacy until the infant reaches the age of 18 and can give a valid receipt. If a will includes legacies to infants, a substantial legacy should be dealt with in the will by setting up a trust; a modest legacy is dealt with by providing that the receipt of the parent or guardian will be a valid discharge to the PRs.

16.4.6 Maintenance

Where the estate includes trusts for minor beneficiaries, **s31 TA 1925** (as amended by **s8 ITPA 2014**) gives power to the PRs to make payments from the income of the estate to the parent or guardian, or to apply the income or any part of it for the maintenance, education or benefit of the minor. For the power to apply, there must be no prior life interest. Even if the life tenant is willing to consent to a payment of income, trustees have no power to do so under **s31**.

To the extent that the PRs do not distribute the income for the benefit of the child, it must be accumulated. Accumulated income is available for maintenance in later years. **s31(2)** provides that an adult or a married minor beneficiary who has a contingent gift is entitled to income, including the accumulations. It should be noted that the power in **s31** applies only if the gift carries interest or income (see **12.2**).

NB Before **ITPA 2014** came into force in October 2014, the previous version of **s31** had contained a number of restrictions and limitations on the trustees' power to maintain. These limitations were commonly removed in professionally drafted wills to give the trustees more flexibility. Wills containing such clauses will be encountered for some years to come.

16.4.7 Advancement

Under **s32 TA 1925** (as amended by **s9 ITPA 2014**), PRs may advance up to the **whole** of a beneficiary's vested or presumptive entitlement to them or for their benefit. The consent of anyone with a prior interest is required, and the beneficiary must bring the advancement into account when the estate is distributed (so that the amount they receive in the end is reduced by the amount they have received already). The advance must be for the benefit of the beneficiary and could take the form of a further trust for their benefit. The trustees are able to advance cash and/or other assets to beneficiaries the value of which are to be brought into account as part of the beneficiary's share if and when he or she becomes absolutely entitled. Note also that a wide definition of "benefit and advancement" was given by the House of Lords in ***Pilkington v IRC [1962]***. If the beneficiary who is given the advance dies, there is no duty to refund the advance.

Before **ITPA 2014** came into force, the previous version of **s32** limited the trustees to advancing up to **one-half** of the beneficiary's share. Professionally drafted wills commonly removed this restriction so that the trustees could advance up to the whole value of the beneficiary's share.

Professionally drafted wills will usually provide that the receipt of the parent or guardian of the beneficiary, or even the beneficiary if aged 16 or over, will be a good receipt for the PRs.

16.4.8 Power to carry on a business

This is important where the deceased was a sole trader because there is otherwise no mechanism for continuing the business after their death. If they carried on a business in partnership, the partners can continue the business and, if the business was incorporated (even if a one-man company), the company will continue to exist and the business can be conducted through the medium of the company.

If the will is silent, the PRs have power to continue the business with a view to sale as a going concern (***Re Crowther [1895]***). The sale should take place during the executor's year. There is no implied power to retain the business other than with a view to sale. If the business was given to the trustees in the form of a trust of land, whether express or implied on intestacy, a power to postpone sale is implied, which may be used to postpone sale indefinitely, provided that this is in the interests of the beneficiaries (***Re Chancellor [1884]***).

The will should express the testator's intentions as to who is to inherit the business and to what extent the PRs have power to continue it. Even if the will includes a trust of land, there will always be an implied power to postpone. It is also advisable to appoint special PRs to deal with the business – the general PRs may not be competent or willing to do so.

When running the business, the PRs are authorised to use only those assets that were used in the business at the date of the deceased's death (***Cutbush v Cutbush [1839]***). This may present cashflow problems for the business, because the PRs may not use assets from the rest of the estate; therefore, the will should authorise the PRs to use assets from the rest of the estate for the business (although, in practice, they should exercise caution in so doing and bear in mind the risk of suffering losses).

The PRs are personally liable on all contracts they enter into while running the business. They can reimburse themselves from the estate in two situations:

- if the business was being continued with a view to sale (in which case the right to indemnity takes priority over the creditors of the estate and the beneficiaries); and
- if the will authorised the continuance of the business for the benefit of the beneficiaries and not with a view to sale, in which case the creditors of the estate take priority.

If the will did not authorise the continuance of the business and the PRs do continue it (not merely with a view to sale), each business creditor has a choice. If they authorise the continuance of the business by the PRs (mere knowledge or acquiescence is not enough), the PRs' right to reimbursement takes priority over any claim by that creditor, even if the PRs had no authority to continue the business (***Re Oxley [1914]***).

Any profits made by the business will go for the benefit of the creditor. A creditor who did not agree to the continuance of the business may treat the continuance as improper, in which case the creditor is entitled to payment out of the assets used in the business at the deceased's death, and that the creditor's right of indemnity takes priority over the PRs' right to reimbursement. Any profit made by the business will, in this situation, accrue for the benefit of the estate (***Dowse v Gorton [1891]***).

It should be remembered that all business liabilities owed at the date of death will be liabilities of the estate and may be satisfied out of any part of the deceased's assets.

Where a PR is entitled to indemnity from the estate under the above rules, the creditor may, instead of proceeding against the PR under their contractual obligation, proceed by subrogation against the assets of the estate. This is particularly useful where the PR is insolvent.

16.4.9 Remuneration

Professionally drafted wills normally include a clause permitting professional trustees, including lawyers, to charge for their professional services. Until **TA 2000** came into force there were two key problems which made the inclusion of such a clause particularly important.

Express trustee charging clauses were construed restrictively by the courts. First, in the absence of express words, no payment could be charged by a trustee for work that could have been done by a lay trustee. This construction has now (subject to any inconsistent provision in the trust instrument) been removed by **s28(2) TA 2000**, which permits trustees to charge for work that could have been done by a lay person.

A second construction was that the charging clause was treated as a testamentary gift to the trustee; a trustee who also signed the will as a witness to the testator's signature would, by virtue of **s15 WA 1837**, lose their gift, that is, their payment. **s28(4) TA 2000** removes this construction so that a payment clause is no longer treated as a gift to the trustee but is now a debt on the estate.

s31 TA 2000 provides that PRs are entitled to reimbursement for all expenses that they properly incur.

s29 TA 2000 would appear, on the face of it, to remove the need for professionally drafted wills to include a charging clause. **s29** provides that, in the absence of a charging clause, a professional trustee may claim reasonable payment provided that the other trustees agree in writing. In practice, however, will-writers continue to include charging clauses which provide that the professional trustees do not have to obtain the written consent of the other trustees. It is also desirable that the beneficiaries and lay trustees are very clear, from the content of the will, that the professional trustee can charge for their services.

Where no charging clause has been included, the court does have an inherent jurisdiction to award payment to a trustee who has done work over and above what was contemplated. The court has this power even if there is a trustee charging clause that is inadequate for meeting the costs of services rendered. Remuneration can therefore be awarded in addition to that claimable under the trust instrument (***Re Duke of Norfolk Settlement Trust [1982]***).

16.4.10 Delegation

Under **ss11–20 TA 2000**, trustees may delegate certain specific powers. Trustees may agree such remuneration for the appointed agent as they think fit. The terms of appointment of the agent must not allow for a substitute to do the work. Further, the liability of the agent of the trustees must not be restricted and the appointment must not give rise to any conflict of interest. A policy statement should be included in any agreement appointing an agent – this is a statement giving guidance as to how the agent ought to exercise their tasks. When delegating, trustees have to comply with the statutory duty of care in **s1**. Note that, under **s23**, trustees are absolved of liability for the acts of the agent provided that they appointed the agent pursuant to the statutory duty of care and fulfilled their review and intervention obligations.

Reflective Questions

The powers and discretion of trustees have been extended considerably in recent years. Looking at the changes to particular powers, do you think that too much discretion has been given to the trustees? Are there additional risks for beneficiaries? How significant do you think the simplification of the rules is in terms of reduced legal costs?

16.5 Summary

(1) Executors gain authority from the will. The grant of probate merely confirms the executors' authority. The property of the deceased vests in the executors when the testator dies.

(2) Administrators gain authority from the grant so there is no authority to act until the issue of a grant. On the death of the deceased, the property vests in the Public Trustee so, until a grant is issued, the administrators have the power to do only what is necessary to obtain the grant.

(3) The duties of the PRs are:

- to collect and safeguard the deceased's assets;
- to pay the debts of the deceased;
- to distribute the estate to the beneficiaries correctly entitled.

(4) The powers of the PRs are found in **AEA 1925**, **TA 1925** and **TA 2000**. Additional or modified powers may be given by the will.

AEA 1925:

- **s39**: PRs have power to sell, mortgage or charge personal property. In respect of real property, they have all the powers of trustees under **TLATA 1996**;
- **s41**: PRs have the power to appropriate assets of the estate in full or partial settlement of any legacies (unless the asset is the subject of a specific legacy);
- **s42**: PRs may appoint trustees where there is an infant beneficiary;
- **s44**: PRs are not bound to distribute the estate until one year after the deceased's death.

TA 1925:

- **s31**: If property is held for an infant beneficiary and there is accrued income, the PRs may apply the income for the maintenance, education and benefit of the infant;
- **s32**: PRs have the discretion to apply up to the whole of the capital for the advancement or benefit of a beneficiary (adult or child) who has a vested or contingent interest in the capital.

TA 2000:

- **s1**: imposes a duty to exercise such care and skill as is reasonable in the circumstances;
- **s3**: gives authority for the PRs to make any kind of investment;

- **s5**: requires PRs to take advice before making investment decisions unless it is reasonable not to do so;
- **s8**: gives power to purchase land as an investment, for a beneficiary to live in or for any other reason;
- **ss11** and **12**: provide for delegation of certain powers to an agent, for example, a solicitor;
- **s28**: removes the restrictive interpretations of trustee payment clauses;
- **s29**: permits professional trustees to be paid if no payment clause exists, the trustee is a professional trustee and the other trustees agree in writing to the payment;
- **s34**: gives the power to insure.

CHAPTER 17

The Administration of the Estate

Aims of the Chapter:

By the end of this chapter, you should be able to:

- identify the assets a personal representative should sell;
- explain the rules for payment of debts, distinguishing between solvent and insolvent estates; and
- explain how legacies are paid and the remaining assets are distributed.

17.1 Introduction

Chapter 16 discussed the duty of the PRs to collect in all the assets of the estate which vest in them and to take proper steps to preserve them. Having obtained the grant, the PRs will need to register it with the holders of assets in the estate, which will enable sufficient assets to be released to them and, if necessary, sold, to realise enough cash to pay the debts (including administration expenses and any loan taken out to pay inheritance tax) and pecuniary legacies. The net proceeds and any unrealised assets can then be distributed under the terms of the will or intestacy.

In this chapter, we will consider what the PRs will need to take into account in deciding which assets to sell. We will then review problems which occur concerning the payment of debts in relation to a solvent and an insolvent estate. In particular, we will look at the statutory order in which such debts may be paid, as well as the relevant case law. We will consider the difficult case law relating to the payment of legacies. Finally we will look at the law which relates to the distribution of the assets, including practical steps which can be taken to deal with missing and bankrupt beneficiaries, assents (formal transfers to beneficiaries) of personalty (non-land possessions) and land, and identifying the end of the administration period after which PRs will normally become trustees if they have not already distributed all the estate.

17.2 What assets should the personal representatives sell?

While PRs generally have a free choice in deciding which assets in the estate they should sell to raise cash for the discharge of debts and payment of legacies, there are a number of considerations that they should bear in mind.

(1) The terms of the will or intestacy – in particular, they should not sell an asset which is the subject of a specific gift to a beneficiary unless it becomes apparent that there are no other assets available and so the specific item must be sold (see the rules on payment of debts in a solvent estate at **17.4**).

(2) The wishes of the beneficiaries – usually, PRs are under no obligation to consult beneficiaries about the administration of the estate, so it is the PRs alone who can decide, for example, which residuary assets should be sold if necessary. However, there is little point in PRs selling, say, a holding of shares in XYZ plc if one of the residuary beneficiaries would like to take those shares in satisfaction of their entitlement (under the power of appropriation (see **16.4.3**)) and there are other shareholdings which could be sold instead.

(3) The taxation consequences of the disposal – there may be inheritance tax or capital gains tax implications in deciding which assets to sell. For example, if land or certain qualifying investments have gone down in value since the date of death within a certain period, any loss made on a sale of that asset by PRs might enable some inheritance tax to be repaid back to the estate.

(4) In some cases, the PRs may have little choice – for example, if the property is subject to an option where the person having the benefit of the option can exercise their right to buy regardless of whether the PRs wish to sell. An existing

right of pre-emption has a similar consequence in that the PRs may have to sell to a particular individual (rather than on the open market), either as a result of the death itself or if the PRs decide to sell the asset. Options and pre-emption rights are often found when the deceased was a shareholder in a private family company so that the deceased's shares can be acquired by other members of the family who also hold shares in the company.

Once the PRs are in a position to pay the liabilities, they must consider the rules on the payment of debts.

17.3 Problems with payment of debts

The underlying law governing payment of debts can seem a little illogical. You might think this would generate an abundance of case law, but there is, in fact, very little, and most of what exists is relatively old. The reason is that, in practice, there is often little need to resort to the legal rules, either because they may not be relevant on the facts, or their application has been avoided by a suitably drafted will that provides clear guidance for the PRs.

The key to understanding the rules for payment of debts lies in understanding why the rules exist at all. So, one of the ways of getting to grips with the topic is to appreciate the problems which the rules are there to solve.

First, the rules are different depending on whether the estate is **solvent** or **insolvent**. Also, there are different rules for debts which are **secured** on property (e.g. a mortgage), as opposed to **unsecured** debts (e.g. council tax or the electricity bill).

17.3.1 When is an estate insolvent?

An estate is **insolvent** if the assets of the estate are insufficient to pay all the debts and liabilities (including reasonable funeral, testamentary and administration expenses) (**s421 Insolvency Act 1986** (**IA 1986**)).

In effect, it is as though the deceased was in a position to be made bankrupt at the time of death.

If the estate is insolvent, there are two implications.

(1) There will not be enough to pay all creditors in full, and so some creditors may not get all that is due to them, receiving just a proportion of their debt. The issue here is that some debts are paid in priority to others as determined by **IA 1986** and the **Administration of Insolvent Estates of Deceased Persons Order 1986** (**AIEDPO 1986**).

(2) There will be nothing for beneficiaries. In other words, whatever the will says about legacies becomes irrelevant, as would the intestacy rules if the deceased died intestate.

17.3.2 When is a debt secured or unsecured?

The issue of secured debts arises when a person dies owing debts which are secured against their property. This is achieved by the borrower mortgaging or charging property, usually their house or other land (but it could be shares, a business interest, a life assurance policy, etc.) in favour of the lender. Many non- lawyers mistakenly believe that taking a loan from a bank or building society, say, which is secured, is somehow safer and better than a personal loan, which is unsecured.

In fact, the only person who is secure is the lender. Part of the lender's security lies in the fact that it has a privileged position in the event of the debtor dying before the loan has been paid off. The lender's right to enforce the loan by selling the borrower's property is preserved on the borrower's death. Consequently, the lender can recover the debt from the asset on which it is secured, regardless of other debtors and the beneficiaries, and also regardless of whether the estate is solvent or insolvent. See **17.4.1** as regards secured debts in a solvent estate and **17.5.1** in one that is insolvent.

17.4 The solvent estate

An estate is solvent if the assets of the estate are sufficient to pay all the debts and liabilities (including reasonable funeral, testamentary and administration expenses). There may or may not be additional assets to pay any legacies.

Consider a situation where Toby leaves a will and his whole estate is given equally to his three sisters or, alternatively, he dies intestate and his three sisters are entitled to the whole estate under the intestacy rules. In either situation, none of his three sisters can lay claim to any particular asset or part of his estate, so the PRs can use any asset or part of the estate to raise cash to pay the bills. The three sisters will wait until the debts are paid and then the PRs will distribute any remaining assets, or proceeds, to them equally.

However, now consider a different will made by Joan:

- Clause 1 says "I give £30,000 to A";
- Clause 2 says "I give £10,000 to B";
- Clause 3 says "I give my house, Redacre, to C";
- Clause 4 says "I give residue to R".

Joan's assets total £280,000, including Redacre worth £200,000.

Her debts total £100,000, including a mortgage of £40,000 secured on Redacre.

It is clear that the estate is solvent and there is enough value in Joan's assets to pay the debts, but how will payment affect the entitlements of the beneficiaries? The point is that A, B, C, and R all have different interests under Joan's will, and the way in which the debts are paid might mean that some of them may not get everything the will promises.

For example, the sum total of the pecuniary legacies and Redacre is £240,000 and if the PRs were to set aside assets to allow these gifts to take effect, that leaves only £40,000 of remaining assets to pay £100,000 of debts. So, where is the balance of £60,000 to come from?

Since creditors must be paid before the beneficiaries, it is obvious that the PRs must resort to the assets earmarked for A, B and C and so it is apparent that some, if not all, of these entitlements cannot take effect as the will intended. The PRs must consider the appropriate rules to determine where the burden (incidence) of the debts should fall among A, B and C and what, if anything, they will take under Joan's will. For example, do they share the burden of the outstanding debts equally or in some other way? Does the fact that the mortgage debt is secured make any difference and, if so, who might be affected?

One thing you should already have noted from this example is that there will be no residue passing to R. There will clearly be nothing left once creditors have been paid and the reduced entitlements of A, B and C have been satisfied.

The way in which PRs should approach such a problem is:

- first consider the position regarding any secured debts charged on property during Joan's lifetime (in this case, the mortgage); then
- look at the incidence of the unsecured debts.

After considering the relevant rules in the text that follows, we will consider their application to Joan's estate in **17.4.2.2**.

17.4.1 Secured debts

17.4.1.1 s35 Administration of Estates Act 1925

In order to show that a debt is secured against land as a mortgage or charge, the correct conveyancing paperwork must have been completed at the time the loan was made. Other forms of loans can also be secured debts, for example, where the testator's business (in their sole name) has been lent money secured on the assets of the business (e.g. a loan secured (charged) against a forestry contractor's equipment).

Of vital importance is **s35 AEA 1925**, the basic effect of which is that when a person dies owning property (either land or some other asset) that is subject to a secured loan or debt, the person who receives that property under the will takes over the responsibility for repaying the loan or debt. So, if a testator, such as Joan in the above example, makes a gift of Redacre as a specific gift, and it is subject to a mortgage at the date of her death, C is entitled to receive the property but will take it subject to the existing liability for the mortgage. This means that if C wants Redacre, C must assume responsibility for paying off the mortgage and cannot insist that the mortgage debt is lumped in with Joan's other debts and paid from other assets in the estate.

Where **s35** applies in this way, the specific beneficiary may be forced into selling the property to pay off the mortgage debt unless, of course, they have funds available (perhaps another entitlement under the will) that will meet the liability.

Before looking at some cases involving the application of **s35**, note two important points.

(1) **s35** is subject to a contrary intention shown by the testator. This may make it clear that the mortgage debt is not to be borne by the specific beneficiary but, instead, is to be treated in the same way as the unsecured debts (see **17.4.1.2**).

(2) **s35** does not affect the rights of the secured creditor because it is there simply to determine the incidence of the mortgage debt between the specific beneficiary and other beneficiaries of the estate. So, regardless of whether or not **s35** has been excluded by a contrary intention, the creditor can still enforce payment against the estate in the normal way.

In ***Re Birmingham, Savage v Stannard [1959]*** the testatrix died at a particularly inconvenient moment during the conveyancing process as she was buying a house. She had exchanged contracts to buy the house just before she died but before completing the purchase (a stage in the conveyancing process which can be a few days or even weeks later). During this transitional period, after exchange of contracts and before completion, the seller of the property, who will only have received the deposit at this stage, has a contractual right to receive the balance of the purchase price. This right to receive the balance is described as a **lien** because it is associated with the subject matter of the purchase, that is, the house. The court treated this lien as a secured debt charged on the property. As a result, the beneficiary who received the house under the codicil to the will was obliged to pay off the balance of the purchase price, not the residuary beneficiaries. The conveyancing costs for the house purchase (solicitors' fees, estate agency commission, etc.) were not treated as being secured against the house itself. They were therefore payable as normal unsecured debts from the residue.

When an individual asset, such as a house, is charged with a debt that exceeds the value of the asset (a house might have a mortgage worth more than its value ("negative equity")) the balance of the debt must be made up from the general estate (usually from the residue). This will apply even if the beneficiary receiving the gift of the charged property is also receiving as separate gifts other charged properties owned by the testator that do have some value in them after payment of the debts secured on them (***Re Holt [1916]***).

Where the testator has made one composite gift, for example, "all my land", of several charged properties, one of which is subject to a secured debt where the value exceeds that of the particular property, this deficit must be paid by the beneficiary who has received the composite gift, assuming that the other charged properties have sufficient value in them after payment of debts to meet this deficit (***Re Baron Kensington [1902]***).

Where the secured debt (e.g. a mortgage) is a single debt expressed to be secured on two separate properties, and the two properties are expressed in the will to pass to a specific beneficiary and to the residue, respectively, the beneficiary of the property passing as a specific gift remains responsible for the loan secured on that property. The decision by the testator to secure the loan on both properties is not treated as expressing a contrary intention under **s35**. The residue of the estate in these circumstances will not therefore be responsible for this secured debt (***Re Neeld [1962]***).

Crucially, regardless of the terms of the will, the creditor retains the right to go to court to force the sale of the asset and recover the sums owed. The creditor will not be concerned about arguments over which beneficiary should be ultimately paying the debt. The PRs in these circumstances will be responsible for ensuring that the correct net financial effect (a process known as "marshalling") is carried out in accordance with the rules described above (see **17.4.2.4**).

Finally, where the will gives X a right to purchase from the estate (an option) a property that is subject to a secured debt at a fixed price or in accordance with a formula, then X, if choosing to exercise this right, will be entitled to receive the property free from that debt. Since X is not a beneficiary as such but a purchaser, the PRs must pay off the debt or mortgage from assets in the residue before completing the sale to X (***Re Fison's Will Trusts [1950]***).

17.4.1.2 Contrary intention reversing the effect of s35

The rule in **s35** may be varied by deed, will or some other document so that the secured debt is not borne by the specific beneficiary. Usually, the variation is in the will and may take one of three forms.

(1) An **express exoneration or relieving provision** where the gift of the property is stated to be "free of mortgage" or "free of charge". In this case, the charge

is treated as an unsecured debt and the will normally provides for it to be paid from residue.

(2) A **general direction** to pay all debts **from a particular fund** such as the proceeds of a life assurance policy or from the proceeds of a shareholding. **s35** provides that this does vary the normal rule, even though there is no specific reference to the actual secured debt. If the fund is insufficient to meet the debt in full, the balance of the debt will be borne by the mortgaged property (***Re Fegan [1928]***).

    NB A basic general direction to pay debts from residue (as opposed to a particular fund) does not show a contrary intention unless there is also some reference to the secured debt. In ***Re Valpy [1906]*** the will directed that all the debts except the mortgage on a specified property (mortgage A) should be paid from residue. There was, in fact, another mortgage on a different property (mortgage B) and the court held that by specifically excluding mortgage A, the testator had, by implication, included mortgage B in the general direction and so varied **s35** in relation to mortgage B, which could be paid from residue.

(3) A **specific direction** to pay the secured debt from **residue** – for example, "I direct my executors to pay from residue all my debts, funeral and testamentary expenses including any mortgages subsisting at my death on any freehold or leasehold property forming part of my estate."

Unusually, perhaps, **s35** permits the testator's contrary intention to be shown by evidence from outside the will. If the variation of **s35** is shown by a document other than a will, it must show that the gift is to be free of charge and how the charge is borne. In ***Ross v Perrin-Hughes [2004]*** the claimant (R), the father and executor of the deceased (D), sought a declaration as to the true construction of a gift of property to the defendant, P, who had been D's partner. D had purchased the freehold reversion and the lease of a maisonette, the lease having been purchased with an endowment mortgage, so there was a life policy to cover the mortgage debt. Following D's death, R had used the proceeds of the policy to discharge the mortgage, but nonetheless contended that, in accordance with **s35**, P took the lease subject to the mortgage and so had to reimburse the deceased's estate. Cosmin J held that P had a right to take the lease free of the mortgage because the fact that D had taken steps to ensure discharge of the mortgage by other means (i.e. by taking out a life policy to cover it) before he made the will was enough to establish a contrary intention within **s35**.

A further issue in this case was that although D had used an ambiguous term in his home-made will describing the property as "my apartment", there was evidence to indicate that he intended the property to be a gift to P and that meant both the leasehold and the freehold reversion. This part of the case was decided in accordance with the rules on admitting extrinsic evidence in **s21 Administration of Justice Act 1982** (**AJA 1982**) (see **14.5.2**).

See **17.4.2.2** for an example of the application of **s35** where there are also unsecured debts to pay.

17.4.2 Unsecured debts

Testators can dictate their own rules by will as to how debts are to be paid. While such directions will not have any consequence for creditors, who can enforce payment in the usual way, the testator's directions will show how the incidence of debts is to be borne by the beneficiaries. If there is no express provision in the will for the payment of unsecured debts, then assets must be applied in paying the debts according to the order referred to in **s34(3) AEA 1925** and set out in **Part II Sch 1 AEA 1925** (the **statutory order**).

17.4.2.1 The statutory order

The statutory order in **AEA 1925** sets out the order of priority in which the property constituting particular interests and gifts in a will is to be used for paying the deceased's unsecured debts. When looking at the statutory order, keep in mind that it is for general application, and not every will is likely to contain interests or gifts necessarily corresponding to those in the order. Also, remember that before attempting to apply the statutory order to a will, you should always consider if the will contains sufficient contrary intention to lay down its own rules about paying debts and so exclude the order (see **17.4.2.3**).

The statutory order is as follows.

(1) Property of the deceased undisposed of by the will, subject to the retention of a fund sufficient to meet any pecuniary legacies.

See ***Re Worthington [1933]*** at **17.6.2** for the meaning of "undisposed of by the will". For the purpose of the statutory order, a pecuniary legacy has the meaning attributed by **s55(1)(ix) AEA 1925**, and means any annuity, general legacy and a demonstrative legacy insofar as not discharged out of the designated fund (see **Chapter 12**).

(2) Residue disposed of by the will subject to a fund for the pecuniary legacies insofar as not provided for as in (1).

(3) Property that the deceased had specifically given for the payment of debts.

(4) Property of the deceased charged with the payment of debts.

The difference between (3) and (4) is very subtle. Property is **given** for the payment of debts if there is no direction in the will as to what is to be done with any surplus after payment of debts. In contrast, property is **charged** with the payment of debts if the will does specify what is to be done with any balance after the payment of debts. If the debts are paid before these classes are reached, then this property falls into residue.

The relative position of these two classes – that is, after the residue – has led some to think of the statutory order as being a little illogical. You would surely expect that if the testator has directed his mind to the question of debts by providing for property within (3) and (4), then those two classes should be at the top of the list. See **17.4.2.3** to see how the courts have approached this peculiarity.

(5) The fund, if any, retained to meet the pecuniary legacies set aside in (1) and/or (2).

(6) Property specifically devised or bequeathed rateably according to value.

"Value" means value to the testator (***Re John [1933]***). If different properties are the subject of specific legacies, in apportioning liability between the different specific legatees, the value of any mortgage debt borne by a legatee because of **s35** would be deducted from the value of the mortgaged property.

(7) The property appointed by will under a general power rateably according to value.

A general power of appointment is where a testator has given a beneficiary property, often on trust, with a power to state who should receive it on the death of the beneficiary. Beneficiaries can make this decision in their will. General powers of appointment are very rare in practice.

The assets listed in the statutory order are not comprehensive. The following assets are also available for the payment of debts:

- funds payable to the estate upon the exercise of an option (***Re Eve [1956]***);
- property subject to a *donatio mortis causa*;
- property subject to a general power of appointment exercisable by deed if it had been exercised (***Re Phillips [1931]***).

Property may appear to fall into more than one category (overlap). For example, if the testator leaves the residue in two parts and one part lapses, that part would appear to overlap both categories (1) and (2). In such a case, the property is to be treated as falling into the higher category only (***Re Kempthorne [1930]***).

There is no distinction between realty and personalty. Property undisposed of by the will is the primary fund for the payment of debts. This will include a lapsed share of residue (***Re Lamb [1929]***).

The statutory order may be displaced by a contrary intention on the part of the testator (see **17.4.2.3**).

17.4.2.2 Practical applications of the statutory order

(1) **Where there is a lapsed share of residue**

If there is a lapsed share of residue and the will does not contain a clear indication that the statutory order is excluded, what does one do?

Suppose T leaves a £2,000 legacy to X and his residuary estate to Y and Z in equal shares. At death, the estate is worth £50,000 and there are unsecured debts of £10,000. Y has predeceased T; there are no exceptions to the rule of lapse applying, and so Y's share is property undisposed-of by the will, which devolves on partial intestacy.

First, identify the residuary property and then identify the undisposed-of share. The residuary estate is identified as £50,000 (i.e. the whole gross estate because there are no specific gifts in T's will) and is then divided to value the lapsed share (£25,000) (***Re Sanger [1939]***). However, category (1) requires deduction of a pecuniary legacy fund (as does (2)), so the undisposed-of share will be reduced to £23,000, from which the debts of £10,000 will be paid, so reducing it further to £13,000.

It should be apparent that the undisposed-of "equal share" is left to pass on partial intestacy and has been reduced to £13,000 by the debts (and the legacy), while the other "equal share" taken by Z is £25,000. (See **17.4.2.3** as to how the result is different if the statutory order is excluded.)

(2) **Where residue is insufficient**

Now go back to Joan's will (see **17.4**). Her estate has a secured debt in it, so we can consider how this applies alongside the statutory order.

By way of reminder, her will said:

- Clause 1: "I give £30,000 to A";
- Clause 2: "I give £10,000 to B";
- Clause 3: "I give my house, Redacre, to C";
- Clause 4: "I give residue to R".

Joan's assets total £280,000, including Redacre worth £200,000.

Her debts total £100,000, including a mortgage of £40,000 secured on Redacre.

Since there is no contrary intention to vary either **s35 AEA 1925** or the statutory order, Joan's PRs will apply the rules as follows.

The mortgage (the secured debt)

The burden of the mortgage debt will fall on C as the specific beneficiary of Redacre (**s35**). So, C will be required to pay £40,000 if they wish to take the property. In practice, C might have to sell Redacre (or re-mortgage) to raise the necessary cash if they do not otherwise have it available.

The unsecured debts

These will amount to £60,000 and the statutory order will be applied as follows.

(1) Since there is no undisposed-of property in Joan's will, this category is not applicable.

(2) This is residue disposed of by the will subject to a pecuniary legacy fund. The residue for this purpose will be Joan's estate less the value of Redacre, which is the subject of a specific gift. That gives £80,000, and from this a fund must be set aside to pay the two pecuniary legacies due to A and B. The fund required is £40,000, which therefore leaves the amount of residue in category (2) as £40,000. This sum can be used to pay the unsecured debts of £60,000 as far as it will go. Since there is a shortfall of £20,000, it is necessary to move to the next categories in the statutory order (having noted there will be no residue available for R under Joan's will).

(3) Property given by the will for the payment of debts. There is none in Joan's will.

(4) Property charged by the will for the payment of debts. Again, the will is silent.

(5) The pecuniary legacy fund that was set aside when at category (2). This fund was worth £40,000. Since there is a balance of £20,000 of debts to pay, there is no need to use the entire fund – and so the good news for A and B is that there will be some money left over to give them something. A and B will get a proportion of their respective legacies corresponding to the value that each was intended to receive. Since there is £20,000 left in the fund to pay £40,000 worth of legacies, A and B will each get 50 per cent of what it says on the face of the will. So A will be given £15,000 and B will take £5,000.

    These two legacies have been the subject of abatement, which was discussed at **13.6.1** when looking at the reasons for the failure of gifts in wills.

    Since all Joan's debts have been accounted for, there is no need to progress further down the order. If the value of the unsecured debts left to pay had been greater than the pecuniary legacy fund in category (5), then there would be a need to move on to (6), at which point it is the subject matter of a specific gift that becomes vulnerable.

You might want to go through this example again, but this time assume that Clause 3 had said "I give my house, Redacre, to C free of mortgage". Remember that this will effectively reverse **s35** so that the secured debt is not borne by C but is instead paid in the same way as the unsecured debts. So work through the statutory order again but with unsecured debts to pay now totalling £100,000. You should end up with C as the specific beneficiary in category (6) having to bear the burden of the balance of the unsecured debts (£20,000).

C does have to pay something, as in the original example, but the difference is that A and B receive no benefit because their legacies have now abated to nothing. The effect of Joan having made C's gift free of mortgage is that A and B have lost their legacies at the expense of half of the mortgage debt, with the other half being borne by C. In the original example, C had to bear the whole mortgage debt.

17.4.2.3 Contrary intention and alteration of the statutory order

As explained at **17.4.2**, the statutory order for the payment of debts may be varied by the testator. As long as the creditors are paid, they will not care which beneficiary suffers the burden.

The first question to consider is whether a direction to pay debts from a non-residuary fund or a charge of debts on such a fund places that fund in category (3) or (4) (see **17.4.2.1**) or whether it amounts to a contrary intention that excludes the statutory order altogether, so making the fund in question primarily liable. The case law says:

- a mere giving or charging of property does not displace the order. If it did, there would never be any property in these categories. Something more is required to displace these categories from (3) and (4) in the order (***Re Gordon [1940]***);
- a direction to pay debts from specified property, coupled with an intention to exonerate other property, will alter the statutory order, as in ***Re James [1947]***, which was followed in ***Re Meldrum's Will Trust [1952]***. The testator bequeathed a bank account to his daughter after the payment of legacies and debts and left the residue to his son and daughter. It was held that the intention to pay the debts from the bank account, coupled with a later gift of residue, showed an intention to exonerate the residue.

So, case law shows that, if the will includes a residuary gift, the court is likely to hold that a direction to pay debts from a non-residuary fund or a charge of debts on such a fund excludes the statutory order altogether because the testator has shown an intention to exonerate residue which would otherwise be used to meet the debts.

Testators may vary the order in other ways.

They may direct that debts are to be paid before the residue is ascertained, in which case the order is varied. In the example in **17.4.2.2**(1) the £10,000 of debts would have to be paid before the value of the residue could be divided into the Y fund and the Z fund, so both those funds would be of equal value. Alternatively, testators may charge the debts on the whole of the residue before saying how residue is divided. In this case, the residue is identified in the usual way but the debts are again paid before the value of each share is identified.

In ***Re Kempthorne [1930]*** the testator left all his property, after payment of debts and legacies, to be divided among his brothers and sisters. Two predeceased him. The trial judge held that the mere fact that the testator had directed debts to be paid did not vary the statutory order, but the Court of Appeal disagreed. The wording of the will, by using the word "after", showed an intention that the debts should be paid **before** the residue could be ascertained.

In ***Re Harland-Peck [1941]*** the testator left property "subject to the payment of funeral, testamentary expenses and debts", to two persons, one of whom predeceased the testator. The Court of Appeal held that the debts were charged on the residue as a whole, thereby altering the statutory order.

In both these cases, the debts were effectively borne rateably by both the lapsed and effective shares of residue. These decisions should be contrasted with ***Re Lamb [1929]***, where the testator directed all his debts to be paid (but did not say from where) and, after making certain bequests, left residue to be divided between four beneficiaries as tenants in common. One of the residuary beneficiaries predeceased. It was held that there was no contrary intention to exclude the statutory order, because the will did not indicate which fund was to be used for payment of the debts, so, applying the statutory order, the lapsed share was liable.

The professionally drawn will should always indicate which fund is to be used for payment of debts – normally, the will directs payment from residue as a whole before division.

Finally, testators can elect to keep the statutory order but prescribe that the categories are to be constituted differently within the order, for example, by indicating that property specifically devised or bequeathed should include only gifts of realty.

17.4.2.4 Marshalling

In administering the estate, the PRs may find themselves having to apply assets out of order to pay debts. This might be the case if PRs are being forced by creditors to pay debts promptly – remember, creditors are not concerned with legal niceties other than those that apply to their right to have their debt paid by the estate. This means that, at the end of the administration, the PRs must **marshal** the assets, that is, arrange them in such a way that the correct beneficiary bears the burden of the liabilities according to the rules which apply. Marshalling means that a disappointed beneficiary may seek reimbursement from a beneficiary whose share should have been used for the payment of debts.

17.5 The insolvent estate

If the estate is insolvent, the beneficiaries get nothing. The PRs must determine in which order the debts should be paid – until the money runs out.

The debts must be paid in the order set out in the **Insolvency Act 1986** (**IA 1986**) and the **Administration of Insolvent Estates of Deceased Persons Order 1986** (**AIEDPO 1986**). Priority is given to reasonable funeral, testamentary and administration expenses, even over preferred debts (**art 4(2) AIEDPO 1986**) and thereafter the order of debts in bankruptcy.

17.5.1 Secured creditors

Secured creditors are those who have lent money to the deceased on the security of property by way of mortgage, charge or lien (see **17.4.1**). Secured creditors enjoy priority over all other creditors and over payment of the funeral, testamentary and administration expenses to the extent that they rely on the security.

Their usual course of action would be to realise the security to meet the debt. In cases where the security may be insufficient to meet the debt, other courses of action can be considered.

(1) To realise (i.e. sell) the security and if there is a shortfall, claim the balance of the debt as an unsecured creditor.

(2) To set a value on the security and prove for the balance. This may be advisable if, for example, the creditor wishes to keep the property, or if to dispose of the property as in (1) would involve high costs. Care must be taken in valuing the security. If the creditor puts too low a value on it, the PRs can insist on the creditor redeeming it at that value and prove as an unsecured creditor for the balance. If too high, the creditor will prove for an insufficient balance.

(3) To surrender the security and claim the whole of the debt as an unsecured creditor. This would be rare but might be done where, for example, the security proves to be worthless.

17.5.2 Unsecured creditors and the order in bankruptcy

If PRs are administering an estate that is, or might be, insolvent, they must observe the correct order for payment of creditors, which cannot be varied by the testator.

The order prescribed by **IA 1986** and **AIEDPO 1986** is:

- funeral, testamentary and administration expenses; then
- the bankruptcy order.

If the PRs do not follow this order, they will be liable for any superior debts left unpaid. Consequently, if there is any possibility that the estate may turn out to be insolvent, the PRs should observe this order when paying the debts.

(1) **Funeral, testamentary and administration expenses**

These take priority over all debts owed to unsecured creditors. As between the expenses themselves, the funeral expenses (which must be reasonable) have priority.

(2) **Specially preferred debts**

These are rare, but could include unpaid expenses incurred by the deceased in attempting to prevent a bankruptcy before their death, such as the costs of an arrangement under **IA 1986** entered into by a debtor in order to settle debts and so avoid bankruptcy proceedings.

(3) **Preferred debts**

These are listed under two categories:

- contributions due to occupational pension schemes;
- remuneration due to the deceased's employees – wages outstanding for the four months before death to a maximum of £800 and accrued holiday pay are the main items under this head.

Both categories of preferred debts rank equally. If the assets are insufficient to meet them, they will abate proportionately according to value.

(4) **Ordinary debts**

These are all debts (including arrears of tax owed to HM Revenue & Customs) not falling within any other category.

(5) **Deferred debts**

These are debts owed in respect of credit provided by the spouse or civil partner of the deceased at the latter's death.

All debts must be proved at their value at the date of death and include interest accrued up to that date. If a precise value cannot be reached, one must be estimated. Interest on ordinary and preferred debts, for the period from death to payment, runs at 8 per cent or the rate specified in the agreement, whichever is the greater. This interest ranks after the ordinary debts. No additional priority is acquired by a creditor who sues for their debt.

17.5.3 Liability for not following the bankruptcy order

The bankruptcy order of priority cannot be varied by the deceased's will – PRs are obliged by **s25 AEA 1925** to comply with the order of payment of debts in an insolvent estate. It is therefore a breach of duty to pay a debt of a lower class before paying a debt in a higher class of which they have notice. If the PRs do so, they become personally liable to pay all debts in the higher class because payment of the inferior debt amounts to an admission that there are enough assets to pay all debts. However, if they pay an inferior debt without undue haste and without notice of a superior one they will not be personally liable (but this does not apply if the PRs pay a beneficiary without notice of the existence of a debt).

PRs must pay all debts in the same class rateably (*pro rata*) and without any preference of one over the other. If PRs pay a debt (including a PR's own, unless the grant was taken out as creditor) in good faith without reason to believe that the estate was insolvent, they are not liable to other creditors in the same class if the estate later turns out to be insolvent (**s10(2) AEA 1971**). This protection does not apply if the liability was known, but not its extent. To be safe, PRs should always administer an estate as if it were insolvent.

17.5.4 Insolvent estates and joint property

Joint property, whether land or pure personalty, is not available to the PRs to pay debts because it does not devolve on them.

If an estate is insolvent, under **s421A IA 1986**, if all other assets have been used up, the creditors may seek an administration order no later than five years after the death appointing a trustee in bankruptcy who has the power to seek recovery of the deceased's share of jointly owned property from the surviving joint tenants.

In determining whether to make an order under this section, and the terms of such an order, the court must have regard to all the circumstances of the case, including the interests of the deceased's creditors and of the surviving joint tenants. Unless the circumstances are exceptional, however, the court must assume that the interests of the deceased's creditors outweigh all other considerations.

17.5.5 Some additional points regarding insolvent estates

Since beneficiaries will get nothing in an insolvent estate and, often, one or more beneficiaries are appointed as executors (or have the best right to apply for administration on intestacy), there may be little, if any, incentive for them to obtain a grant. A creditor can always obtain a grant under **rr20** or **22 NCPR 1987** as appropriate. If those entitled in priority will neither obtain a grant nor renounce, a creditor can use the citation process to clear them off or ask the Registrar or District Judge to pass them over under the power in **s116 Senior Courts Act 1981** (**SCA 1981**) (see **15.2.3**).

PRs or creditors can petition for a trustee in bankruptcy to be appointed following an insolvency administration order made by the bankruptcy court. **AIEDPO 1986** provides that whether the estate is being administered by PRs or by a trustee in bankruptcy, the same rules, broadly speaking, will apply, although there are some practical advantages if a trustee is appointed.

17.6 Payment of legacies

Like payment of debts, this is an area that has caused difficulties, having been described by Salt QC in ***Re Taylor [1969]*** as "*tortuous*" and "*notoriously obscure*". It is concerned with which share of the estate is to be used for the payment of general legacies – it may be undisposed-of property or residue generally, it may be personal property only, or real property may also be liable. While **s34 AEA 1925** deals with the payment of debts, it does not state expressly that it applies to the incidence of legacies, although there are references in the statutory order categories (1) and (2) to the retention of a pecuniary legacy fund for the payment of legacies.

The unresolved question is to what extent, if at all, **AEA 1925** has altered the pre-1925 rules on the incidence of legacies. Answering this question is not easy and the case law since 1925 is not conclusive. However, as with the problems concerned with the statutory order for payment of debts, in practice, the issue of how pecuniary legacies should be paid is usually resolved by the terms of the will.

17.6.1 Pre-1925 rules

Before 1925, general legacies were payable only from residuary personalty (including any that was subject to a gift which had lapsed). If residuary personalty was insufficient, real property could not be used and the legacies abated. This rule was subject to a contrary intention expressed in the will. Two rules evolved in relation to contrary intention:

- ***Greville v Brown [1859]***, where real property and personalty were included in a single residuary gift. The real property would be liable for the payment of legacies if personalty was insufficient; and
- ***Roberts v Walker [1830]***, where the will clearly directed legacies to be paid from residue as a whole, real property and personal property were liable rateably.

17.6.2 Post-1925 rules – undisposed-of property

After 1925, a statutory trust with a power of sale is imposed on undisposed- of property (**s33 AEA 1925**) where no express trust arises under the will, and **s33(2)** appears to envisage that debts and legacies will be treated in the same way, that is, the legacies will be payable primarily out of the lapsed share. Since 1 January 1997, the statutory trust for sale in **s33**, as originally enacted, has become a statutory trust with a power of sale and, to the extent that there is land in the estate, it will be a trust of land (**TLATA 1996**), but the same principle would seem to apply.

So, in ***Re Worthington [1933]***, after certain legacies, the testator left the residue to A and B in equal shares. A predeceased the testator, and the Court of Appeal held that the residue should be divided first and the legacies paid from the undisposed-of property, being A's lapsed share. ***Re Worthington*** was followed in ***Re Gillett [1950]***.

If the will imposes an express trust for sale (or, since 1 January 1997, an express trust of land) and there is a lapsed share of residue, the express trust in the will excludes the statutory trust imposed by **s33**, which means that **s33** does not apply to make the legacies payable from the lapsed share (***Re McKee [1931]***). Instead, the legacies would be payable out of the general residue before division.

If all the beneficial interests under a trust for sale of residue fail (perhaps through lapse), the express trust is of no effect and the statutory trust under **s33** takes effect, again making the general legacies payable from the lapsed shares.

17.6.3 Post-1925 rules where s33 Administration of Estates Act 1925 does not apply

Where **s33 AEA 1925** does not apply and the will is silent on how general legacies are to be borne, the question is whether **AEA 1925** altered the old rules. This question is relevant in a number of situations including:

- if there is a lapsed share of residue, but it is subject to an express and effective trust, thereby excluding **s33**;
- if there is a lapsed share of residue to which **s33** does apply, but it is insufficient to meet all the general legacies;
- if there is no lapsed share of residue and so, again, **s33** does not apply.

The authorities are divided as to whether the old rules have altered. If the old rules have altered, the effect is to make any undisposed-of property primarily liable, followed by residue as a whole. Unlike the old rules, real and personal property would be liable rateably.

Re Thompson [1936] and ***Re Anstead [1943]*** suggest that the rules have **not** altered. In ***Thompson*** the estate consisted of residuary personalty and realty. The testator left various legacies and gifts of residue.

It was held that there was no rateable apportionment. The whole of the residuary personalty should be used first and any shortfall made up from the realty. It is noteworthy that the court's decision may well have been influenced by estate duty considerations, because if the legacies had been paid rateably, additional estate duty would have been borne by the legatees to the extent that their benefits were attributable to realty. However, this decision was followed in ***Re Wilson [1967]***.

Thompson and ***Anstead*** were concerned with whether residuary personalty was primarily liable for payment of legacies or whether real property and personalty were liable rateably. In ***Re Beaumont [1950]*** and ***Re Taylor [1969]*** the court took the same view. These two cases were concerned with whether, if there was an express trust for sale of residue (which excluded **s33**) and an undisposed of share of the residue, that share was primarily liable for payment of legacies under the statutory order or whether residuary personalty as a whole was primarily liable. The court held that there was no change in the law and that residuary personalty as a whole was liable.

The cases that support the view that the law **has** changed are ***Re Midgley [1955]***, ***Re Gillett [1950]*** and ***Re Martin [1955]***. In ***Midgley*** it was held that legacies were payable from a lapsed share of residue, although it was commented on that it was a tortuous way of legislating. In ***Gillett*** it was conceded that the statutory order applied.

All the cases are first-instance decisions, so there is no definitive answer to this question, although the majority of the decisions favour the old rules, as do some academic writers.

It is unusual for the law to be changed without express mention, and **s34(3) AEA 1925** expressly refers only to debts. If the law has not changed, the reference to the pecuniary legacy fund in the statutory order means only that, before dealing with the incidence of unsecured debts, one must apply the rules on legacies and take the legacy fund from undisposed-of property or residue, as appropriate, before applying the rules on the incidence of unsecured debts.

In view of the uncertainty in the law, it is important that the will contains an express direction on where the general legacies are to be paid from. Generally, this is from residue before division into shares.

17.7 Distribution of the assets

When the deceased's assets have been collected in and realised and all the debts and expenses have been either paid or provided for, the PRs are in a position to distribute the estate to those entitled, under the valid provisions of the will or according to the rules of intestate succession.

There are no time limits as to when distribution must take place. **s44 AEA 1925** says that a PR is not bound to distribute the estate before the expiration of one year from the death (although it is possible for distribution to take place within the year). A legatee could not compel distribution of a legacy during the executor's year, or even afterwards, if there is a good reason for non-payment, but the PR must deal with the estate promptly. Undue delay could render him liable to a *devastavit* action, brought by an aggrieved beneficiary or creditor.

17.7.1 Ascertainment of the beneficiaries

The PRs must ascertain the persons who are entitled under the will or intestacy. They must correctly identify the beneficiaries, applying the rules of construction, and locate them. On intestacy, they must correctly identify the class of relatives entitled to inherit and identify and locate each member of the class.

In particular, if a principal beneficiary has predeceased or otherwise failed to inherit their entitlement, the PRs must consider who is entitled under any substitution provision. While an express provision on the face of the will should be readily apparent, remember that **s33 Wills Act 1837** (**WA 1837**) can imply a substitution in some cases (see **13.4.3**), as can the application of the statutory trusts arising on intestacy (see **10.4.2**).

Finding beneficiaries

The PRs can adopt certain courses of action in tracking down beneficiaries.

(1) Enquiry: the PRs can pursue their own enquiries in order to find missing beneficiaries and next of kin on intestacy. They could, for example, engage the services of a genealogist, while a practical alternative is to take out missing person's indemnity insurance.

(2) Insert a notice under **s27 Trustee Act 1925** (**TA 1925**): this has been mentioned in relation to protection from the claims of creditors (see **16.3.2.1**). Protection can also be afforded to PRs from a later claim by a beneficiary (e.g. under a class gift) of whom they did not have notice at the time of the distribution (***Re Aldhous [1955]***). However, protection will be available only against claims from beneficiaries the PRs did not know about. **s27** will not afford protection in the case where a beneficiary is known but cannot be found, although **s27** advertisements may still be helpful in trying to locate the missing person and such advertisements will invariably be insisted upon by the court if applying for a ***Benjamin*** order.

(3) Apply for a ***Benjamin*** order (see **16.3.3.1**): if a beneficiary is known but cannot be found, then application can be made for a ***Benjamin*** order, where the court will order distribution on the terms of the order, for example, on the footing that a named beneficiary has predeceased.

Although the PRs will be protected from personal liability if **s27** applies or they obtain a ***Benjamin*** order, neither will prevent missing beneficiaries who subsequently appear from pursuing their rights and recovering their share from those who have received distributions. A beneficiary can take action to recover from the wrongly or overpaid beneficiaries through tracing, or an action for a refund as in ***Re Diplock [1948]*** (see **18.8**).

17.7.2 The rights of the beneficiaries pending distribution

Prior to distribution, the PRs hold the assets on a limited trust. In ***Commissioner for Stamp Duties (Queensland) v Livingston [1965]*** Viscount Radcliffe said:

"[W]*hatever property came to the executor by virtue of his office came to him in full ownership, without distinction between legal and equitable interests . . . He held it for the purposes of carrying out the functions and duties of administration, not for his own benefit . . . Certainly, therefore, he was in a fiduciary position with regard to the assets that came to him in the right of his office, and for certain purposes and in some aspects he was treated by the court as a trustee."*

The trust is limited in scope. It does not, as a general rule, give the beneficiaries an equitable interest in their entitlement in the same way as a beneficiary under an express trust has an equitable interest. As Viscount Radcliffe pointed out in his judgment: *"The assets as a whole were in the hands of the executor, his property; and until administration was complete no one was in a position to say what items of property would need to be realised for the purposes of administration or of what the residue, when ascertained, would consist or what its value would be."*

What is the nature of the beneficiary's interest? Pending distribution, the beneficiary has a chose in action to ensure that the estate is properly administered. A chose in action is the right to bring an action to compel the due administration of the estate. The chose is assignable by the beneficiary in the same way as any other chose in action (***Re Leigh's Will Trusts [1970]***).

Re Hemming, Saul & Co [2008] confirmed that the right of a beneficiary pending distribution is a chose in action. In this case, the effect of this rule was to vest the chose in action in the trustee in bankruptcy of the insolvent beneficiary. It is a common practice for solicitors to carry out bankruptcy searches against the names of beneficiaries in order to identify whether or not payment should be made to a trustee in bankruptcy.

17.7.3 Assents

When PRs assent to certain property passing in accordance with the terms of the will or intestacy, they are indicating that they no longer need the property for the purposes of the administration and the property can pass to the beneficiary.

17.7.3.1 Assents to personalty

There is no set form as to how the assent is to be made where the property is other than land. A PR can indicate orally, in writing or by conduct that the asset is no longer required for the administration (***Attenborough v Solomon [1913]***).

The transfer of property does not occur by reason of the assent but by virtue of the dispositions in the will. The assent merely makes the dispositions operative.

The effects of the assent of a specific gift of personalty are as follows.

(1) The gift relates back to death, therefore the beneficiary has the right to the income and profits arising from the date of death. The assent is operative in respect of the legacy and not the legatee. The significance is that in a situation where the legacy has been given to the wrong person (e.g. a later will is found altering the destination of the gift), the assent perfects the title to the rightful legatee from the death.

    This is illustrated by ***Re West [1909]***, where the executors assented to the person named in a codicil. A later codicil was subsequently discovered, bequeathing the legacy to a different person. The beneficiary under the later codicil successfully sued the executors. The fact that the assent had been made to the wrong person made no difference, for the assent was to the bequest and not to the beneficiary.

(2) The assent vests the property in the beneficiary, who becomes responsible for it. A consequence is that any costs of transport or packaging of the chattel and insurance in transferring the asset must be borne by the beneficiary, for example, in a delivery of china in ***Re Sivewright [1922]***. Often, however, the terms of the will may reverse this rule by proving the gift is "free of costs of transfer and delivery", in which case such costs are paid by residue.

(3) ***Re West*** shows that the beneficiary is entitled to take legal proceedings for the recovery of the chattel. This right exists only in respect of specific gifts, general or residuary legacies.

    Title to the property passes when the assent is made. In the case of a chattel, such as a painting, title will pass immediately. In the case of a chose in action, such as shares in a limited company, the PRs become trustees for the beneficiary where it is necessary to comply with other requirements of the transfer. For example, in the case of company shares, the title will pass to the beneficiary only when the beneficiary's name is entered on the share register (***Re Grosvenor [1916]***). (The same principle applies to land pending the registration requirements at the Land Registry.)

17.7.3.2 Assents to land

s36 AEA 1925 governs assents to land and applies to estates or interests in land that devolve on the PRs which they then wish to transfer to a person entitled. The person entitled might be an adult beneficiary who is absolutely entitled under the will or could be trustees to hold on the trusts of the will. An assent will also be used if PRs are exercising their power of appropriation (see **16.4.3**) and the beneficiary has consented to take the land in satisfaction, or part satisfaction, of their interest under the will or intestacy.

Unlike a normal transfer or conveyance of land, which must be by deed to pass a legal estate, an assent need only be in writing. It must be signed by the PRs and must name the party in whose favour the assent is made (**s36(4)**).

If the title is already registered at the Land Registry, the assent needs to be on form AS1. Since an assent now triggers an application for compulsory land registration if the title is currently unregistered, form AS1 is used then.

Prior to 1964, conveyancing practitioners thought that the provisions of **s36(4)** did not apply where the PR and the beneficiary were the same person because there was no passing of the legal estate, merely a change in the capacity in which the estate was held. This view was held to be incorrect by the court in ***Re King's Will Trust [1964]*** (see **17.7.7**). Until the assent has been made, the PR holds the legal estate as PR and so does not have the ability to deal with it as beneficial owner.

The assent operates to vest the legal estate in favour of the person named in the assent as from the date of death (subject to complying with Land Registry requirements). **s36** contains provisions intended to protect beneficiaries and subsequent purchasers. If the deceased's title was already registered at the Land Registry, this protection was not needed and since any unregistered title that is the subject of an assent will now be subject to first registration anyway, these provisions are far less important than when first enacted.

s36(5) entitles beneficiaries to require the PRs to enter a notice of the assent on the probate or letters of administration at the expense of the estate. This was intended to give protection to the beneficiaries if the PRs subsequently tried to deal with the property in favour of another. In such a case, the purchasing party would not have the protection afforded by **s36(7)**. On the other hand, if the beneficiaries have not insisted on a **s36(5)** notice, they will not be protected against a subsequent sale.

In the case of a subsequent purchaser (i.e. from the assentee) for money or money's worth, **s36(7)** gives protection by providing that an assent of a legal estate is sufficient evidence of the assentee's title (and therefore their right to sell the property) unless notice of a previous assent or conveyance has been placed on, or annexed to, the probate or letters of administration.

s36(10) authorises the PRs to assent subject to a mortgage.

If the PR is slow to make the assent, the beneficiary can apply to the court for directions under **s43(2) AEA 1925**. Again, the executor's year rule applies.

If land is conveyed to the PRs after the death – for example, where the deceased died between contract and completion of the purchase – then an assent that is merely in writing will not suffice and the land will have to be transferred by the PRs by deed as required in a normal conveyancing transaction (***Re Stirrup's Contract [1961]***).

17.7.4 The power to set off legacies against debts

Where a beneficiary who is entitled to money from the estate owes money to the estate, the PR may set off or retain the money owed by the beneficiary against what is due. For example, if X is entitled to a pecuniary legacy of £5,000 under the will of the deceased but, at death, X owes the estate £2,000, then, before X can obtain the legacy, they must pay the £2,000 or the PRs can deduct the £2,000 and pay over the net £3,000.

The right of set-off applies only where there is a gift of money and not where the subject matter is, for example, a chattel (***Re Savage [1918]***). The beneficiary must owe money and not something else, and the money must be due and payable. If, for example, the debt is being repaid by instalments, then the set- off can only apply against those instalments due and payable. In ***Turner v Turner [1911]*** the debt was owed by two partners jointly but the legacy had been left to one of the partners. The right of set-off was not available.

The right is not available if the beneficiary has predeceased the testator but the legacy has been saved from lapse, for example, by the operation of **s33 WA 1837**, as in ***Re Binns [1929]***.

The right of retainer gives the PRs the right to recover the debt without the need for incurring court costs. In ***Courtenay v Williams [1844]*** the PRs could set off against a statute-barred debt.

17.7.5 Bankrupt beneficiaries

PRs who pay a legacy directly to a bankrupt beneficiary may become personally liable to the beneficiary's trustee in bankruptcy (who is responsible for protecting the interests of the beneficiary's creditors). Under **s306 IA 1986**, all the property of the bankrupt person, including their rights to claim a share in the deceased's estate, vests in the trustee in bankruptcy.

Under **s279 IA 1986**, a bankrupt person will normally have the bankruptcy automatically discharged after a year. Essentially, this means that the bankrupt person has the debts cleared. If the discharge was before the date of the deceased's death, the PRs may pay the beneficiary their share of the estate. If the discharge was after the date of the death but before distribution of the estate, the PRs must pay the share to the trustee in bankruptcy.

In order to avoid liability, PRs should carry out bankruptcy searches at HM Land Registry Bankruptcy Unit against the names of the beneficiaries - https://www.gov.uk/government/publications/bankruptcy-official-search-application-k16 (see **17.7.2** and ***Re Hemming, Saul & Co [2008]***).

17.7.6 The administration period

There is no statutory definition of the end of the administration period. In practice, the final distribution of the assets to the beneficiaries and the handing over by the PRs of signed estate accounts would mark the end of the period. It is important to fix a time for the end of the period because, in many cases, the PR is appointed both executor and trustee. When the period has ended, the person becomes a trustee if still holding assets and is then subject to different rights and liabilities. In addition, their tax position may change (see **17.7.7**).

Administration ceases and trusteeship begins:

- in the case of land, when PRs assent to themselves as a trustee (or to others);
- in the case of pure personalty, either on an assent or completion of the administration period, whichever is first.

It is largely a question of fact when the administration period has ended.

Note the following points.

(1) The PR can be sued after the end of the period for acts committed during the period.

(2) In special cases, a grant may be obtained after the administration period, for example, to an infant who is of age, where the PR must account to the beneficiary for the work done, or where a reversionary interest falls into the estate long after the administration period has ended.

(3) The PRs may still have to act as such in relation to any assets or liabilities discovered at a later date.

17.7.7 Personal representative or trustee?

PRs wind up the estate and distribute the assets. Trustees hold assets until a special event occurs, for example, the end of a life interest or the meeting of a contingency. There are a number of reasons why it may be important to decide whether someone is acting as PR or as trustee.

Authority: this is the right to be able to deal with assets and pass good title. For PRs, authority is joint as to land, and joint and several as to pure personalty. So, all the PRs must execute an assent of land to transfer title to a beneficiary. However, just one of several PRs can validly transfer title to, say, the deceased's bicycle by either selling it or transferring it to a beneficiary. On the other hand, trustees must always act jointly, whether dealing with land or pure personalty (see ***Attenborough v Solomon [1913]*** below).

Sale: a sale by a sole or last surviving PR is sufficient to overreach equitable interests, whereas for there to be such overreaching by trustees, the disposition must be made by all the trustees, being at least two in number, or a trust corporation.

Appointment: a new trustee can be appointed by the other trustees or the PR of the last surviving trustee. However, PRs cannot appoint an additional PR (though the court can do so on request); if a sole or last surviving PR dies and the chain of representation is broken, a grant *de bonis non* is necessary.

Tax: rates, allowances and the rules applying to income tax and capital gains tax are often different depending on whether the person receiving income or making a capital gain is a PR or trustee at the relevant time.

Limitation of actions: in the case of claims against PRs, beneficiaries generally have 12 years from the date on which the right of action accrued. This will usually be the date of death, but could be later, for example, if the action relates to an estate asset that only came to light some years later. In the case of a claimant under a disability, the limitation period will not start to run until the disability ends. No limitation period applies if the PR is fraudulent or is in possession of estate assets or proceeds.

Claims against trustees must usually be made within six years of the date when the right of action accrued.

A grant to a PR that is limited in time, for example, *durante minore aetate* (for as long as a child is a minor) expires at the end of the period, otherwise, the office of PR lasts for life. A person may be PR and trustee at the same time, but cannot hold the same item of property in both capacities simultaneously.

In ***Attenborough v Solomon [1913]*** the testator appointed two sons as executors and trustees and left part of his estate to them and part in trust for his daughter.

The testator died in March 1878 and, by March 1879, all the debts and legacies had been paid. Silver plate in trust for the daughter had always been in the custody of one of the sons. In March 1892, the son pledged the plate to a pawnbroker who did not know it was trust property. The son died and his brother took action against the pawnbroker, claiming that he had no title to the plate. The House of Lords held that the executors considered that they had done all that they could as executors in 1879, nothing else was done as executors and therefore the chattels vested in them as trustees. The individual son could not, therefore, give valid title to the lender despite the fact that there was no formal assent.

In ***Ponder v Ponder [1921]*** the wife was PR of the estate of her husband. She paid all the debts and divided the estate according to the pre-1926 **Statutes of Distributions**. At that stage, she had assumed the character of trustee and therefore could exercise the statutory power to appoint new trustees.

This was questioned in ***Harvell v Foster [1954]***. The testator appointed his daughter as executrix but, at his death, she was a minor. Letters of administration were granted to her husband, limited during her minority. An administration bond (something similar to an insurance policy then required to guarantee due administration) was given. The husband received the net residue, misappropriated it, and disappeared. When the daughter came of age, she had the bond assigned to her and took action on it to recover the estate. The Court of Appeal, relying on the wording of the bond, said that the husband had not "well and truly" administered the estate. The court commented on ***Ponder v Ponder***: one cannot say that once the PR has distributed the residuary estate, they are no longer a PR. On these facts, the husband remained liable as PR until he correctly distributed the estate he held on trust for his wife, so the wife could recover under the bond.

In ***Re King's Will Trusts [1964]*** the court held that a PR who had completed the administration of the estate should, as regards realty, formally assent to himself so that the title to the property now vested in him as trustee. Previously, conveyancing practitioners had followed ***Ponder*** and accepted that the PR had the power to appoint trustees if acting in the capacity of trustee. The decision in ***Re King's Will Trusts*** has been criticised but it was followed in ***Re Edward's Will Trust [1981]***.

As a result of the decision in ***Re King's Will Trusts***, it is most important for PRs who are also beneficiaries to assent in their own favour. If a PR dies without doing so, a further grant will be needed to the deceased's estate (which will be a *de bonis non* grant, unless the chain of representation applies) in order to assent to or sell the property, because legal ownership of the property remained in the PR "as PR" and not as beneficial owner.

17.8 Summary

(1) Sale of assets – the PRs should have regard to the terms of the will, the wishes of the beneficiaries, the taxation consequences of disposal and the possibility of options and pre-emption rights binding on them.

(2) Solvent estates:

- **s35 AEA 1925**: where a debt is charged on property during the deceased's lifetime, the property charged will be liable for payment of the debt unless a contrary intention is shown;
- **s34** and **Sch 1 AEA 1925** give the statutory order of funds available to pay debts but the testator can provide for the order not to apply.

(3) Insolvent estates – the order of priority of debts is specified in **IA 1986** and **AIEDPO 1986**:

- funeral, testamentary and administration expenses;
- preferred debts;
- ordinary debts;
- deferred debts.

(4) Pecuniary legacies must be paid out of available property. Ideally, the will should determine what property should be used but, if not, the pre-1926 rules will apply unless **s33 AEA 1925** has altered them. Under **s33**, if there is undisposed-of property, a statutory trust is imposed on the lapsed share and the legacies are paid primarily from that. Where the will provides an express trust and there is a lapsed share of residue, the express trust excludes the statutory trust.

(5) Ascertainment and confirmation of known beneficiaries can be carried out by:

- PRs pursuing their own enquiries;
- advertising under **s27 TA 1925**;
- a ***Benjamin*** order.

(6) Assents: the process of property passing from the PRs to the beneficiary:

- assent to personalty – there is no set form;
- assent to land – by **s36 AEA 1925**, this must be in writing and signed by the PRs. It must also name the person in whose favour it is given.

(7) PR or trustee? A PR winds up the estate and distributes the assets. A trustee holds assets until a special event occurs, such as the end of a life interest.

CHAPTER 18

Liability of the Personal Representatives

Aims of the Chapter:

By the end of this chapter, you should be able to:

- define *devastavit*;
- describe breach of trust;
- identify the duty to account to the court;
- describe the defences available to PRs; and
- outline situations where beneficiaries should take action against the recipients of assets.

18.1 Introduction

This chapter deals with what happens when PRs fail to perform their duties as they should. The beneficiaries named in the will are not able to lay claim to any property comprised in the estate until the administration has been completed. When things go wrong, creditors, beneficiaries and, on occasion, the next of kin need to have a remedy. PRs are also entitled to defend themselves and, in appropriate cases, to be relieved of liability. Many of the relevant principles come from the general law of trusts and the applicable statutes.

In particular, we will examine the broad category of breach of duty known as "*devastavit*" which covers misappropriation of assets and maladministration of the estate. We will also look at breach of trust and the duty of trustees to account to beneficiaries. The powers of the court to take over the administration of an estate will also be examined. In addition, we will look at the defences available to PRs and the rules relating to limitation (time periods within which claims against PRs must be made). Finally, we will briefly review the options available to beneficiaries and creditors to sue the recipients of assets.

18.2 *Devastavit*: breach of duty by a personal representative

Any breach of duty by a PR is called a *devastavit*. There are three main areas of liability: misappropriation of assets, maladministration and a failure to safeguard assets.

(1) **Misappropriation**

Examples are where a PR uses estate assets for their personal use (***Re Morgan [1881]***) or enters into collusive sales.

(2) **Maladministration**

(a) Misapplication – applying estate assets, albeit in good faith, otherwise than in the order provided by the will or statute – for example, paying an ordinary creditor before a preferred creditor. PRs who had no notice of the preferred creditor will not be liable (***Re Fluyder [1898]***) unless they would have had notice if they had advertised under **s27 Trustee Act 1925** (**TA 1925**) (***Chelsea Waterworks v Cowper [1795]***).

(b) Unjustified expenses – PRs should incur only reasonable expenses. For example, a PR will be liable in *devastavit* if they spend more than is "reasonable" on funeral expenses. This is a question of fact in each case.

(c) Wasting the assets – giving away an asset of value or paying debts that the PR is not bound to pay (e.g. where they are statute-barred).

In ***Thompson v Thompson [1821]*** the asset was a leasehold property which had a greater value than the rent payable. The PR was liable when he surrendered the lease without consideration instead of selling the asset at a premium. The converse would apply if the PR fails to surrender an uneconomic lease, where the rent exceeds the value (***Rowley v Adams [1839]***).

(d) Failure to pay debts promptly so that the creditor sues, failure to recover assets so that the claim becomes statute-barred and delay in obtaining probate (***Re Stevens [1897]***) would all amount to *devastavit*.

(e) Failure to collect in the estate assets with due diligence.

(f) Failure to distribute the estate to those correctly entitled.

Misapplication can arise if the PR does not take enough care in determining who is entitled under the terms of the will or application of the intestacy rules and ends up giving property to someone who was not actually entitled to it. For example, if the will says "£10,000 to my housekeeper", the person entitled in this situation would be the person answering the description of "my housekeeper" at the date the will was made (***Re Whorwood [1887]***) (see **13.2.2**(4)). So if, instead, the PR pays the housekeeper employed by the testator at the date of death, the PR will be liable to the rightful beneficiary for misapplication.

The PR might be an executor distributing under a will in which there is undisposed-of residue passing on partial intestacy. The executor ascertains that the closest class of relatives entitled under the partial intestacy are the deceased's brothers and sisters of the whole blood because there is no spouse or civil partner, no issue and the parents died years ago. The PR locates a brother who tells the executor that there are also two sisters still alive. So, the executor distributes the residue in three shares on the basis that these are the deceased's siblings who are entitled. What the executor has not been told, because they did not ask the right questions when making enquiries, is that the deceased had another brother who died a few years ago and who left a son who is still alive. Consequently, the executor should have set aside four shares and paid one to the son being the issue of the predeceased brother. Since this was not done, the executor will be personally liable for misapplication to the son to the extent of what the son ought to have received.

Very often, liability for misapplication can be avoided by the PRs seeking protection from liability. So, rather than trying to work out for themselves what the will means and running the risk of getting it wrong and so paying the wrong person, the PRs might consider seeking guidance from the court in the form of specific relief (see **18.5**). Again, if there is the possibility of the existence of other relatives within a class who might be entitled, the PRs should seek protection by inserting statutory advertisements (see **16.3.3.1**).

(3) **Failure to safeguard assets – negligence**

PRs cannot be held liable for loss in the absence of evidence of a failure to take reasonable care (***Job v Job [1877]***). They would not be liable if assets were lost in a robbery. The burden of proving loss as against the PRs rests with the party alleging the loss.

18.3 Breach of trust

PRs may also be appointed as trustees by the express provisions of a will. It is important to ascertain when they are acting in their capacity as PRs (when they can be liable for *devastavit*) and when they are acting as trustees (when they will be liable for breach of trust). The concept of breach of trust is wider: for example, a PR who makes an unauthorised profit from the estate even though the estate itself does not suffer loss, makes an unauthorised investment or fails to observe the terms of the will would be liable.

The acts of a co-representative will not make the other PRs liable unless their wilful default results in their not obtaining property into their joint control. This means that PRs will not be liable for the default of a fellow PR unless they were aware of that PR's activities.

ss11 and **12 Trustee Act 2000** set out the powers of PRs to appoint agents. **ss21–23** lay down their obligations to keep such appointments under review and the limits of their liability for agents who have been duly appointed in accordance with the duty of care described in **s1** and applied in various situations in accordance with **s2** and **para 3 Sch 1**.

18.4 Duty to account

By virtue of **s25 Administration of Estates Act 1925** (**AEA 1925**), the PRs owe a duty when called upon by the court to exhibit an inventory and account of the estate. They make the promise to do this when applying for the grant by way of a statement of truth or oath form lodged with the Probate Registry. This duty can be enforced by any beneficiary or creditor and will require the PRs to produce an account of the receipts and payments made. This will reveal the state of the administration and whether any breach has been committed.

Where appropriate, the PRs may be called upon to account on the footing of wilful default (i.e. for what they would have received but for their wilful default).

18.5 Administration by the court

Any person interested in the estate who is not satisfied with its progress or who is otherwise concerned about matters not being dealt with correctly may issue proceedings for administration by the court. The applicant may be, *inter alia*, a PR, beneficiary or creditor. Application would be to the Chancery Division of the High Court under **s61 Senior Courts Act 1981** (**SCA 1981**) and the **Civil Procedure Rules 1998**. There must be a duly constituted PR before the court would consider taking the administration because there must be a defendant to the proceedings. This person cannot be an executor *de son tort* because their duty is not to administer the estate, merely to account for what they have received.

If no grant of administration has been made, creditors and beneficiaries interested in the estate may apply to the court for the appointment of a receiver to protect the estate pending the appointment of a PR. If there are proceedings pending in the estate, a better course of action is to apply for the appointment of an administrator pending suit under **s117 SCA 1981**.

An administration order may take the form of an order for full administration, in which case the PRs may act only as directed by the court, or the court may grant specific relief (e.g. as to the interpretation of the will). A full administration order will rarely be made, partly because of the expense. If such an order is made, the court will direct the following accounts to be prepared:

- an account of property not specifically devised or bequeathed that has come into the hands of the PRs;
- an account of the debts, funeral and testamentary expenses;
- an account of legacies;
- an account of any property of the deceased that remains outstanding.

Apart from an order calling to account, the court could appoint a person to act as a judicial trustee. This is an officer of the court who can act with the PR or alone.

The PRs themselves may apply to the court for specific relief, for example, on the meaning of a particular clause in the will or for a summons for the court to pronounce on the validity of the will. An example of the former is the case of ***Spurling v Broadhurst [2012]*** (see **14.5.2**) where the executors of a will sought a declaration from the court on the meaning of a residuary gift in circumstances where the words used were open to at least four different interpretations. An example of the latter is the privileged will case ***Re Jones (Deceased) [1981]*** (see **4.2.2**) where the court was asked to consider the validity of the words uttered to the warrant officer.

In ***Perotti v Watson [2001]*** the court concluded that, although the claimant had legitimate complaints about the way in which the defendant solicitor had administered the estate of his late uncle, the most pragmatic course of action was to allow the administrator to continue. The judge had awarded the administrator three-quarters of his costs, by way of indemnity, out of the estate, and the Court of Appeal reduced this figure by £2,500. Further, the court subsequently granted the defendant his legal fees, since the will had no charging clause.

18.6 Defences of personal representatives

PRs are personally liable where *devastavit* is proved, but certain defences may be raised.

(1) A clause in the will restricting the liability of PRs to wilful wrongdoing limits the liability so far as the beneficiaries are concerned, but does not affect the rights of the creditors of the estate at death. In ***Armitage v Nurse [1998]*** a clause in a will excluding the executors from liability for everything short of actual fraud was held to be valid.

Professional bodies including the Law Society and the Society of Trust and Estate Practitioners (STEP) require their members to bring such limitations of their liability to the attention of clients, for example, prior to the client executing a will in which the professional is appointed as an executor or trustee. It is, in fact, questionable whether the inclusion of any clause limiting liability for acts of negligence by a professional executor or trustee is justified at all (see (2)). While such protection may be appropriate for lay people acting in such a capacity, more often than not a relative or friend, it is thought by many that a professional, who is being paid a fee for their reputed expertise, should not be able to avoid liability. There is further weight for this view given that the professional will usually have the benefit of professional negligence insurance to cover any loss should it arise.

(2) By **s61 TA 1925**, the court can grant relief against a claim by a beneficiary or creditor where the PR/trustee has acted honestly, reasonably and ought fairly to be excused against a claim.

Relief was granted on terms to the administratrix in ***Evans v Westcombe [1999]*** (see **16.3.3.1**). The administratrix of a small estate took legal advice (from the probate partner) as to the proper distribution of the estate, in circumstances where her brother had not been heard of for more than 30 years. She took out missing beneficiary insurance cover, as being a cheaper option than an application for a ***Benjamin*** order. This would have realised about £20,900 for the brother, when he reappeared, where half the estate had been worth £21,000, but he claimed to be entitled to interest also. The sister asked to be relieved against liability for any breach of trust under **s61 TA 1925**, in view of the fact that she had taken and followed advice. The breach alleged was that she had received trust property (her brother's share) and converted it to her own use. It was held that she had acted reasonably. Nevertheless, the claimant was entitled to interest. The judge held that fairness required the sister to satisfy the interest claim out of a property derived from the estate, which remained at her disposal. Enforcement was stayed until sale and the sister was relieved of other liability for interest and to render accounts and enquiries. Points to note are as follows.

(a) Reliance on legal advice is not a "passport to relief" under **s61**.

(b) PRs of small estates are not to be discouraged from seeking practical solutions to difficult administration problems which avoid incurring the expense of an application to court.

The court is less likely to allow paid professional PRs to rely on a clause in the will limiting their liability or to grant them relief under **s61**, although in ***Bogg v Raper [1998]*** it was held that an exemption clause was valid where it limited the liability of the trustees and executors of an estate and that no special procedures were required.

(3) Protection may be afforded by the **s27 TA 1925** notice (see **16.3.2.1**).

(4) Where a beneficiary or creditor who is *sui juris* and with full knowledge of the facts acquiesced in the breach, the onus of proving acquiescence rests with the PRs. The PRs can protect themselves by obtaining a written release from the beneficiary for acts done in the course of the administration of the estate, but this release is ineffectual if it has been obtained fraudulently or by means of undue influence. Such a release is usually obtained on completion of the administration.

(5) Under **s62**, the court can order PRs to be indemnified for loss where a beneficiary or creditor has consented to the breach of duty.

Under this provision, the court may order the beneficial interest of a beneficiary to be impounded to indemnify the PRs, where the beneficiary consented in writing, instigated or requested the breach. This is relevant where the beneficiaries who did not consent sue the PRs. The moral is to obtain a written release or consent from all the beneficiaries.

(6) The right to take action may be barred by the **Limitation Act 1980** (**LA 1980**). In the case of creditors, the limitation period is six years for a debt due under a single contract; the period runs from the date on which the right accrued (**s5**). In the case of a judgment debt, the period is 12 years from the date on which the judgment became enforceable (**s24**). The periods may be extended by acknowledgment of the debt by the PRs, either by part payment or in writing.

(7) PRs may plead that they have duly administered all the assets which have come into their hands by entering the plea *plene administravit*.

(8) A modified form of the defence in (7) is to plead *plene administravit praeter*, that is, they have duly administered the assets that have come into their hands with the exception of assets of a stated value which they still hold. These two defences are available against a creditor and mean that the claim can be satisfied only from future assets or those which the PRs admit to holding.

(9) Under the **Inheritance (Provision for Family and Dependants) Act 1975** (**I(PFD)A 1975**), the PRs are protected from liability for distributing the estate provided that they wait six months from the grant before doing so and no prior claim has been made (**s20(1)**).

(10) For rectification of the will, the PRs are protected from liability if they wait six months from the grant before they distribute the estate and no prior claim has been made (**s20(3) Administration of Justice Act 1982** (**AJA 1982**)).

(11) Under **s48 AJA 1985**, PRs can plead that they have relied upon the opinion of a barrister on any question as to the meaning or interpretation of the will. The opinion must be written and given by a barrister of at least 10 years' standing. The opinion cannot be acted upon until the court so orders and the court will refuse where there are contentious issues which need to be aired before the court.

(12) Where the estate includes leasehold property, the PRs may be liable not only for liabilities outstanding at the date of death, but for the deceased's continuing liability under privity of contract (if the deceased was an original tenant under a lease granted before the **Landlord and Tenant (Covenants) Act 1995** came into effect). They will also be liable for liabilities arising during the administration period, only to the extent of the deceased's assets, so long as they did not enter into possession. **s26 TA 1925** protects the PRs in relation to these liabilities. They may satisfy all liabilities to date, set aside a fund to meet future known liabilities for a fixed amount and then assign the lease.

If the PRs entered into possession, **s26** does not apply and the PRs must rely on an indemnity from the beneficiaries or set aside an indemnity fund from the estate which must be retained until all claims are extinguished.

(13) Where the estate is subject to contingent liabilities, the PRs must set aside an indemnity fund, or obtain an indemnity from the beneficiaries or insure against the risk of the liability being enforced.

18.7 Limitation of actions

In the case of creditors, actions in contract must be commenced in the usual way within six years of the cause of action, and 12 years in the case of proceedings on a covenant.

In the case of the beneficiaries, action must be commenced within 12 years from the date on which they became entitled and within six years to recover arrears of interest (**ss15** and **22 LA 1980**). The period can be extended where there is a future interest, or the facts have been concealed by fraud (unless by reasonable diligence the beneficiary should have discovered the fraud). The period does not apply where there has been fraud by a PR or where a PR is in possession of estate assets or their proceeds, unless the beneficiary is barred by *laches* (delay) once they have discovered the facts.

In ***Green and Others v Gaul and Others [2006]*** it was held by the Court of Appeal that the limitation period of 12 years for claims by beneficiaries ran from the end of the executor's year.

18.8 Action against the recipient of assets

Action against the PR will be the first course of action by the creditor or beneficiary, though the PR may not own sufficient assets to cover the value of a claim. In that case, the choices are as follows.

(1) A tracing action to follow the assets to those who have received them, other than a *bona fide* purchaser for value without notice of any defect. This action does not depend on the solvency of the recipient but is rather an action against the asset in question. For the action to succeed, the asset must be identifiable, and it must not be inequitable to trace in the circumstances.

(2) Pursuit of those who have received assets wrongly by way of a personal claim, as in ***Ministry of Health v Simpson [1951]***. Enquiries must be made to see that the recipient is solvent and that the claim is worth pursuing.

This claim is a personal claim against the overpaid beneficiary or creditor for a refund of the amount overpaid. The remedy is available only if the remedy against the PR has been exhausted. **LA 1980** applies, so that the right to claim is lost after 12 years.

A leading example of tracing is the lengthy judgment of the Court of Appeal in ***Re Diplock [1948]***, where property was left by will to named charities for charitable **or** benevolent purposes. After distribution of many of the assets, the will was successfully challenged on the basis that the gift was void and should have read "charitable **and** benevolent". As a result, a succession of tracing actions commenced on behalf of those entitled on intestacy. The court said that where, for example, property had come into the hands of an innocent volunteer who had mixed the property with their own, perhaps, for example, by extending a house, it would be inequitable to allow a tracing action to succeed. Tracing is not barred by limitation but, being an equitable remedy, the party seeking the relief must act promptly, and if guilty of *laches*, the right to take action will be lost. To the extent that tracing was not available, and the PRs were not able to make refunds, the overpaid beneficiaries were ordered to refund the overpayment.

18.9 Summary

(1) Breach of duty by a PR is known as *devastavit*. There are three main areas of liability:

- misappropriation;
- maladministration;
- failure to safeguard assets.

(2) Where PRs are acting as trustees, they may be liable for breach of trust.

(3) **s25 AEA 1925** states that PRs must, when called on by the court, exhibit an inventory and account of the estate.

(4) Any person interested in the estate may issue proceedings for administration by the court.

(5) Defences available to PRs:

- there may be a clause in the will restricting liability;
- **s61 TA 1925**: the court can grant relief if a PR has acted reasonably.

(6) Creditors must take action within six years, or 12 years for proceedings on a covenant. An action by a beneficiary must be commenced within 12 years, or six years where the action is to recover arrears of interest.

(7) There may be situations where it is inappropriate for beneficiaries to take action against PRs. In these cases, beneficiaries may be able to take action against the recipient of assets – tracing or pursuing those who have received assets wrongly.

Index